Records Management: Controlling Business Information

Irene Place, Ed.D.
Professor Emeritus
School of Business Administration
Portland State University

David J. Hyslop, Ph.D.
Associate Professor of Business Education
Bowling Green State University

Reston Publishing Company, Inc.
Reston, Virginia
A Prentice-Hall Company

Library of Congress Cataloging in Publication Data

Place, Irene Magdaline Glazik, 1912-
  Records management, controlling business information.

  Bibliography: p.
  Includes index.
  1.Business records.   2. Files and filing (Documents)
I. Hyslop, David.   II. Title.
HF5736.P63   651.5   81-12049
ISBN 0-8359-6606-2   AACR2

Copyright © 1982 by Reston Publishing Company, Inc.
A Prentice-Hall Company
Reston, Virginia 22090

10   9   8   7   6   5   4   3   2

PRINTED IN THE UNITED STATES OF AMERICA

Contents

Preface

Maintaining useful records is a problem for everyone, but especially for business. Electronic computers with vast data storage capacities have not eliminated filing problems, as originally hoped, although they have introduced processing changes. Records that were previously maintained as paper documents may now be stored in magnetic or graphic form and manipulated by high-speed equipment, but paper documents continue to be created and used in offices.

No matter how records are kept, whether as paper documents manually stored in filing cases or as magnetic spots in computer data libraries, three basic records management problems persist. They are (a) how to control the output of an abundance of information and documents, (b) how to separate useful information from unneeded documents, and (c) how to organize and maintain remaining records so that they are readily available in an easily accessed form as needed.

As an organizational resource, information serves many functions in a firm's operations. Information and business records help managers communicate and make decisions. Today's managers have an abundance of information to read, process, and preserve, but to be of maximum value the information must be organized and managed effectively. Glowing claims made for computers and a paperless society have recently overshadowed fundamental knowledge accumulated over the years about filing classifications and indexing procedures. Since a paperless society is not yet a reality, this book about information management and control does not neglect the previously accumulated base of records management knowledge. Principles, classification systems, and filing practices derived from years of experience are included as well as a discussion of more recent computer-based procedures. The general principles act as a point of departure for anyone interested in managing business records, whether in small or large organizations. Since they are basic, they apply to small organizations as well as corporations.

Records Management: Controlling Business Information presents guidelines and procedures for controlling business information from its creation through distribution, retention and retrieval, storage, preservation, protection, and final disposition. It tackles these phases of records management directly and realistically, using guidelines derived from decades of experience with filing and data processing systems.

This book covers every phase of business information maintenance from classification systems, retention and disposition procedures, equipment and supplies, micrographics and other automated systems, the development and evaluation of records management programs, and the growing responsibilities of records managers themselves. It contains fourteen chapters presented in four parts. Part I, Management Aspects of Information Control, examines information management in terms of planning, program development, and evaluation techniques. Part II, Classification Systems, reviews five classification methods (alphabetic, numeric, subject, geographic, and chronologic). Part III, Control of Information and Records, presents techniques and procedures for improving processing operations. Chapters on forms management and inactive records highlight specific techniques for controlling records. Part IV, Micrographics and Automation, explores technical aspects of records management and presents an overview of various ways to reduce document size. The last chapter, Automated Information and Records Systems, presents information about electronic media including word processing.

Because *Records Management: Controlling Business Information* is a teaching/learning text, designed for records management students or those preparing for other business careers, chapters include discussion questions and learning activities that give students opportunities to formulate and discuss ideas. A glossary in the Appendix enables students to study related terminology and to strengthen their awareness of records management concepts and career opportunities. Another Appendix section describes the Certified Records Managers program (CRM) for those interested in becoming professional records managers. A short bibliography for those who wish to prepare for the CRM examination is part of this section.

Some end-of-chapter learning activities include work organization and judgment-making situations that involve assumptions and decision making. These are included because, in our opinion, a records management text should supply opportunities to practice concepts presented in it that are used in developing comprehensive records management programs.

An accompanying workbook highly recommended for use with this text is *Records Management Projects,* authored by Dennis Bauer. This workbook presents ideas, assignments, and related projects for records management students to complete that correspond to the chapters of the book. By completing these assignments, students can apply and practice concepts presented in the text. Each project is placed on a separate page to permit the teacher to collect and evaluate the student's progress on the assignment.

Irene Place, Ed.D.
David J. Hyslop, Ph.D.

I

MANAGEMENT ASPECTS OF INFORMATION CONTROL

1

The Process of Controlling Information

INTRODUCTION

Within any organization, whether large or small, there is a need to have information created, used and stored in an efficient manner. All organizations need information to effectively achieve goals; those that can control and use this information see the results of their actions in many ways.

Information and business records of all types make an organization function today. In this context, information can be viewed as any knowledge which is communicated for some designated purpose. It is a vital link among employees in an office or between the firm's managers and the customers or clients it serves. Information can and does serve many purposes—and without the right information at the right time, an organization can flounder and pursue directions that will not assist it in achieving its goals.

Much emphasis is placed on the role of information in our society today and how necessary it is that we manage it. Our twentieth century technology has created a vast array of equipment and processes to control and distribute information. Increasingly, it is a responsibility of office employees to manage and use information effectively. Hence, the need arises for studying the process of controlling information and arriving at practical and wise decisions in managing this process.

WHAT IS INFORMATION MANAGEMENT?

The field of information management deals with all of the plans and activities that need to be performed to control an organization's records. It includes the managerial functions of planning, organizing and controlling as they apply to all types of business records and information. The terms "records management" and "information management" may be used interchangeably, as they are similar in nature. Some may prefer using information management as it denotes all types of documents (both paper and nonpaper, such as electronically-stored records) along with data processing activities. Either term can be used to express the process a document goes through while being used. Both terms contain the word "management" indicating the need to control the process to achieve desired goals. Throughout this text, the two terms will be used interchangeably when describing various procedures and activities of business records.

Definition of Terms

In order to understand the processes that occur in information management, some of the important terms are defined below (see also Glossary in Appendix).

Information. Consists of all data and words that an organization needs to function effectively. Can include paper and electronically-based records and all types of numeric or graphic records. (May also be called **record** or **document.**)

Information Management. The process of controlling organizational information from the creation of the information through its final disposition. (May also be called **records management.**)

Filing. The physical process of preparing records to be filed and placing them into their respective storage containers. Filing is one of the activities that occurs as part of records management.

Record. Includes any format upon which information is placed, stored, used or distributed. The most commonly used records are forms, correspondence, reports, and printouts.

Records Cycle. The steps that a record passes through from its creation to its final use. These steps, which are discussed fully in Chapter 3, include (1) creation of record, (2) survey and use, (3) storage and retention, (4) transfer, and (5) disposal.

Records Control. The management steps in which records are systematically processed so that they are used effectively and contribute toward achieving some goal.

Filing and Records Management

People who are not familiar with information management concepts may incorrectly assume that filing and records management are identical concepts. They are not. Filing is always a *part* of records or information management; a single activity that is necessary as part of a much larger process. Filing entails knowing and using the various filing methods (alphabetical, numeric, subject, geographic and chronological) and physically processing documents so they are stored and used efficiently. On the other hand, records management is concerned with all management and control activities and processes associated with documents and could include the following:

Forms control
Reports management and control
Correspondence control
Active files management
Inactive files management
Micrographics
Records management manuals
Vital records control
Directives management
Mail management
Records inventory and appraisal
Records retention and disposition
Archive management and control
Copy reproduction control (Reprographics)

Thus, records management should be thought of as a comprehensive, organized and coordinated set of activities in which an organization controls its information, from the creation of this information through final disposition of it.

THE GOALS OF INFORMATION MANAGEMENT

All organizations produce and use information for some purpose. If information has no value or use, then steps that are taken to control it are unnecessary and should be eliminated. We too often hear of cases where information is either collected or stored by an organization or agency but is never used in any meaningful way. This situation produces "paperwork explosions" and is responsible, in part, for "red tape" problems we experience when trying to conduct business.

What are some of the goals to be achieved by managing information? Although the goals will vary from organization to organization, some important goals are given below.

1. To furnish accurate and complete information when, where, and to whom required in order to manage and operate the organization effectively.
2. To control the creation of information so that only needed and meaningful information is originated.
3. To process and handle information as efficiently and effectively as possible.
4. To provide records control at the lowest possible cost without incurring unnecessary expenses.
5. To render maximum service to the user of the records so that this person can quickly and easily obtain whatever information is required.
6. To have all necessary information available and in a useful format so that sound and timely decisions can be made.
7. To fulfill the requirements of external agencies and organizations by providing them with whatever information is needed or requested.
8. To process and retain only those records that have a specified value to the organization or have a legal requirement to be retained.

Even though the above statements may apply to any organization, it is important to stress that *each* office must construct its own set of goals for handling information. Furthermore, each organization must determine the priority of these goals so that the most important of them receive greatest emphasis and the least important, less emphasis. Goals can and will change according to the overall purpose of the organization, the type of records it maintains, the volume of information processed, the need for information, the method by which records are processed and maintained and, finally, the type of equipment or automation used in the records process. As you might imagine, goals and activities of information management for a small organization, such as a neighborhood grocery store, vary greatly from those of a large, multinational corporation, such as General Motors or Exxon.

PROBLEMS IN CONTROLLING RECORDS

Unfortunately, not all managers and administrative workers see the importance of controlling records. Some may relegate the record management process to the "back burner" and complete only the minimum activities of control. Filing may not be viewed as an essential activity either, and may also receive little emphasis and be assigned to the most inexperienced person in the office. Or an office supervisor may feel there are too many other "more important" tasks to do and, accordingly, pursue records control activities only when all other work is done—which may rarely occur.

If an organization is to actively pursue sound principles and procedures of information control, problems such as those listed above must be examined and attacked so that solutions may be found. Managers and administrative personnel have to see and understand the value to be gained through records control. They must experience what benefits good records control can bring to their jobs, the office and the entire organization. And in times of expanding information requirements and capabilities, they must visualize that controlling information will become even more important in future years.

Some of the difficulty in originating and implementing an information management program stems from the lack of top management support for such a program. Support at all levels is necessary. From the president of the firm to all office employees, each individual must support the goals and practices of information management. A good program is comprehensive, implying that *all* organizational units (such as marketing, accounting, production, etc.) participate in the process of originating and implementing a program. Even in a small office, each person must be included in the process in order to make the program acceptable and valuable. Organizations that tend to have their records management program not on a comprehensive basis can suffer some serious problems when departments or people must communicate and share information, some of which may not be in an appropriate form or place.

Another difficulty some organizations experience regarding records control is the failure to see the cost involved in maintaining records. They may perceive that failure to control information is relatively "costless" and that by completing records management activities, they are spending unnecessary dollars which could be better spent elsewhere. This is hardly the case! Think, for example, of the cost involved if an employee must spend 30 minutes (or more) trying to locate a record which should be available in seconds. Or a case of a customer who, after calling or visiting an organization to obtain some document, is unable to do so and, therefore, is denied any assistance. Or the office that maintains a policy of retaining every record in existence for as long as possible. What about the cost of maintaining unneeded records? How about the cost of the equipment and office space that is necessary to house the records? These are very real and, unfortunately, unneeded costs an office will incur if records are not controlled.

Excessive costs may be incurred if either too few or too many records are maintained. If too few records are available, information may not be available when and where needed, and the decision making process may be hampered. On the other hand, if too many records are maintained, high costs for labor, equipment and storage space will be incurred, and operation inefficiencies will eventually hurt the organization. Obviously, a program of controlling only needed records will yield the best efficiency and effectiveness for the organization—at the lowest cost.

APPLYING INFORMATION CONCEPTS IN THE OFFICE

Information management should be applied to all organizations, as they all have a need for information in their day-to-day functioning. Information today is plentiful; we have the capabilities of creating, storing and retrieving vast quantities of information. As offices and organizations become more automated, and as scientists and technicians improve our communication equipment, we will have far greater potential for creating and using information.

A key question surrounding our technological advances and the growth of information activities is that of creating a value for and justification of information. There is no value in information that does not serve a purpose. Any activity that is undertaken to control information is meaningless if the information has no value or use. So a beginning point in applying information management concepts to an office is to establish the need for and value of the information. Key questions that may be asked are:

What purpose or function does the information serve?
How does the information assist in meeting office or organizational goals?
Who will use the information?
Is the cost (time and expense) of collecting, storing and using the information justified in relation to the value received by having the information available?

Once an office establishes that the information is necessary, appropriate management control activities, as given in the remainder of this book, can be originated and implemented for the organization.

As organizations vary in size, personnel, procedures and purpose, so will the information control activities they conduct. A small office, for example, may be concerned primarily with active files maintenance and mail and correspondence control, while a larger office may focus on activities such as forms controls, directives management or other activities that were listed earlier in this chapter. Another example: a large organization may have the need to prepare an elaborate records management manual with various policies and procedures, while the small office has only a short set of instructions outlining its records management policies and procedures. Even though these offices vary, if they are both effectively managing and controlling their records, then what they are doing is satisfactory—even though it is not the same.

Further, some organizations (for example, health care organizations, police or fire protection) may need instant and easy access to records while other offices may not require instant retrieval capabilities. Each one should then design a retrieval system that is unique to its needs and goals—as long as it can be effectively used.

THE CHANGING NATURE OF INFORMATION MANAGEMENT

Although many changes have occurred in recent years, many more exciting changes in information management are on the horizon. We are witnessing a revolution in office work as a result of new equipment and technology, new processes and new information requirements. The office of the future is fast approaching, if not here. In fact, in 1979, the first so-called "paperless office" opened in Washington, D.C.[1] Although not entirely paper free, most operations are performed without the use of paper documents. Another office (insurance) in Philadelphia, Pennsylvania, has as its goal to be "Paper Free in 1983," when all information processing activities will be performed in some automated fashion.

A variety of new systems are changing information processing policies and procedures. Consider, for instance, some of the newest of these:

Voice systems (including transcription)
Text editing and word processing
Optical character recognition
Reprographics
Micrographics
Facsimile communications
Graphic systems
Telecommunications
Electronic mail
Photocomposition

---

[1]Micronet, Inc., Washington, D.C.

As we introduce these new concepts into offices throughout the country, the entire field of information management will be revolutionized—for the better. Offices will become more efficient and process information more quickly than most of us can imagine. We will be able to accomplish this processing at many locations—not only at the "main office"—and at a time convenient to whoever is requesting or needs the information.

THE CAREER FIELD OF INFORMATION MANAGEMENT

The demand for employees in records management, like the demand for workers in other phases of office work, is strong and should continue to remain so. According the the 1980 *Occupational Outlook Quarterly* published by the Bureau of Labor Statistics, U.S. Department of Labor, some of the fastest growing jobs are those in the clerical and administrative fields, including those in records management. A projected increase for clerical workers from 1978 to 1990 is 28.4 percent, one of the largest of any occupational group.[2]

The skills needed to work in the field of information management will vary depending on whether the person works in a supervisory or nonsupervisory position. Many career opportunities exist for the employee hired into an administrative job to advance into a supervisor's position in records management.

Some basic skills needed by all records personnel include accuracy, good reading and scanning abilities, recording skills (such as handwriting, typing, keyboarding) and the ability to make good decisions. Other skills that may be necessary for a particular job could include

Good memory
Ability to use coding systems
Good technical vocabulary
Manual dexterity

Figure 1–1 gives a summary of the major positions available in records management, along with listing major duties and responsibilities, personal attributes, qualifications and career mobility for each

---

[2]Bureau of Labor Statistics, U.S. Department of Labor, Washington, D.C., *Occupational Outlook Quarterly*, Spring 1980, p. 5.

job. Records personnel also enjoy the flexibility of being able to change into related office or administrative roles, if they so wish. Some organizations, especially smaller firms, would not have all of the positions shown in Figure 1–1 but would have some records management jobs that might involve some duties and responsibilities contained in several of those positions.

PROFESSIONAL ASSOCIATIONS

Appendix B lists some of the records management (and related) organizations and publications that a records employee would find beneficial in furthering his or her career and professional competence. The most relevant publication for records personnel is *Information and Records Management*, a monthly publication containing a wide range of articles on every aspect of information management.

The primary organization for records specialists is the Association of Records Managers and Administrators (ARMA) headquartered in Prairie Village, Kansas. (See Appendix B for complete address.) This national organization provides a variety of professional experiences such as seminars, workshops, conventions, etc., to keep records management personnel updated and current on the latest policies and procedures in the field.

Some experienced records personnel may be interested in the Certified Records Manager (CRM) designation, administered by the Institute of Certified Records Managers (P.O. Box 89, Washington, D.C. 20044). To achieve the CRM designation, individuals must have at least three years of full-time or equivalent work experience in records management, have the necessary educational requirements[3] and pass a six-part CRM examination. (See Appendix A, The Certified Records Managers Program.)

The attainment of this designation, although not a requirement for initial or continued employment, indicates that an individual has achieved a high level of competence in the information management field, and should contribute greatly to his or her career aspirations and promotional opportunities.

---

[3]A baccalaureate degree from an accredited university is required; or the candidate may substitute two years of records management experience (in addition to the required three years) for each year of college. For example, an individual with two years of college would need a total of seven years experience—the required three years plus two for each of the two years of college.

CAREERS IN RECORDS MANAGEMENT

Level	Job Title*	Duties and Responsibilities	Personal Attributes	Qualifications	Career Mobility
Collegiate and University	**RECORDS MANAGEMENT DIRECTOR**	responsible for development & implementation of all company records management policies and practices maintains **Records Management Manual** which details the policies and procedures of the program directs & coordinates personnel and resources	must relate well to people successful supervisor and consultant effective in selling concepts of records management thoroughly versed in the profession of records & information management	ED — minimum of Bachelor's Degree or intensive course work in areas such as business law, accounting, data processing, systems analysis, personnel, records management. Advanced degrees helpful. EXP — 5 years senior records management experience as supervisor or consultant	higher level staff position such as Manager of Office Services
	RECORDS MANAGEMENT ANALYST	surveys, analyzes, recommends department filing systems, procedures, equipment for economic and efficient procedures & utilization reviews, evaluates, recommends changes of retention schedules conducts periodic department inventories participates in training personnel	must relate well to people effective in selling concepts of records management thoroughly versed in the profession of records & information management	ED — minimum of Bachelor's Degree or intensive course work in areas related to records management EXP — 2 years experience as junior records analyst or records center clerk	functional area supervisor or Assistant Director
	RECORDS MANAGEMENT COORDINATOR	coordinates with corporate records management staff the various facets of the records management program responsible for maintenance & operation of divisional or subsidiary company level records management program in cooperation with corporate director for records management	must relate well to people successful supervisor and consultant effective in selling concepts of records management thoroughly versed in profession of records & information management	ED — minimum of Bachelor's Degree or intensive course work in areas related to records management EXP — 2-5 years records management experience in any advanced phase	Corporate Records Manager
	REPORTS MANAGER	responsible for development & implementation of all company reports management policies and practices develop & implement efficient techniques to assist department and line management in identifying, reviewing, & establishing controls on reports	has high aptitude for identifying problem must relate well to people must be firm, flexible, aggressive, & determined should be self-disciplined & career motivated	ED — college graduate EXP — 5 years of experience, preferably in paperwork management & work simplication	supervisory position higher level line or staff position
	FORMS MANAGER	plans, implements, coordinates forms control program throughout company provides technical assistance regarding design, use, specifications, cost, procurement of forms prepares & maintains control records for company standardized forms	high aptitude for identifying problem communicates effectively knowledge of hardware and software standards in the records management field knowledge of principles of standard office practices knowledge of forms design	ED — college graduate EXP — 5 years experience, preferably as forms analyst in forms control section of a system; administration or industrial engineering organization	supervisory position higher level line or staff position

Education Level	Job Title	Duties	Personal Traits	Education/Experience	Career Path
Junior/Community College	RECORDS CENTER SUPERVISOR	operates and maintains a corporate records center; selects & supervises records center clerks and support staff; responsible for vital records protection. storage. disposal	work effectively with all levels of personnel; able to supervise effectively; able to coordinate resources available for an effective program; good organizer & decision maker; has an analytical mind	ED — minimum 2 years of college or vocational training in business or related areas; EXP — 2-5 years in records center operations	Records Management Analyst; Assistant Records Management Director; Records Management Director
	REPORTS ANALYST	provides on company-wide basis, most efficient methods of reports creation, improvement & control through review of reports procedures & systems; designs and formats reports to obtain maximum information required at minimum cost; participates in training personnel	possess report writing skills; relate well to people and be able to make suggestions without antagonizing them; creative; self-motivated	ED — minimum 2 years of college; EXP — 3 years experience as report writer, preferably in one of the functional departments of a company	Reports Manager; higher level line or staff supervisory position
	FORMS ANALYST	investigates and analyzes forms requirements; designs, drafts, & prepares finished art work masters analyzes, revises & consolidates existing forms; maintains records required to document and control all company forms	relate well to people & make suggestions without antagonizing them; ability to establish priorities of work; broad background in all types of forms design, office equipment, and printing services	ED — minimum 2 years of college; EXP — 5 years experience, preferably in general business functions & management methods, graphic arts, duplicating, or other related fields	Forms Manager
High School	RECORDS TECHNICIAN	operate. control. maintain technical files center of a reasonably complex nature; organizes & maintains file in conformance with system & standards developed by corporate records management; oversees disposal of unneeded records at the proper time	analytical mind; ability to grasp difficult question and derive answers using records at hand; decision maker; good planner and organizer	ED — high school diploma and advanced work in office procedures; EXP — 2-5 years file or records experience in difficult records area; NOT AN ENTRY-LEVEL POSITION	Divisional Records Coordinator
	MICROGRAPHICS SERVICES SUPERVISOR	operates a central micrographics program; works closely with records analyst & other corporate members in development of micrographic applications; trains micrographics technicians	mechanical aptitude to maintain equipment; ability to translate micrographics systems specifications into work procedures to prepare film requirements; good organizer and planner. decision maker; analytical mind	ED — high school plus additional training in micrographics; EXP — 3 years experience as micrographics technician (may substitute vocational training for experience)	Records Center Supervisor; higher level line or staff position
	MICROGRAPHICS TECHNICIAN	operates various types of cameras; operates film processor; tests developed film for overall quality; operates microform preparation equipment conforms to production standards	good mechanical aptitude; handle confidential data with utmost discretion; make sound judgments; ability to analyze problems; ability to plan and organize work	ED — high school plus technical training in microfilming; EXP — previous records experience helpful but not necessary	Micrographics Services Supervisor
	RECORDS CENTER CLERK	assists in accessioning. reference. retrieval. & disposal activities of center; assists with vital records; searches, sorts, & files records as requested by users	relate well to people; mechanical aptitude; ability to analyze data for answers to questions; handle confidential requests with discretion; analytical mind	ED — high school where some training in records management and office procedures received; May be an ENTRY-LEVEL POSITION	Records Center Supervisor; Records Technician
	RECORDS CLERK (File Clerk 1) (File Clerk 2)	sorts, indexes, files, and retrieves all types of records; may enter data on records; may search & investigate information in files; classifies materials & records; transfers records & disposes of records according to retention schedule	relate well to people; mechanical aptitude; ability to analyze data for answers to questions; handle confidential requests with discretion; analytical mind	ED — high school where some training in records management, filing and office procedures received; ENTRY-LEVEL POSITION	Records Technician; Records Supervisor

*Job Titles and Descriptions
1976 Dictionary of Occupational Titles

Education Committee
Association of Records Managers and Administrators

FIGURE 1-1. Careers in records management.
(Courtesy Association of Records Managers and Administrators)

REVIEW QUESTIONS

1. What is information management?
2. What is the difference between filing and records management?
3. By what other word could the term information be called?
4. What are some of the types of business records in an office?
5. What are some of the activities which should be completed as part of information control?
6. Why would the records control activities an office undertakes vary, depending on whether it is a small or large office?
7. What are the important goals any office should accomplish in its information management?
8. Why might some organizations experience difficulty in controlling records?
9. How can an office determine the cost of its records?
10. In what ways can the creation of information be justified?
11. What are some changes that will occur in the use and processing of information in future years?
12. What skills are needed by persons working in records management? How might the skills change depending on the position a person has?
13. What is the CRM designation? How is it earned?

LEARNING ACTIVITIES

1. List the most important goals of records control. Try to construct a ranking of these goals, from most important to least important. Justify your ranking.
2. What are some of the most important changes you feel will occur in records management over the next ten years? How might the nature of information change in this period?
3. What are some of the problems a small office (three to ten employees) might have in controlling records? What might this office do to overcome these problems?
4. Select two or three organizations within the local area with which you are acquainted—for example, a retail store, fast-food restaurant, bank, etc. Describe the records each of these organizations may need and use.

2

Development of an Information Management Program

Information, like other resources, must be carefully managed or controlled within the business enterprise. The concept of an information management program implies that activities and procedures be coordinated and systematically used at all levels within the firm. Accordingly, the focus of this chapter is on those elements that are essential in developing an effective and efficient information management program.

CREATING AN INFORMATION MANAGEMENT PROGRAM

Initial steps in planning any program are to determine the present conditions of operations, to re-examine program objectives, and to assess previous successes or failures. A thorough study of current information processing practices gives a person sufficient knowledge of how good the procedures are. Helpful information can be obtained by conversations with records personnel and users or by observation while records are being processed or used.

A study of information processing practices can assume two points of reference: (1) the positive aspects of present operations and (2) the aspects that are presently deficient and need improvement. By focusing on both, records personnel can balance their perspective and avoid focusing on primarily the negative aspects, a common tendency of many persons. A simple list can be used to record present operations and isolate activities that need special attention.

Standards or guidelines with which present procedures can be compared should be the goals of the office or organization. As stated in Chapter 1, these goals include service to the user of the records, reduced costs, and other measures of efficiency and effectiveness. Some goals may be general, but each should be clearly stated and reflect what is important to the organization's existence and success. Once determined, these goals can be used in the analysis process, especially in trying to isolate critical activities that must be performed successfully.

Advantages of Having a Program

By looking at information processing activities as they presently exist in an organization, and then analyzing them as part of a total program, several important advantages are evident:

1. Costs can be reduced, as each information processing activity is measured and evaluated against its contribution to some predetermined goal, and even eliminated if it cannot be justified.

2. Standardization of policies and procedures will occur, making it easier for records personnel to perform their jobs, work with others in a coordinated manner, and provide services to records users in a consistent fashion.

3. Equipment may be replaced or eliminated, as it is no longer needed.

4. Work activities become more efficient and/or effective, as each worker develops a better understanding of his or her job, other jobs in the organization and the goals to be achieved.

5. Responsibility and authority for records operations can be clearly defined, enabling users of the information processing program to receive prompt, accurate service; thus allowing records supervisors to control operations and pinpoint any problems that might occur.

6. Paper and nonpaper records become standardized, allowing for better control when creating or using these records, especially in the case of forms. Through standardization, information can be obtained and processed in similar ways, perhaps permitting some form of automated processing.

Procedures for Creating An Information Management Program

To have an effective program, several key steps should be completed to determine the nature and scope of a proposed program. As mentioned earlier, the initial step is to determine the present state of records activities by assessing how well they are meeting goals. However, prior to this step is the determination of *who* will conduct the investigation. Several possibilities exist, each with distinct advantages and disadvantages. As illustrated in Table 2–1, these possibilities include the use of (1) internal consultants, (2) a committee approach or (3) external consultants. Selecting any one of these three possible choices is a decision that each organization must make dependent on the availability of personnel, financial resources, and the size and scope of the records operations. A large corporation, for example, may decide to use an external consultant while the small firm may not have the financial ability to do so. Additionally, large organizations may employ records specialists on its staff who are fully qualified to conduct investigations while a small organization may not have qualified personnel.

Two advantages of using a committee approach to conduct the inquiry are worth special mention. By having several key persons serve together in the study and design of an information management program, a high degree of commitment to and acceptance of the final program can be achieved. Further, the committee approach, since the

TABLE 2–1.   Selecting personnel to conduct a records study

Choices	Major Advantages	Major Disadvantages
1. Internal Consultants	1. Know the organization its procedures and goals 2. Should be able to obtain information quickly 3. Recommendations should be realistic and workable	1. May have bias point of view 2. Small firms may not have qualified personnel 3. May not have support of top management or other functional areas of organization 4. May not be able to devote full time to study
2. Committee Approach	1. Brings together people from different functional areas 2. Decisions and recommendations should reflect entire organization 3. Acceptance and implementation of program should be easier	1. Time consuming 2. Inability to pinpoint responsibility within committee 3. Decisions may result that do not reflect "balance" between departments or functional areas
3. External Consultants	1. Well trained and qualified 2. May bring expertise from what other organizations are using 3. Able to devote full time to study	1. May take considerable time to complete study 2. May be expensive 3. Recommendations may not be well accepted 4. May not have good understanding of information processing procedures and goals

personnel represent different backgrounds and processing needs, can result in a program that represents a wider variety of the needs of the enterprise and tries to balance them in an effective way.

After selecting appropriate personnel to complete the study, information must be obtained that accurately depicts the scope and condition of information processing activities. That is, a study should be carefully structured so that *all* vital information is obtained and reviewed prior to making recommendations.

This information may be obtained through a variety of techniques: (1) personal interviews with records personnel, (2) written questionnaires completed by all personnel involved in processing activities or (3) structured observation of personnel as they perform their jobs. Each technique has several important attributes which yield effective results; therefore, it is difficult to recommend which is best. The size of an organization, the volume of information processed and the number of records personnel are some variables which affect the selection of any one of these three techniques.

THE INFORMATION MANAGEMENT SYSTEM

The concept of an information management program can be likened to what is known as a system today. A system can be defined as a combination of components that interact to achieve some goal or objective. Stated another way, a system is a composite of various processing activities that are interrelated while being performed as they proceed toward achieving a predetermined goal.

There are various types and "levels" of systems depending on how complex an organization is and how many activities are undertaken. A system, for example, may describe the activities performed to achieve a widespread corporate goal, such as increased profits or increased market share. A system may be divided into subsystems, which still contain all the characteristics of the larger system. An example of these various levels for a financial institution (such as a bank or savings and loan association) might be:

System. Maintaining customers' financial records

Subsystems. Preparing monthly checkbook statements Handling checkbook deposits

Under the systems approach, each system or subsystem consists of a set of activities that must be done in order to achieve some purpose. Thus, bank officials perform certain operations while processing checkbook deposits for customers. These tasks—in total—comprise a subsystem and are part of the larger subsystem, preparing monthly checkbook statements. Finally, the activities performed while preparing monthly checkbook statements can be thought of as a part of an overall system, maintaining customers' financial records.

A similar conceptual approach can be used in analyzing other information processing activities. For example, an information system may be defined as the combination of activities and procedures by which people communicate with each other, either orally or in printed form. Further, information systems can be divided into two types: external information systems and internal information systems. (Both may be termed "subsystems" of the overall system of information management.) The *external information system* consists of those activities and procedures used to communicate effectively with people outside the organization. Examples of documents falling into this category would be purchase orders, city tax forms, workmen's compensation records, business insurance forms, customer orders. Conversely, the *internal information system* is composed of activities and procedures used to communicate within an organization or office. Some examples of documents of this type might include payroll records, personnel folders, accident/safety records, office equipment records.

In general, the value of using the systems approach in analyzing work operations is to provide a basis upon which component operations can be evaluated and altered if need be. Since the focus of systems is on end results, the evaluative process helps determine the value of each activity and provides a measure of how well it contributes to some specified goal of the parent system. Thus, the systems approach is useful when creating an information processing program or when evaluating an existing program. According to Quible's analysis[1], other objectives for using the systems concept are:

1. To improve the efficient utilization of the organizational resources
2. To control operating costs
3. To improve operating efficiency
4. To help achieve the objectives of the organization
5. To assist in carrying out the various functions of the organization

Another use of the systems approach is to divide information management into three subsystems: (1) communication, (2) processing and (3) storage of information. According to Porreca et al., these three subsystems could be viewed as interrelated subsystems of an office

---

[1]Zane Quible, *Introduction to Administrative Office Management* (Cambridge, Mass.: Winthrop Publishers, Inc., 1980), pp. 497–498.

system, as shown in Figure 2–1. The intersection of the three subsystems implies their interrelatedness, and that a change in one will result in a change in the other two. Therefore, as records personnel use such analytical devices, they get new points of view and deeper understandings of the relationship among office systems, which will help them develop valid and workable recommendations.

ORGANIZATION OF THE PROGRAM

To have an effective information management program, principles of staffing and organization must be used. This section of the chapter examines staffing requirements and organizational relationships and gives some guidelines to follow in determining an effective organizational structure.

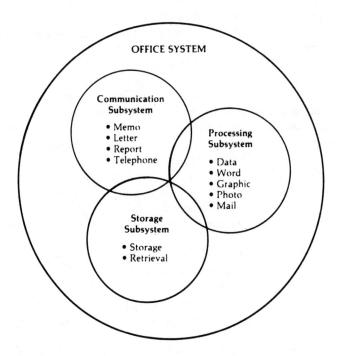

FIGURE 2–1. Office system. (*Source:* Anthony Porreca, Helen Petree, and Carolyn Sheddan, "The Office Systems Concept," *Business Education Forum,* March 1979, p. 7)

Staffing Requirements

To conduct any business endeavor, someone must be given the authority to carry out activities within the organization. Therefore, one person must be designated by top management as responsible for administering the information program (rather than using a committee approach). Although the title of the person may vary in different organizations, the individual must possess the backing and support of top management if success is to be achieved. Some firms call this person a records manager, while other firms use titles such as office manager or administrative services manager.

Ideally, the records manager should assume overall direction and control of all information processing activities. In a small organization, one person may be designated to fulfill these responsibilities, while in larger firms, the records manager may supervise other records personnel and delegate certain responsibilities. Some duties of the records manager in a large organization are described in Figure 2–2.

---

1. Plans, recommends and carries out new methods and procedures to improve records management, records disposition, records center, reference services, and microfilm services.

2. Confers with management, supervisory, law and tax people; establishes distribution, retention, filing and security policies for each type of record.

3. Provides staff assistance to Records Disposition Committee; maintains complete record of disposition policies established and revised; and implements records disposition program.

4. Provides complete companywide analytical service of filing systems and equipment, records centers, retention policies and records disposal; and installs new filing systems and records centers to improve filing and retrieval efficiency, to save office floor space and to reduce operational costs.

5. Operates records center for semi-active and inactive records; maintains index; provides complete reference service; and applies official policies for retention and disposal.

6. Studies applications and efficiencies of microphotography; recommends new methods and equipment; and operates microfilm service center.

FIGURE 2–2. Responsibilities of a records manager.

In large firms, several levels may be present as shown in Figure 2–3. In this example, the records manager, who reports to the vice president of administrative services, supervises the work of the line supervisors, of which there may be several. Each line supervisor may be responsible for one (or more) information processing functions, such as forms control, mail management, inactive records control, etc. Also, the line supervisor has direct control over the work of operating personnel, which might include record clerks, secretaries or others who perform administrative tasks in the processing system.

Under the information management concept, records managers must be provided with sufficient authority (the power to make decisions and obtain compliance from others) if they are to be successful. Thus, supervisors who occupy this position must be knowledgeable in all operations of the business and be respected as competent and trustworthy by others. Further, records managers must possess the abilities to plan, organize, delegate and control. They must also be able to motivate others and build an effective team of information specialists.

In addition to their professional qualifications, they must also possess the interest and desire to achieve good operating efficiency. Their knowledge of records procedures and policies must be excellent. Keeping current on new trends and practices in information processing, especially those involving electronic processing, storage and distribution, is essential to all records managers. Finally, they must be able to communicate effectively.

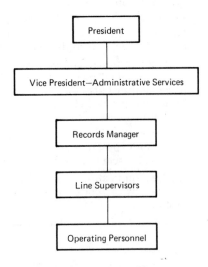

FIGURE 2–3. Organizational levels.

Like the records manager, a line supervisor must also possess the managerial skills of planning, organizing, controlling, delegating and motivating. This person must be a specialist in the phase of records of which he or she is given control and must know how to perform a variety of tasks and to train others to perform their tasks. For example, a line supervisor with the primary responsibility of mail management would need to know:

U.S. Postal Services laws and regulations

Procedures for receiving, processing, and routing incoming mail

Methods of distributing intraorganizational mail and correspondence

Procedures for obtaining, packaging and rating outgoing mail

Personnel and departments within the organization so that correct routing and distribution of mail is achieved

Operating personnel, although they do not have supervisory responsibilities, are important members of the information processing "team." They must be chosen carefully and have the ability to perform a variety of information processing tasks—both accurately and quickly. Reading skills, effective communication skills, and good recording skills are necessary. An interest in filing and pride in work well done are also key qualifications, since they affect the speed and accuracy with which work is done.

Structure of the Program

The structure of any program will vary greatly, in part, based on the size of the organization and the number of documents processed. In the small enterprise, for example, no separate organization structure may be created or be needed to manage information. In these cases, line supervisors may assume responsibility for the function as part of other assigned responsibilities. One caution should be stated here: if an individual is assigned responsibility for information management as a secondary or collateral assignment, there may be a lack of proper control or emphasis on this function if the individual feels it is not the most important job to complete. Thus, information management activities may receive little or no attention and may not be a coordinated, effective program.

On the other hand, a common organizational arrangement for a records management program in large firms is to develop a separate structure exclusively responsible for records control. One popular structure is known as the *administrative services concept*, in which processing activities are centralized and placed under the control of one person, usually a department head or vice president. Figure 2–4 presents one possible structure under this concept. In this case, the

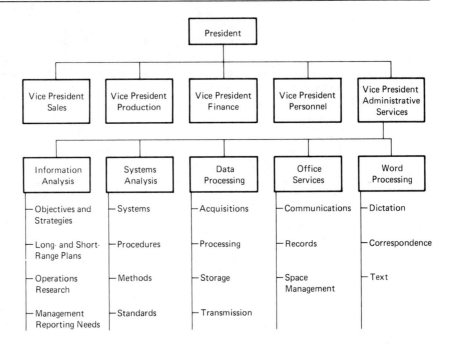

FIGURE 2—4. Organizational structure using the administrative services concept.

administrative services executive serves as a vice president and has the same level of authority as other vice presidents. Included within this person's control are information processing and administrative activities, which are separated into five functional areas. Several important advantages can be achieved by using the administrative management concept:

1. Centralization of information processing activities can result in the coordination of work and efficient work processes.
2. Control of activities is clearly defined as the responsibility of one person—the administrative services supervisor.
3. Specialized attention and visibility can be given to information processing as it occupies an important hierarchical position in relation to other parts of the organization.
4. The cost of activities can be carefully monitored, and perhaps reduced, as duplication of effort, excessive equipment costs and personnel expenses can be examined and kept at an acceptable level.

Another type of organization chart that might be appropriate for a large firm is shown in Figure 2–5. In this chart, two types of lines are used to depict formal relationships. The solid lines show significant command or "line" authority, which indicates a direct supervi-

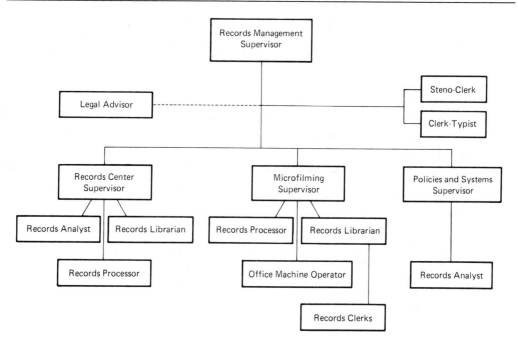

FIGURE 2–5. Records management organization chart.

sor-subordinate relationship. For example, in Figure 2–5, the micro-filming supervisor is directly supervised by the records management supervisor; while the librarian serves as the immediate supervisor for the records clerks assigned to the microfilming operation. A dotted line, such as shown for the legal advisor, signifies a "staff" or functional relationship. This relationship is one of advising or assisting, rather than carrying out direct responsibilities as is part of the line structure. In the example in Figure 2–5, the legal advisor can assist the records supervisor by providing legal advice on records operations, such as retention requirements, privacy of information, federal reporting requirements or the like. Although this staff person serves as an assistant to the supervisor, no direct authority or control exists between the two positions. Further, the legal advisor may also serve as a staff person to other managers within the organization.

The use of organization charts such as those just described can be helpful in many ways. First, a clear determination of responsibilities can be set up, with every processing activity assigned to an appropriate person. Second, the chart can be used to analyze the degree of "balance" that exists to ensure that work assignments are divided fairly and equally, and that no one person has extreme control or authority over others. Third, the chart provides an easy and quick reference about how an organization operates, which can be used in orienting and training new employees or others who work with the firm.

Centralization Versus Decentralization

Over the years, organizations have tended to follow a practice of either centralizing or decentralizing operations and facilities. Recently, there has been a trend toward more centralization of some activities, such as the use of word processing centers or the adoption of the administrative services concept. However, equipment advances may in the future encourage more decentralization, as people will be able to process information at various geographic locations and to transmit such information quickly and easily through electronic media.

Centralization refers to the grouping of similar activities under the jurisdiction of one individual usually at one location. With *decentralization*, activities are performed under the supervision of several individuals at various locations. Centralization or decentralization can occur in three possible ways:

1. The physical location of processing facilities, including equipment, furniture and supplies.

   Centralization: All facilities are at one geographic location.

   Decentralization: Various facilities are used at different geographic locations.

2. The processing of information, including creation, storage and destruction.

   Centralization: All information is processed (companywide) at one central site.

   Decentralization: Information is processed at various geographic sites.

3. The management of the information processing system and activities.

   Centralization: One supervisor has control over all activities at all processing sites.

   Decentralization: Control is assumed by several supervisors, each one responsible for managing the program at a particular site.

Because of the variety of ways an organization may centralize or decentralize, firms may use elements of both in combination and not practice exclusive use of either one. A form of centralization, however, is usually found in most firms, especially those with offices or branches throughout the country or world. In many instances the corporate headquarters serves as the "centralized" processing facility, since information flows into the headquarters from various sites at other locations.

A commonly used method of centralization is that of controlling the creation of records, especially forms, at one location. Sears, Roebuck and Company, for example, centralizes forms control activities at its Chicago headquarters, thus requiring all retail or distribution outlets to use standardized forms and records in their merchandizing operations. Many other organizations, including the federal government and most state governments, also centralize records creation, use and control in their operations.

The final decision on which type of structure to follow should be made on an individual basis, dependent on many factors unique to any firm. However, there are several advantages and disadvantages to centralized control which can assist the records supervisor in creating an appropriate structure. Some of the advantages of centralization include:

1. Uniform work methods and procedures are used.
2. Uniform services are provided to records users.
3. Fewer duplicate documents or procedures are used.
4. Equipment purchase and use can be minimized.
5. Employees can be better utilized, since they can perform tasks in their areas of specialization.
6. Work can be better coordinated, thus avoiding wasted time or "down" periods where little is accomplished.
7. All related information is maintained at one location, simplifying the processing and retrieval functions.
8. Responsibility can be easily placed, allowing for effective management of operations.
9. Documents can be standardized, permitting efficient processing and analyzing operations.

The disadvantages of centralization could include:

1. Because of having a single physical location, personnel (from other areas) may experience delays or confusion in obtaining information.
2. Internal control of work activities and procedures can become complicated as jobs are highly specialized and personnel complete only a small segment of the operation.
3. The information maintained and processed at the central location may not be in the best possible format or structure for use by personnel at other locations.
4. Some records and documents do not lend themselves to centralization.

USE OF MANAGERIAL PRINCIPLES

Coordinating the work of people in an organization requires the use of traditional and validated management principles. Without these, goals may not be achieved, and services provided to information users may become disorganized and confusing. Some of the most widely-used management activities are those of planning, organizing, directing, controlling and delegating. These functions represent the major activities of a records supervisor, both in degree of importance and in the time necessary to complete them. While the operating personnel in an information processing system do not normally have supervisory responsibilities, they still must plan, organize and control, to a degree, the work that flows through the system. A records supervisor, on the other hand, must do both: plan, organize and control the work process, and also manage the activities of people supervised.

Planning

Planning, as the name implies, means the formulation of a course of action for the future. Many activities associated with planning can be categorized as short-range plans or long-range plans. Generally, short-range plans are those of a year or less, while long-range plans can be defined as more than a year. There is no exact rule about how far in advance plans should be made; but most firms operate at least a five-year plan. Some even plan for up to 20 years in the future, especially when major capital expenditures are involved or other significant activities occur.

Responsibility for planning rests with information managers, although subordinates may be involved in formulating plans. This activity can be done in a variety of ways, either informally or formally. For example, an informal approach may be used in some firms where various personnel meet and participate in goals of the firm; while other organizations, using a more formal method, prefer to have plans prepared at the chief executive officers' level and then distributed to other personnel. Planning, however, is necessary at all levels in the organization, and the plans made at each level should be coordinated as they are used.

Major planning areas for a records supervisor can include (1) manpower analysis, (2) cost control, (3) equipment purchases, (4) records procedures and (5) user service—and others. Perhaps the most common planning tool is a budget, which directly affects almost every phase of the information management system. Planning is important because it

Helps offset uncertainty and change

Helps focus attention on objective work goals

Aids in controlling costs and unnecessary expenses

Facilitates control and follow-up

One way of effectively adopting the planning process is to use the familiar "what, why, who, when, where, how" approach. Specifically, this involves posing the following questions and then developing appropriate responses:

1. *What* action is necessary to achieve the objective?
2. *Why* is the action necessary?
3. *Who* will be responsible for taking the action?
4. *When* will the action be taken?
5. *Where* will the action take place?
6. *How* will the action be taken?

Some key elements to consider in the planning process are

1. Do the plans reflect the important goals of the organization?
2. Are the plans realistic?
3. Are the plans put into written form?
4. Are the plans communicated to employees?
5. Are the plans really used?

Organizing

The second basic function of a supervisor is organizing. Organizing is the ability to arrange, in a systematic way, the firm's personnel, equipment, work areas and work processes. Organizing involves determining how work is to be structured, assigning authority and responsibility relationships, and determining individual job duties. In short, it involves the *work*, the *people* to do the work, the *place* and *other resources* needed to accomplish the work, and the *relationship* among these elements. Like planning, this step requires conscientious and thorough completion, or work activities and results will be less than desired.

Some basic principles of organization found in most management texts are

1. An individual must be given sufficient authority (the power to make decisions, to obtain compliance) that is equal to the amount of responsibility or accountability expected from him/her.

2. Each necessary information processing function should be assigned, and the person receiving the assignment should clearly understand what is expected.

3. Lines of authority and responsibility (called the *chain of command*) should be determined to reflect balance in authority and workload and express supervisor-subordinates relationships.

4. Individuals should not be supervised by more than one person (*unity of command*).

5. The number of persons reporting directly to a supervisor should not exceed the number that can be effectively directed by that supervisor (called *span of control*).

6. Each worker should have a clear understanding of the duties and responsibilities of the job he performs, and the duties should be put into written form (*job description*).

7. Responsibility for action should be decentralized to the greatest possible extent to the persons primarily accountable for the actual performance of work (*principle of delegation*).

8. The work environment should be constructed to permit efficient work operations and to maintain a comfortable and convenient place of work for employees and clients.

Organizing, like planning, is a key factor in managing operations because of its affect on productivity and employee morale. A well-organized firm is more capable of reaching its plan than one not so well organized. Several of the key questions that can be posed during the completion of this function are

1. Are employees given ample authority to complete their assigned jobs?
2. Do employees accept responsibility for this assignment?
3. Do employees know and understand their job duties and assignments?
4. Is the workload evenly distributed?
5. Does the work environment help influence results?

Directing

The directing function is one of providing guidance and direction to subordinates in the completion of assigned duties. Good directing means getting the right resources to the right job with the right instructions. The result of effective directing is high employee motivation.

A records supervisor may spend considerable time directing, depending on the nature of the job, the number of people supervised, and the type of work operations. Directing can assume a variety of roles—assisting employees, communicating effectively, providing appropriate incentives, training employees and solving problems as they occur.

Controlling

The process of observing and regulating performance in accordance with a specified plan is called controlling. It is a critical function and may require more time than any of the functions discussed earlier.

The controlling process involves several steps:

1. Reviewing goals and objectives
2. Establishing standards of work performance
3. Measuring employee performance
4. Comparing employee performance with standards and goals
5. Analyzing and evaluating deviations in work performance, if any
6. Determining corrective action
7. Implementing corrective action

Controlling can also be thought of as a process of observing and analyzing work activities to see if they are being completed as planned. As such, the control process requires a degree of feedback to the supervisor on how subordinates are performing. This feedback can be in the form of oral reports, written reports, personal observation, or any other form of communication designed to apprise the supervisor regularly of "how things are going" on the job.

Since control involves examining employee performance, careful attention to the use of human relations skills must be a part of the process, especially if performance is not meeting standards. However, it is important that employees receive prompt and accurate feedback on their performance, or they may feel what they are doing is satisfactory. New employees especially are anxious to receive feedback in order to change their behavior if it is not in line with what the supervisor wants.

Within information processing activities, there are four aspects of an individual's performance which serve as the basis for control. They are (1) *quality* of work, (2) *quantity* of work, (3) *costs* incurred and (4) use of *time*. Historically, the major concern of control was with the quantity of work produced, as measured over a period of time. Today, however, greater concern—and control—is given to the costs of information processing activities and the quality of the work performed. Administrative and processing costs have been steadily increasing and represent, as some office specialists write, an area that needs much more "cost awareness" and control.

Perhaps the most difficult aspect of control is the quality of work, as it is difficult to define exact standards of quality. Some supervisors relate quality to accuracy, neatness, thoroughness or other factors; but there is a degree of subjectivity in any definition of quality. Therefore, supervisors within one organization may have varying quality expectations, making the use of this aspect of control somewhat less than totally objective.

Greater depth of the control process, including performance evaluation and standards, is presented in Chapter 4 of this text.

Delegating

Effective assignment of work is one of the most important supervisory functions affecting the success or failure of a manager. Delegating tasks is usually a necessity: one manager cannot handle all the duties that are assigned on a daily basis. Furthermore, delegation of tasks helps build the performance levels of subordinates, while also serving as a tool to increase employee motivation and participation. When employees are given meaningful responsibilities through delegation, they tend to respond with feelings of belonging and self-esteem. The results of effective delegation usually are high performance and morale, and a staff of subordinates well-trained in their respective jobs.

Records managers should be keenly aware of the payoffs in delegating assignments and should create a work climate in which subordinates readily accept greater responsibility. Whenever possible, the supervisor should examine daily activities and analyze which might be appropriately delegated.

REVIEW QUESTIONS

1. What are some of the goals of an information management program?
2. Who should be given responsibility for developing a records program? What type of resource persons might be available to assist in developing the program?
3. Under what conditions might an organization choose to use external consultants to develop an information management program?
4. What is an information system? In what ways can systems be divided?
5. How does an internal information system differ from an external information system?
6. What are some of the goals that can be achieved in using the systems concept?
7. What are some of the primary responsibilities of a line supervisor in a records management operation?

8. How can the administrative services concept help in inspiring information processing efficiency?

9. How does an organization chart help in developing a records management program? What are some of the uses of an organization chart?

10. In what different ways can an organization practice centralization or decentralization in regard to records management?

11. What are some of the major reasons why a firm might wish to centralize processing activities?

12. Define the following terms: planning, organizing, controlling. Why is successful completion of these functions important in developing an effective records program?

13. What are some of the activities accomplished during the organizing phase of management?

14. Define the following concepts:
    a. authority
    b. responsibility
    c. chain of command
    d. unity of command
    e. span of control

15. How can the controlling process be used to help achieve desired results?

LEARNING ACTIVITIES

1. Ronald Kraft, as Records Manager for Upton Corporation, wishes to review his filing and storing operations with the notion of adopting some micrographic system. At present, no department within the firm uses any type of micrographics, but the Accounting and Supply departments are interested in obtaining such equipment. Mr. Kraft's immediate subordinate, Dave Sherman, is also interested in pursuing micrographics and has stated he will gladly conduct a study to determine if the company should use some type of microfilming.

    a. In your opinion, who should conduct this study?
    b. What would be the advantages and disadvantages of having Mr. Sherman conduct the investigation?
    c. Under what conditions might Mr. Kraft choose to hire an external consultant?

2. When they were a small company, Parnell and Associates had a staff of three persons who maintained and processed this consulting firm's records. However, as the organization grew, more records personnel were hired; and the functions of the records department expanded greatly. Their present organization chart is shown in Figure 2–6.

However, in actual practice, the forms clerk also works for the assistant supervisor in processing a variety of forms that come into the office and eventually go to the financial section. Some confusion has existed in recent days because of overlapping job responsibilities and unclear authority-responsibility lines. For example, the microfilming employees work part of the day in data processing and complain they are overworked. Conversely, the correspondence secretaries complain of not having enough work and state they should be reassigned to another department—either financial records or data processing. Finally, many of the employees are upset with the leadership given by the assistant supervisor, claiming he's always too busy to help them with their problems.

a. Comment on the present organization structure used here.

b. What organization principles appear to be violated?

c. What suggestions do you recommend for the company to improve their organizational effectiveness?

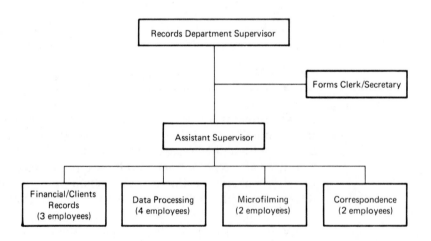

FIGURE 2–6. Parnell and Associates organization chart.

3

The Records
Management Process

Business records, once created, move through a series of steps until they are no longer needed and can be disposed of. We call this series of steps the *records cycle*, and this chapter reviews each step in the cycle in detail.

To introduce the concept of the records cycle, let's consider an example of a business form which might include some activities as described here. First, suppose the form's purpose is to gather information on a person who wishes to obtain credit at a local clothing store. The record is *created* when the individual requesting credit completes the form. Once completed, an office clerk takes the form, verifies its completion and forwards it to the credit manager, who in turn decides to extend credit. A file is then opened for this new customer, and the credit application is stored within the file. However, prior to being filed, the form is coded with the correct filing information and is assigned a retention time—say five years in this case.

During the next several months, the credit application may be *used* by someone in this office as the new customer uses his credit. At the end of one year, however, the credit clerk *transfers* the record to another location, as it is no longer actively used in the office. The credit application remains stored at this other location until the end of the five years, the predetermined retention time. Then the application is obtained from the file and *disposed* of by some means (perhaps shredding) that insures the record is destroyed. Thus, the last step in the cycle is completed.

A visual representation of the credit application process is given in Figure 3–1. Although this example may seem somewhat simple to

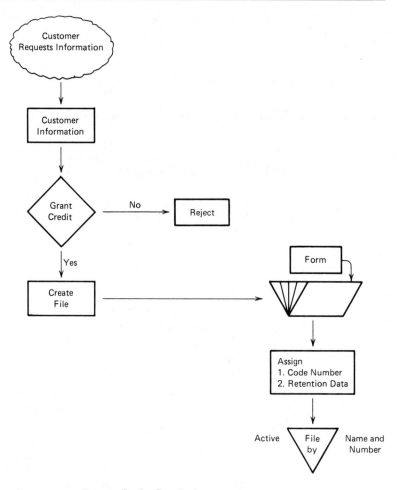

FIGURE 3–1. Credit form process.

visualize and understand, in practice, there may be more difficult steps to complete. For example, at various times in the cycle, some decisions must be made:

Why is this particular record used? Can its use be justified?

Where is the record filed? How is it filed? How can I be sure it will not be lost or misplaced?

How long should I retain the application? Why should I keep it for this period of time?

When will the record be transferred from active to inactive status? How will transfer occur? Who will be responsible for transferring the form?

When will the form be destroyed? How will it be destroyed? Who is responsible for destruction?

The basic steps through which all documents pass is given in Figure 3–2. Within each step, specific tasks must be completed by records personnel to exert control over the record. The remainder of the chapter examines each of these steps and presents various techniques for appropriate management control.

STEP ONE: CREATION OF RECORDS

This step in the records management cycle involves determining the type and volume of records that shall be originated by an organization. There are two ways in which records may come into the creation stage: they may be received by the firm from an outside organization or individual; or they may be created internally by one or more of the company's personnel. The creation of external records—such as letters, reports, forms—is not within the control of a firm since the records are created by someone else. However, the creation of internal documents can be controlled—based on the needs of the firm.

Several key questions can be posed in trying to determine effective strategies for controlling the creation of records. First, *who may create records?* Someone within the organization should be assigned the responsibility to monitor the creation of records. In a small office, the office supervisor may assume control; while in a large firm, responsibility may rest with a records management committee composed of several members. A key to creation control in the large firm is to centralize the control function and allow new records to be created only when a centralized department or committee authorizes such creation.

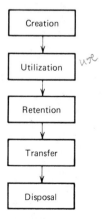

FIGURE 3–2. The records cycle.

A second question is: *How are records created?* This question examines the form (or format) a new record takes and the method in which it is created. For example, a new record may be in letter, report, memo or form *design* and may be created manually, mechanically or electronically. Good creation control requires standardization in format and the use of cost-conscious methods of creation.

Last, the question must be asked: *Why is the record being created?* This is the most vital of all elements in creation control, for if the document cannot be justified, it should not be created. And if the record is not created, then all other steps are avoided—an unquestioned solution to many firms' records problems.

Justifying the creation of a record can be achieved by one or more techniques:

1. *Evaluating the purpose or goal to be achieved by having the record.* Asking *what* will the record be used for, or what goal will the record help achieve can provide some evaluation. Someone within the organization should be able to substantiate *why* the record should be created. We recognize that some records must be created to meet a legal or contractual requirement—and, if so, their justification is taken for granted. However, other records (that might be called "discretionary," because they may or may not be created depending on an organization's preference) should be subject to close scrutiny prior to creation. If the record serves no visible purpose, or if the purpose it may serve is not of great importance, then creation can be avoided.

2. *Measuring the cost of the record.* Another means of justifying a record is to measure its estimated cost if created. Although it may be impossible to obtain exact costs, a reliable and approximate estimate may be obtained by considering the following possible costs:

Printing and duplication
Processing
Storing
Routing and distribution
Equipment and supplies
Overhead
Other costs

When processing a record, related costs should be estimated to arrive at a final figure. As an example, the Dartnell Corporation in Chicago, Illinois, calculated average business letter costs in 1980 to be $6.63.[1] This figure included costs for

---

[1]Dartnell Institute of Business Research, Chicago, Illinois, 1981

Time of dictator

Time of secretary

Nonproductive time

Overhead

Filing

Mailing

Materials

3. *Evaluating how efficient and effective the proposed record will be.* This last factor combines both of the above methods and asks: Is the cost of the record worth the value received from its use? Is the record in the best possible format to reduce processing and related costs? Can the record be used by everyone concerned without creating problems of interpretation, completion or use?

In other words, the record is critiqued to see if it is in a highly useable form and can easily be used to fulfill its intended purpose.

STEP TWO: UTILIZATION OF RECORDS

This step in the cycle is concerned with developing efficient procedures in order that records may be used, stored and retrieved effectively. After the record is created, several activities occur in the storage and use of the record:

The record is correctly classified and coded for filing.

After initial use, the record is appropriately stored.

As needed, the record is retrieved for later use.

The procedures for completing these activities are important for control and are covered in detail in Part II, Chapters 5–9, and Part III, Chapter 10, Correspondence Control.

Records Inventory

One other control activity that can be used during this step is to complete a records inventory. During this inventory, records personnel can obtain a summary of records used in the office and evaluate their actual use. While the creation stage evaluated the *proposed* goal and cost of the record, the inventory can determine the *actual* goal and cost.

Several guidelines should be followed in completing this inventory. First, only official records are surveyed. Extra copies, personal copies or miscellaneous copies of documents are *not* surveyed as it is important to control only the official records of the organization. Second, only those records whose value and use are highly important to the goals of the firm should be surveyed. Too much time and effort would be required to inventory every document; therefore, the greatest benefit will occur if only those documents which are frequently and repetitively used are surveyed. Last, a designated time should be selected for completing the inventory—once a year would be appropriate for most offices. Perhaps the best time would be at the end of either the calendar, fiscal or operating year, whichever one is used by the organization.

The inventory should be completed in as short a time as possible. A person (or several people) should be assigned this responsibility and can complete the inventory by these methods:

Conduct a physical count of the records

Interview records personnel and complete the inventory

Send a written questionnaire to employees requesting them to complete the inventory

A small office may find the first method, the physical count, the easiest and quickest to use but it usually does not allow for enough participation from other involved personnel. Therefore, the interview or questionnaire methods might be preferred by large firms as the volume of records might prohibit having a physical count.

Once the inventory is finished, the records should be reviewed to see if they are still needed and used. Some key questions to consider are:

What use is made of the record?

How frequently is the record used?

How many people use the record?

How much time and money is spent on processing and using the record?

What would happen if the record were not retained?

STEP THREE: RETENTION OF RECORDS

A common concern of many records personnel today regards the retention of records. Employees seek answers to the questions: How long should I keep a record? By what authority should I retain it? Who can tell me how long to keep a record? Are there legal requirements? Although there are no easy or single answers to these questions, there are some principles and procedures which aid considerably in the final decision.

A retention period is recommended for any type of record. Without one, people tend to save and accumulate every piece of information they think they might need. In offices where space is unlimited, documents may be saved on the basis of "I better save this record; you'll never know when I might need it." Such logic may suffice for a short period of time, but it is hardly an effective way to control information. Like the other steps, establishing retention periods is vitally important and must be completed with care.

A retention and disposition schedule should be completed after a records survey is done, unless a retention schedule already exists. In order to make the retention schedule easier to prepare, records can be sorted into categories or subjects. For example, an organization might use some of the following categories:

> Accounting
> Advertising
> Personnel Records
> Products
> Public Relations
> Purchasing
> Tax
> Transportation

Using record groups or categories makes the process easier because most of the records within the group will have identical retention periods. Thus, someone can quickly decide upon and code the document with its correct retention time.

After records are categorized, they should be classified according to value. One widely-used classification is shown in Table 3–1. Each record classification, then, would assist in determining the retention time. For instance, vital records, because of their value, are never destroyed and have an indefinite life. So if a new document is created and classified as vital, its retention period is automatically determined.

Although Table 3–1 gives four workable classification categories, an organization may wish to use its own system and have different categories. Whatever works should be followed. The important part is that the records are classified and properly coded before being filed.

Another possible method of determining records retention is to consider the value of a record based on either its *historical, legal* or *operational* use. Documents may have historical value if they can be used to record a history of past and present activities of an organization. Special care should be taken in preserving these records as they are retained for a long period of time.

TABLE 3–1. Classification of records.

Type	Definition	Examples
Vital	Records that cannot be replaced and hence should never be destroyed. These records are essential to the effective, continued operation of the organization and should not be transferred from the active section of the storage area (usually the general office area).	Property deeds Legal documents Incorporation documents Contracts
Important	Records that are necessary to an orderly continuation of the business and are replaceable only with considerable expenditure of time and money. Such records may sometimes be transferred to inactive storage but are usually not destroyed.	Tax records Financial records Sales records
Useful	Records that are useful for the smooth, effective operation of the organization. Such records are replaceable, but their loss would involve some delay or inconvenience to the firm.	Letters Business reports Some financial records
Nonessential	Records that have no predictable value to the organization. Since the purpose for which they were created has been filled, they may be destroyed.	Routine correspondence Interoffice memos Seasonal publications

Records may also have a legal use, a common purpose today as many records are required based on local, state or federal laws. Each of the 50 states has statutes of limitations which specify how long records must be retained. Further, The Guide to Records Retention Requirements, published annually by the U.S. Government Printing Office, lists retention periods of records as required by departments or agencies of the federal government. If a firm is unsure about the legal necessity of retaining a record, then legal advice should be obtained before making a final decision.

A third use of records is for operational use. The retention of records for this use is decided by records management personnel based upon their best judgment. Since no formal retention timetable is available, the retention schedule will have to be based on a "reasonable period of time" as decided by the most knowledgeable people within the firm. Examples of operational uses for records are financial, fiscal or administrative. Financial records are those necessary for completing the accounting functions of the business, while fiscal records are those used for tax purposes. Records have an administrative use if needed for making decisions, determining policy, or in explaining organization structure, procedures and operations.

A sample records retention schedule is presented in Table 3–2. This schedule summarizes the retention period for 18 different record groups based on either federal laws or administrative considerations.

TABLE 3–2. Records retention schedule.

LEGEND FOR AUTHORITY TO DISPOSE	LEGEND FOR RETENTION PERIOD
AD—Administrative Decision	AC—Dispose After Completion of Job or Contract
ASPR—Armed Services Procurement Regulation	AE—Dispose After Expiration
CFR—Code of Federal Regulations	AF—After End of Fiscal Year
FLSA—Fair Labor Standards Act	AM—After Moving
ICC—Interstate Commerce Commission	AS—After Settlement
INS—Insurance Company Regulation	AT—Dispose After Termination
	ATR—After Trip
ISM—Industrial Security Manual, Attachment to DD Form 441	OBS—Dispose When Obsolete
	P—Permanent
	SUP Dispose When Superseded
* After Disposed ** Normally	‡ Govt. R&D Contracts

TYPE OF RECORD	RETENTION PERIOD YEARS	AUTHORITY
ACCOUNTING & FISCAL		
Accounts Payable Invoices	3	ASPR-STATE, FLSA
Accounts Payable Ledger	P	AD
Accounts Receivable Ledgers	5	AD
Authorizations for Accounting	SUP	AD
Balance Sheets	P	AD
Bank Deposits	3	AD
Bank Statements	3	AD
Bonds	P	AD
Budgets	3	AD
Capital Asset Record	3*	AD
Cash Receipt Records	7	AD
Check Register	P	AD
Checks, Dividend	6	
Checks, Payroll	2	FLSA, STATE
Checks, Voucher	3	FLSA, STATE
Cost Accounting Records	5	AD
Earnings Register	3	FLSA, STATE
Entertainment Gifts & Gratuities	3	AD
Estimates, Projections	7	AD
Expense Reports	3	AD
Financial Statements, Certified	P	AD
Financial Statements, Periodic	2	AD
General Ledger Records	P	CFR
Labor Cost Records	3	ASPR, CFR
Magnetic Tape and Tab Cards	1**	
Note Register	P	AD
Payroll Registers	3	FLSA, STATE
Petty Cash Records	3	AD
P & L Statements	P	AD
Salesman Commission Reports	3	AD
Travel Expense Reports	3	AD
Work Papers, Rough	2	AD
ADMINISTRATIVE RECORDS		
Audit Reports	10	AD
Audit Work Papers	3	AD
Classified Documents: Inventories, Reports, Receipts	10	AD
Correspondence, Executive	P	AD
Correspondence, General	5	AD
Directives from Officers	P	AD
Forms Used, File Copies	P	AD
Systems and Procedures Records	P	AD
Work Papers, Management Projects	P	AD

Revised and printed by Electric Wastebasket Corp. 1977

Reprinted by permission

TABLE 3-2. *(cont'd.)*

TYPE OF RECORD	RETENTION PERIOD YEARS	AUTHORITY
COMMUNICATIONS		
Bulletins Explaining Communications	P	AD
Messenger Records	1	AD
Phone Directories	SUP	AD
Phone Installation Records	1	AD
Postage Reports, Stamp Requisitions	1 AF	AD
Postal Records, Registered Mail & Insured Mail Logs & Meter Records	1 AF	AD, CFR
Telecommunications Copies	1	AD
CONTRACT ADMINISTRATION		
Contracts, Negotiated. Bailments, Changes, Specifications, Procedures, Correspondence	P	CFR
Customer Reports	P	AD
Materials Relating to Distribution Revisions, Forms, and Format of Reports	P	AD
Work Papers	OBS	AD
CORPORATE		
Annual Reports	P	AD
Authority to Issue Securities	P	AD
Bonds, Surety	3 AE	AD
Capital Stock Ledger	P	AD
Charters, Constitutions, Bylaws	P	AD
Contracts	20 AT	AD
Corporate Election Records	P	AD
Incorporation Records	P	AD
Licenses - Federal, State, Local	AT	AD
Stock Transfer & Stockholder	P	AD
LEGAL		
Claims and Litigation Concerning Torts and Breach of Contracts	P	AD
Law Records - Federal, State, Local	SUP	AD
Patents and Related Material	P	AD
Trademark & Copyrights	P	AD
LIBRARY, COMPANY		
Accession Lists	P	AD
Copies of Requests for Materials	6 mos.	AD
Meeting Calendars	P	AD
Research Papers, Abstracts, Bibliographies	SUP, 6 mos. AC	AD
MANUFACTURING		
Bills of Material	2	AD, ASPR
Drafting Records	P	AD†
Drawings	2	AD, ASPR
Inspection Records	2	AD
Lab Test Reports	P	AD
Memos, Production	AC	AD
Product, Tooling, Design, Enginneering Research, Experiment & Specs Records	20	STATUE LIMITATIONS
Production Reports	3	AD
Quality Reports	1 AC	AD
Reliability Records	P	AD
Stock Issuing Records	3 AT	AD, ASPR
Tool Control	3 AT	AD, ASPR
Work Orders	3	AD
Work Status Reports	AC	AD

44

TABLE 3-2. *(cont'd. on next page)*

TABLE 3–2. *(cont'd.)*

TYPE OF RECORD	RETENTION PERIOD YEARS	AUTHORITY
OFFICE SUPPLIES & SERVICES		
Inventories	1 AF	AD
Office Equipment Records	6 AF	AD
Requests for: Services	1 AF	AD
Requisitions for Supplies	1 AF	AD
PERSONNEL		
Accident Reports, Injury Claims, Settlements	30 AS	CFR, INS, STATE
Applications, Changes & Terminations	5	AD, ASPR, CFR
Attendance Records	7	AD
Employee Activity Files	2 or SUP	AD
Employee Contracts	6 AT	AD
Fidelity Bonds	3 AT	AD
Garnishments	5	AD
Health & Safety Bulletins	P	AD
Injury Frequency Charts	P	CFR
Insurance Records, Employees	11 AT	INS
Job Descriptions	2 or SUP	CFR
Rating Cards	2 or SUP	CFR
Time Cards	3	AD
Training Manuals	P	AD
Union Agreements	3	WALSH-HEALEY ACT
PLANT & PROPERTY RECORDS		
Depreciation Schedules	P	AD
Inventory Records	P	AD
Maintenance & Repair, Building	10	AD
Maintenance & Repair, Machinery	5	AD
Plant Account Cards, Equipment	P	CFR, AD
Property Deeds	P	AD
Purchase or Lease Records of Plant Facility	P	AD
Space Allocation Records	1 AT	AD
PRINTING & DUPLICATING		
Copies Produced, Tech. Pubs., Charts	1 or OBS	AD
Film Reports	5	AD
Negatives	5	AD
Photographs	1	AD
Production Records	1 AC	AD
PROCUREMENT, PURCHASING		
Acknowledgements	AC	AD
Bids, Awards	3 AT	CFR
Contracts	3 AT	AD
Exception Notices (GAO)	6	AD
Price Lists	OBS	AD
Purchase Orders, Requisitions	3 AT	CFR
Quotations	1	AD
PRODUCTS, SERVICES, MARKETING		
Correspondence	3	AD
Credit Ratings & Classifications	7	AD
Development Studies	P	AD
Presentations & Proposals	P	AD
Price Lists, Catalogs	OBS	AD
Prospect Lines	OBS	AD
Register of Sales Order	NO VALUE	AD
Surveys	P	AD
Work Papers, Pertaining to Projects	NO VALUE	AD

TABLE 3–2. *(cont'd. on next page)*

TABLE 3–2. *(cont'd.)*

TYPE OF RECORD	RETENTION PERIOD YEARS	AUTHORITY
PUBLIC RELATIONS & ADVERTISING		
Advertising Activity Reports	5	AD
Community Affairs Records	P	AD
Contracts for Advertising	3 AT	AD
Employee Activities & Presentations	P	AD
Exhibits, Releases, Handouts	2 - 4	AD
Internal Publications	P (1 copy)	AD
Layouts	1	AD
Manuscripts	1	AD
Photos	1	AD
Public Information Activity	7	AD
Research Presentations	P	AD
Tear-Sheets	2	AD
SECURITY		
Classified Material Violations	P	AD
Courier Authorizations	1 mo. ATR	AD
Employee Clearance Lists	SUP	ISM
Employee Case Files	5	ISM
Fire Prevention Program	P	AD
Protection - Guards, Badge Lists, Protective Devices	5	AD
Subcontractor Clearances	2 AT	AD
Visitor Clearance	2	ISM
TAXATION		
Annuity or Deferred Payment Plan	P	CFR
Depreciation Schedules	P	CFR
Dividend Register	P	CFR
Employee Withholding	4	CFR
Excise Exemption Certificates	4	CFR
Excise Reports (Manufacturing)	4	CFR
Excise Reports (Retail)	4	CFR
Inventory Reports	P	CFR
Tax Bills and Statements	P	AD
Tax Returns	P	AD
TRAFFIC & TRANSPORTATION		
Aircraft Operating & Maintenance	P	CFR
Bills of Lading, Waybills	2	ICC, FLSA
Employee Travel	1 AF	AD
Freight Bills	3	ICC
Freight Claims	2	ICC
Household Moves	3 AM	AD
Motor Operating & Maintenance	2	AD
Rates and Tariffs	SUP	AD
Receiving Documents	2 - 10	AD, CFR
Shipping & Related Documents	2 - 10	AD, CFR

46

Coding Records for Retention

After a retention schedule is prepared, records personnel should code new records as they are created with the appropriate retention period. An advantage of coding documents when they are received or created is that the retention decision is made when the document is read or used, thus saving time by eliminating the need to reread it later.

Records may be coded in a variety of ways to meet the individual needs of an organization. A classification code (corresponding to vital, important, useful or nonessential or some other system) may be entered on the document, or a date may show the retention period. Figure 3–3 illustrates a letter with a retention date entered in the upper righthand corner—a good location for easy scanning and filing of the document.

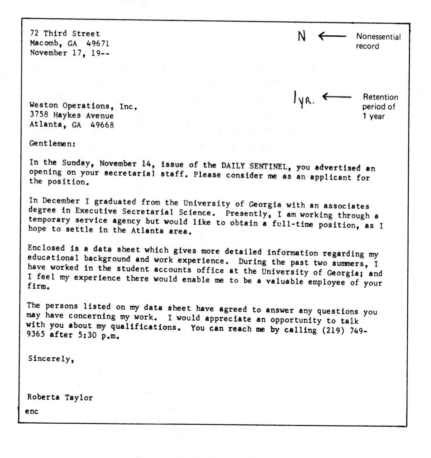

FIGURE 3–3. Sample letter.

STEP FOUR: TRANSFER OF RECORDS

During the retention and storage stages, a record may be retrieved and used frequently. Hence, the record may be called "active" during this period. However, later, the record may not be frequently needed or may be disposed of. The process of reviewing the records, reclassifying them and changing their storage site is called *transfer control*.

Several possible decisions should be made during this step. First, records may be transferred from active status to inactive status—but retained within the office. Or they may be changed to inactive and stored at a distant location (another office or a records center) for the remainder of their retention period. A last possibility is to dispose of a record in accordance with the retention schedule. Figure 3–4 shows three sets of steps the transfer process can encompass, depending on the policies and information needs of the firm. Whichever action is taken will alter the activities to be performed by the records personnel.

Like other steps in the records cycle, the transfer of records must also be carefully planned and carried out effectively. Serious paperwork bottlenecks and space problems can occur if the transfer process is neglected or not completed on time. Through planning, transfer can be accomplished quickly and easily—and with a minimum of disruption in the normal, daily activities of an organization.

To transfer records effectively, several questions can be posed as a starting point in determining appropriate control procedures. The questions are:

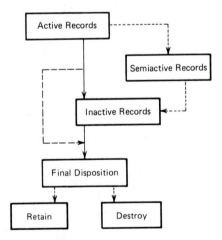

FIGURE 3–4. Transfer steps.

What methods can be used to effect transfer?

When should records be transferred?

Where may transferred records be located?

Who should assume responsibility for transferring records?

Each of these questions is elaborated on in the following section of this chapter.

Methods of Transferring Records[2]

Two methods of transferring records are possible: (1) the *perpetual method*, which provides for continuous transfer of documents, or (2) the *periodic method*, which provides for transfer at stated intervals. Each method has distinct features and either may be used, depending on the type of information maintained and the policies of an organization.

Perpetual Method

The perpetual method calls for constant transfer of records to occur after the processing of a document is complete. It requires careful attention by records personnel not to allow records to accumulate or to be retained in active status when they should be transferred. Because of the nature of office work and the unpredictability of peak work loads, perpetual transfer may not be conscientiously maintained. However, it does allow for efficient processing of records and should help in avoiding lack of space or retrieval problems in an organization. This method of transfer could be used by businesses that maintain and process information for clients, patients, or customers and that are "closed out" when activity is complete. Examples of such organizations could include: hospitals, prisons, law offices or other professional offices (tax, accounting or consulting services).

Periodic Method

The periodic transfer is more complex as it can involve one or more patterns. These patterns may either be a one-period (transfer occurs once a year) or multiple-period[3] (transfer occurs more than once during the year) transfer. In the one-period method, records are transferred from active to inactive status or final disposition at the end of

---

[2]See also Chapter 12, "Inactive Records," (Transfer Methods and Procedures).

[3]Some writers refer to this method as either a two-period or maximum-minimum method.

the year by physically moving all records from one storage location to another. The multiple-period transfer, is completed on a more frequent basis, perhaps monthly, quarterly or semiannually.

The flow of records under the multiple-period method is from active to semiactive to inactive or final disposition (as shown by the dotted lines in Figure 3–4). The following example illustrates this method:

Suppose an organization wishes to use the multiple-period method and transfers records twice a year. Further, suppose this firm follows a calendar year for its information procedures processing. Given these facts, two transfer periods would occur in any year (assume the 1981 calendar year):

One transfer occurs on January 1, 1981, in which records for the previous year are separated:
records from January 1, 1980, to June 30, 1980, are transferred to an inactive status; and
records from July 1, 1980, to December 31, 1980, are maintained as semiactive.

A second transfer occurs on July 1, 1981, when the records are transferred as follows:
records dated July 1, 1980, to December 31, 1980, are transferred to inactive status; and
records dated January 1, 1979, to June 30, 1981, are transferred to semiactive status.

Graphically, these steps are shown in Figure 3–5.

The purpose of this transfer method is to have frequently used records retained within close reach of the users with less frequently used records moved to another location.

Determining Transfer Date

The transfer date for records depends on whether an organization uses the perpetual or periodic method of transfer. If the perpetual method is used, the transfer time is variable and occurs whenever records personnel are finished with the document. However, in the case of the periodic method, transfer will occur at a predetermined time based on organizational policies.

Every organization has some time schedule it follows in the normal course of beginning and closing transactions or activities. They may follow the calendar year (January 1 to December 31), use a fiscal year (July 1 to June 30 or October 1 to September 30), or have alternate dates for an "operating year." An operating year can be any 365-day period (or 366 days in leap year) as long as it does not violate the

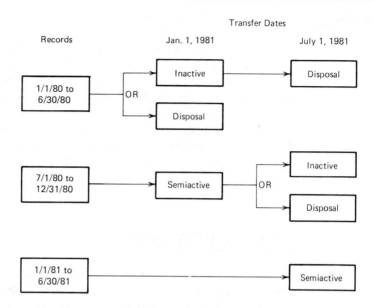

FIGURE 3—5. Illustration of multiple-period transfer method.

policies of any local, state or federal government agency. In any event, whichever year is used has both a beginning and ending date; and the ending date should specify when records are to be transferred. In theory, the transfer should be completed immediately after the close of the year; but in practice, it may take several days or weeks to effect a transfer. The important points are that the transfer date is fixed, that is, personnel cooperate, stay on schedule, and complete the transfer as quickly as possible.

Location of Transferred Records

The amount of space available plays an important part in deciding where transferred records are stored. However, they should be put in a location that permits easy retrieval and still maintains adequate safety and security for the records.

Some organizations store records in a close-by office or storage cabinet. If space permits, the arrangement is satisfactory. However, many times the volume of records dictates storage at a designated location or records center. Larger organizations may operate their own records center where the transferred records can be safely stored and retrieved when needed. Other firms may select to use the services of a commercial record center, which will provide control services for a specified fee. (See Chapter 12, Records Centers)

Responsibility for Transfer Control

The easiest way to determine responsibility for transferring records is to have the policies and procedures for control a part of a records management manual—or at least in written form if a manual is not used. Overall responsibility for transfer activities is normally assigned to the records supervisor or office manager, while other records personnel may be charged with responsibility for carrying out the physical transfer. In a small firm, one person may have total control over this process, while it may be assigned to several people in a large business.

STEP FIVE: DISPOSAL OF RECORDS

The last step in the life cycle of a record is its disposal. A variety of methods may be used to destroy records. These range from simply crushing records and throwing them into a wastebasket to the use of complex, expensive machines. Some methods which could be used include:

> burning
> macerating
> shredding
> chemically treating
> burying

Firms may elect to purchase equipment to destroy records or use the services of a commercial records disposal firm. Records that contain confidential content should be carefully disposed of by a method that insures they are completely destroyed. For these records, an organization may choose to use a "Records Disposal" form showing when, where and how records have been disposed of. However, for most records, documentation is not necessary and such control need not be used.

Disposal of records should occur in a timely fashion which can be easily determined according to retention schedules. Records may be batched or stored for a short time prior to destruction rather than having single documents disposed of on a perpetual basis. However, care should be taken to insure that records do not accumulate beyond control or present a safety or security problem for the organization.

CONTROL ACTIVITIES FOR THE RECORDS CYCLE

Table 3–3 summarizes the major control activities that occur during each of the five steps in the records cycle. This figure can serve as a checklist to insure that responsibility for each activity is assigned.

TABLE 3–3. Control steps in the records cycle.

Step	Control Activities
1. Creation	a. Justify the need for the record b. Measure its possible costs c. Assign responsibility for creation control
2. Utilization	a. Prepare documents for filing b. Obtain appropriate filing equipment and supplies c. Determine retrieval procedures d. Complete records inventory
3. Retention	a. Classify records according to their value b. Establish retention schedule c. Code documents with retention period
4. Transfer	a. Determine transfer date b. Assign responsibility for transfer c. Effect transfer in one of several methods
5. Disposal	a. Review retention schedule b. Select disposal method most appropriate c. Carry out disposal in timely manner

REVIEW QUESTIONS

1. What are the steps in the records cycle?
2. Why is controlling the creation of records important?
3. In what ways can the creation of records be justified?
4. How might control of records be assigned in an organization?
5. What is the purpose of having a records inventory?
6. What methods can be used to complete the records inventory?
7. How is the records inventory used after it is completed?
8. What activities occur during the retention stage of the records cycle?
9. By what methods can records be classified to help in determining their retention periods?
10. What is a retention schedule? How is it used?
11. Why must an organization consider state or federal laws before determining retention periods for records?

12. How should documents be coded for retention?

13. What is the difference between active, semiactive and inactive records?

14. What methods can be used to transfer records? How can an organization determine which method to use?

15. When should records be transferred?

16. What are some of the ways that records may be disposed of?

LEARNING ACTIVITIES

1. Armo Corporation's regional distribution office, located in Nashville, Tennessee, had for years used the perpetual method of transferring records. Most of the records of this corporate office consisted of transportation, purchasing, marketing and personnel records which included:

   bills of lading   price catalogs
   freight bills   sales contracts
   consignment orders   employee contracts
   shipping documents   attendance records
   purchase orders   insurance reports
   contracts
   price quotations

   The new records manager, Alina Mitchell, is concerned with the seemingly unnecessary paperwork generated by the perpetual method. She wishes to examine the periodic method and see if it might help solve her paperwork problems.

   What possible benefits might be gained if this office were to switch to the periodic method of transfer?

   Which of the above records might be better controlled through the periodic method? Justify your answer.

2. The Newhouse Public Relations Company maintains a variety of records including advertising contracts, news releases, layouts, advertising sales contracts, customer referral forms and advertising proposals. Because of uncertainty over how long these records should be retained, the company has stored all records for the past 10 years. Now, with space becoming limited, the company must review these records to determine a suggested retention period. In reviewing the above records, what retention periods would you recommend for each type of record?

4

Evaluating the Information and Records Management System

It would be an enjoyable state of affairs if work, once well planned and organized, could be completed without delays, problems or confusion. However, we usually find this is not the case; and at one time or another, most work activities need to be reviewed to see how well they are progressing.

The evaluation of work and information processing activities can be likened to a review process: it analyzes operations and measures them in terms of efficiency and effectiveness. Evaluation is concerned both with meeting goals (being effective) and utilizing organizational resources such as personnel, equipment and money as best as possible (being efficient). It can be focused on all records activities—from creation of information through its final disposition.

Evaluation is a dynamic tool of control. When used effectively, it provides accurate and timely feedback upon which to analyze operations, make changes or devise new plans. However, if it is to remain an effective tool of control, it must be used thoroughly and conscientiously. It is not enough to evaluate activities just after they are finished or at the end of the operating year. Rather, the greatest amount of control can be obtained when activities are evaluated while being completed, as opportunities for adjustments or changes in operations exist at this point. For example, consider the use of a budget, a popular tool of control for organizational expenditures. If the only time the budget is evaluated is at the end of the year, then changes in operations or spending patterns can be reflected only in the next period—not a very timely situation. On the other hand, if evaluation of the budget occurs frequently within the year (perhaps monthly), then changes can be made while operations and expenditures are being performed.

Determining Activities to Evaluate

It is unlikely that any organization will wish to evaluate all information processing operations. If they did, the "cost" of evaluation may exceed the possible value in improved operations. Businesses should carefully screen their operations and decide which ones represent the most important operations to evaluate. Some possible guidelines to help complete this process are to revise activities by their:

1. *Relative importance.* How important is the activity to the overall goals? How crucial is its timely and accurate completion?
2. *Cost.* How expensive is it (relative to other activities)? What level of resources is required for its completion? What financial hardships might occur if it is not done correctly?
3. *Repetition.* How frequently does the activity occur? How structured and uniform are the work tasks that are a part of the activity?
4. *Time.* How much time is necessary to complete the activity? Does the activity require the time of several persons?

Unlike many manufacturing operations, information processing activities can vary greatly—both in how they are structured and in the methods people use to complete the activities. Those activities that change constantly would be most difficult to evaluate and may not be worth the effort. But many activities, such as filing and retrieving tasks, are somewhat structured in that the records personnel perform similar work methods in completing the tasks. These, then, would be easier to evaluate and could be the basis for improvements in efficiency or effectiveness, since they are done repeatedly.

Each organization can determine the relative importance of information processing activities based on its overall goals or management philosophy. A utility company, for example, would have as an imperative goal the restoration of power any time it is lost by customers within the utility's operating area. Evaluation of information or documents that are processed while restoring power to customers would be a vital concern, since timely and thorough service to customers is a top priority for any utility company.

Some organizations may wish to focus their evaluation on business forms. Forms may require a great amount of time and expense because they are used repeatedly in day-to-day operations. Forms control may yield excellent results since an improvement in processing one form is compounded many times as additional forms are completed.

DEVELOPING PERFORMANCE STANDARDS

The basis for evaluating work is to compare present performance against some predetermined or expected level of performance. The development and use of work standards help give records supervisors guidelines with which employee performance can be compared. With standards, an objective assessment of performance can be made; without standards, a feeling of inconsistency or unfairness may pervade the entire review process.

An acceptable work standard may be defined as: a level of performance in which the quality and quantity of work produced meets the expectation of management, and is a reasonable achievement based on a worker's physical and mental abilities. In this context, work standards represent a "reasonable" level of achievement, which all employees should be capable of meeting. If standards are set extremely high where few, if any, can achieve them, they lose their effectiveness as both a way of measuring performance and of creating a positive motivational climate. If, on the other hand, they are set too low, employees may do less than they are capable of (once they meet standards, they "stop"); and the organization may not be producing at optimum capacity.

A good work standard should specify desired behavior clearly and concisely. It should tell workers (1) what should be done and (2) how well they do the work. Work standards should be developed for most of a person's assigned duties, especially those that represent critical job tasks or require a great amount of time or organizational resources. It is unlikely that standards can be developed for all aspects of a person's job, nor should an attempt be made to do so as the effort may not yield a worthwhile result.

Types of Work Standards

Four basic types of standards can be used for information processing activities. They are: (1) quantity, (2) quality, (3) cost and (4) time standards. Although individual standards can be developed in each of these four areas, they are interrelated and overlap when used in reviewing and analyzing performance. For example, the standards of quantity of work produced and time necessary to complete the task are naturally bound together. Quantity of work always uses time as a constraint or variable, specifying a set amount of work that should be achieved over a set period of time. Likewise, time and costs standards are interrelated as any change in the time required to complete a project changes the costs of that project.

Quantity Work Standards

Perhaps the most commonly used type of standard for administrative or records personnel is the quantity standard. As mentioned earlier, this standard specifies the amount of work that should be accomplished over some period of time. Quantity standards can be developed for many phases of information processing including sorting, pasting, filing, retrieving, distributing or processing operations. These standards can have a measurable impact on organizational effectiveness as they specify acceptable levels of production for records personnel.

Several examples of the use of quantity standards illustrate their adaptability in an organization. For example, a financial clerk in a retail store may be expected to process (i.e., sort documents, post entries to accounts) one hundred customer accounts per hour as a reasonable amount of work to complete. With this quantitative measure, the clerk's supervisor can easily monitor performance and see that goals are achieved. Another example: a file clerk may be expected to sort, code and file five hundred documents per day as the expected output for a certain office. Rather than an hourly quota, the clerk is evaluated on the basis of a total day's output.

Quantity standards are usually quite easy to develop and use. They are quantitative in that a numeric amount of expected output is given. They can be adapted for most information processing activities including:

> sorting records
> coding records for filing
> completing actual filing operations (including retrieval)
> alphabetizing
> completing forms
> answering telephone requests
> posting entries to financial accounts
> preparing reports
> processing automated documents
> typing correspondence
> distributing mail

Quantity standards appear specific but they are not "absolute" in that a person should always achieve the specified number. Rather, they represent "averages," in which a person should approximate the absolute number over a period of time. For instance, if a claims adjuster for an insurance company has a standard of processing 15 claims per hour, it is impossible to expect this person will achieve the exact goal every hour of each workday. Rather, production will vary below or above the standard, depending on interruptions, complexity of the claim, or on ability to contact other people. Therefore, the evaluation of a person's performance should account for a range in output and an "average" production amount should be used as a comparison figure.

Quality Standards

Unlike quantity standards, most quality standards are somewhat inexact and therefore more difficult to develop and use. Even if organizations agree on acceptable quality standards, it is difficult to uniformly administer them, especially as managers vary in their interpretation of them.

Determining quality standards should be a part of controlling information management activities, however. Many offices have been slow in controlling work quality, and the practice of quality control in today's offices has not yet caught up with its manufacturing counterparts.[1] The primary elements in work quality for administrative tasks appear to be those of (1) accuracy, (2) appearance, (3) thoroughness, (4) clarity and (5) effectiveness.

Each business can—and should—develop some quality standards for information processing tasks. The type of standards used should reflect the most important goals of the firm. If accuracy, for example, represents a very important goal, then quality standards reflecting accuracy should be generated.

Cost Standards

These quantitative standards have a popular appeal for most organizations because controlling costs is a vital activity and most costs can easily be measured and analyzed to determine their appropriateness. Costs directly associated with work activities, such as supplies, employees' time, equipment use, etc., are especially easy to control and can be developed into viable standards. Other costs, such as *overhead expenses* (cost of utilities, property rental or purchase, taxes, etc.) are

---

[1]Martin R. Smith, "Quality Control in the Office," *Journal of Systems Management*, vol. 25, April 1974, p. 34.

somewhat more difficult to develop standards for, as many employees may be involved in determining these expenditures, thus making it difficult to relate them to one person's work or output.

Some of the important areas for developing cost standards can include:

equipment use (and maintenance)
telephone/telecommunication services
supplies
employees' time (including overtime)
duplication of work
work scheduling activities
use of business forms
utility costs (lighting, heating, cooling)

Once developed, cost standards need to be reviewed and revised frequently as the cost of doing business escalates. However, the review and revision of cost standards is not a major hurdle to overcome and can be accomplished quickly. Nor do cost standards need to be developed for all areas. Focus instead on the largest cost items, repetitive costs, or those most easily controlled. This is where the greatest possible opportunity for cost reduction lies.

Time Standards

Most time standards are associated with the amount of work produced and, therefore, are really part of a quantity standard. However, two additional uses of time standards are possible: (1) to develop a realistic time estimate for one-time work activities and (2) to determine completion times or dates for work projects. Two examples are: (1) estimating the time needed to inventory existing records and (2) determining the time required for transferring records from active to inactive status. Time standards can be used to determine work loads and to help schedule workers' time so that activities are completed as planned.

How are Standards Determined?

In order to make standards realistic, the basis for their development is observing work operations over a period of time. Three commonly-used objective approaches to measuring work in order to develop standards include time and motion study, work sampling, and predetermined time standards. Other more subjective techniques may be used as long as they yield satisfactory results.

Briefly, *time and motion studies* examine worker motions and activities by the use of a stopwatch. Each activity is timed, grouped according to the task, and then an average time is computed. This average time is used as a standard upon which future activities are measured. *Work sampling* is a less quantitative technique in which representative samples of an individual's work are obtained and then analyzed to develop a reasonable output expectation. *Predetermined time standards* are measures of a variety of processing tasks that are developed by one organization and then used in others that have similar processing tasks. These standards, like those set through time and motion studies, examine each individual motion or work activity and establish average times which become the standards.

Using Work Standards

Excellent control of information processing activities can be achieved through the use of work standards—if they are correctly used. However, they must be developed and used with flexibility and a good understanding of human behavior. Records supervisors are responsible for maintaining work standards but must sustain the support of subordinates if they are to provide a positive motivational impact on the employees.

Supervisors need to assure employees that the standards have been fairly and justifiably developed. Further, supervisors need to administer the standards equally and consistently. Employees who fail to meet them should be counseled to determine reasons for failure and to correct the situation. Employees who meet or exceed the standards should be appropriately recognized and rewarded for their efforts.

Although specific standards will vary with individual organizations, there are some guidelines for developing work standards which can be used by all records managers. Guidelines for developing effective work standards should be:

1. Based on a realistic expectation of what a person should accomplish in a given job.
2. Reflective of the important goals and work activities of the organization.
3. Clearly defined, understood and accepted by each employee.
4. Consistently used in the process of reviewing employee performance.
5. Put in written form *and* communicated orally to employees.
6. Measurable so the employee or supervisor will know exactly when they are met.
7. Totally within the control and ability of the employee to achieve.

8. Flexible, to some degree, based on changes in flow of work, processing procedures or work environment.

9. Periodically reviewed and revised if changes in job duties or work environment exist.

MEASURING EMPLOYEE PERFORMANCE

Evaluating employee performance is a critical component of controlling records management activities, and one that must be done effectively. An experienced supervisor will recognize the importance of this function—not only in regard to achieving productivity but also in relation to giving employees an opportunity to participate in the activities of the organization. Hence, a good performance review can serve several goals while increasing the level of job satisfaction.

As used in this section, the performance review process is defined as the periodic evaluation of performance in comparison with predetermined work standards. It is an attempt to see that results are obtained efficiently and on time, and to pinpoint and correct problem areas as they arise. Simply stated, it is managing for results.

Although primary responsibility for records management results rests with records supervisors, all records personnel are involved in the process. A traditional approach to evaluation has the supervisor determining work goals and concerns, communicating these to subordinates, and then evaluating their performance. Minimal employee participation in the goal-setting process is provided or expected.

More recent approaches stress the active participation of employees in the process. They encourage employees to set their own goals and to determine the best method by which work is accomplished. The subordinate and supervisor, under this concept, act as a team and share in goal-setting and organizing processes. Some organizations opt for a more formal goal-setting arrangement known as Management by Objectives (MBO).[2] Under this system, both parties meet and construct written performance goals which constitute a "formal" contract under which the employee works and is expected to achieve.

Techniques of Obtaining Performance Data

A variety of techniques exist to obtain reliable and representative data to analyze current performance. A *job performance grid*, as illustrated in Figure 4–1, is an example of a form that can be used to obtain per-

[2]This concept has been developed and popularized in the research of Peter Drucker, George Odiorne and others. Consult texts authored by these individuals for further information.

JOB TASK: _____

	Minimum Requirements	Expected Performance	Actual Performance	Deviations in Performance
Quantity Expected				
Quality Expected				
When Required				
Cost Limitations				
Other Expectations (if any)				

FIGURE 4–1. Job performance grid.

formance data. In this grid, standards of performance can be entered first, and then actual performance recorded and deviations (if any) noted. (Some may wish to specify the reasons for the deviations, which could be beneficial in developing strategies to correct deficiencies.)

Another popular technique is to use a production study chart or work activity log, as illustrated in Figures 4–2 and 4–3, respectively. The *production study chart* can be adapted to a variety of processing

PRODUCTION STUDY CHART

Name _____   Date _____

TIME	Receive Calls	Place Calls	Visitors	Transcription	Dictation	Research	Type Reports	Meetings	Open Mail	Distribute Mail	Write Letters	Make Copies	File	Distribute Checks	Miscellaneous
8:00									✓						
8:15	✓								✓	✓					
8:30						✓									
8:45											✓				
9:00	✓	✓													
9:15	✓														
9:30					✓										
9:45					✓										
10:00					✓										
10:15	✓	✓													
10:30															
10:45	✓		✓						✓	✓					
11:00	✓			✓											
11:15	✓			✓											
11:30				✓											
11:45	✓			✓											
12:00				✓											
12:15													✓		
12:30															
12:45															✓
1:00	Lunch														✓
1:15															
1:30															
1:45															
2:00	✓								✓	✓					
2:15	✓		✓												
2:30								✓							
2:45								✓							
3:00								✓							
3:15	✓														
3:30		✓													
3:45											✓				
4:00	✓						✓					✓			
4:15							✓								
4:30	✓													✓	
4:45														✓	
Totals															

FIGURE 4–2. Production study chart.

DAY: _____

Time Period	Job Assignment	Activities Completed	Problems Encountered
8:00-8:30			
8:30-9:00			
9:00-9:30			
9:30-10:00			
10:00-10:30			
10:30-11:00			
11:00-11:30			

FIGURE 4–3. Work activity log.

tasks simply by listing the tasks of the specific employee being reviewed in the horizontal columns provided. Additional columns can be constructed as needed. The totals from several days of observations can then be compared with standards for each task. The *work activity log* serves the same purpose, only it is constructed differently. It is used to list the major activities completed in greater depth than provided in the production study chart.

Concerns in Measuring Performance

Like many other controlling activities, there are several concerns or potential problems which might be experienced when measuring performance. These can include the following:

1. An employee may disapprove of the supervisor's collecting data or closely observing performance. Employees may feel threatened or exposed because someone is monitoring their work activities.
2. Employees, seeking to win approval of a supervisor or to keep standards at a minimum level, may change when being observed and produce either more or less than they are capable of. Either extreme can produce data that are invalid.

3. A representative sample of work activities must be obtained to make the performance review valid and reliable. Obtaining the necessary number of performance samples may require considerable time and cost.

4. Some work activities and tasks are varied and seldom are accomplished in a repetitive or standardized way. Therefore, trying to determine levels of performance for employees who complete unstructured tasks is difficult and inherently inexact.

Some concerns can be eliminated by obtaining the active support of subordinates by informing them of the value and purpose of the performance review. Other concerns may be minimized by giving employees an active role in collecting information and greater responsibility for meeting goals and taking corrective action if goals are not achieved.

EVALUATING DOCUMENT USE

Since the heart of most information processing activities involves processing and using business records and documents, evaluating how these documents are used can be of assistance in improving operations. Three measures of records usage involve determining how frequently they are used, how many are located when requested, and how much time is needed to retrieve the records.

Use Ratio

The measure of how frequently records are used can be termed an activity or use ratio. It is computed by:

$$\frac{\text{number of records requested}}{\text{number of records filed}} = \text{use ratio (\%)}$$

Generally, a ratio of 20 percent or higher is considered satisfactory, although each office should establish a standard, perhaps higher than 20 percent, that seems reasonable.

A high use ratio signifies several things: (1) the records being maintained are used in day-to-day operations, (2) unneeded records are not maintained in the files and (3) filing procedures appear to be followed. A low use ratio may mean that records of marginal value are being created and maintained or that filing procedures are not effective.

Accuracy Ratio

Another important measure of document use is found by using the accuracy or finding ratio, which measures the number of records located when requested. It is computed by:

$$\frac{\text{number of records found}}{\text{number of records requested}} = \text{accuracy ratio (\%)}$$

This measure is a good indication of how well an organization is maintaining records, including following filing procedures and properly training records personnel in filing and retrieving operations. Generally, most accuracy ratios should be extremely high; if not 100 percent, then very close to this number. Anything lower than 95 percent is normally considered unsatisfactory and indicates the need for examination of present procedures.

The ability to locate a record when it has been requested is an important function of any office. In some instances, a misplaced record may mean the loss of a client or customer, poor public relations, or a poor decision because essential facts were not available. Some organizations, such as banks, hospitals, and insurance companies, have unique information needs; and the loss of a document may be crucial to the organization's operations.

One other aspect of using this ratio bears special explanation. The "number of records found" part of the ratio should represent those records located within a reasonable time of the request. Although it is hard to quantify how much time is a reasonable amount, each organization can develop some norm to use here. In most instances, reasonable time should be within five minutes, although retrieval may take longer based on the physical location of the record. However, if the record is not located for a longer than reasonable time or is located after it is "too late" to be used, the document should *not* be counted as having been located when using this ratio.

Efficiency Ratio

A final measure of records retrieval is the efficiency ratio which is used to calculate how long it takes to locate a record. It is determined by:

$$\frac{\text{total time required to locate records}}{\text{number of records requested}} = \text{efficiency ratio (time)}$$

This ratio will indicate the average time required to locate a record after being requested. The final answer may be expressed in seconds or minutes, whichever is appropriate. Since the major cost of information processing is employee expense, this ratio helps records supervisors know how efficient the retrieval process is and how records clerks spend their time.

Using this ratio will require obtaining information on retrieval speed through work sampling. It is impractical to time every record request, nor does every retrieval attempt need to be measured. Through work sampling, a small, representative number of retrieval times can be obtained and an efficiency ratio generated. There is no set standard on how long retrieving a record should take, although one can be developed within each office or file center of an organization. The efficiency ratio may vary from office to office or organization to organization based on:

1. Physical location of the records in reference to the work area of the records clerks.
2. Volume of records maintained at the retrieval site.
3. Degree of filing or retrieval automation used, if any.
4. Training and competence of records personnel.
5. Filing method used to maintain the records.
6. General condition of the files including the use of dividers, guides, file folders, etc.
7. Correctness in filing materials originally, including inspecting, coding, cross referencing.
8. Type of filing equipment used to maintain records.

Obviously, the above factors can have a significant impact on an efficiency ratio. For example, one midwestern utility company, which has customer records automated into a central computer, has an efficiency ratio of approximately 15 seconds, a very good figure. Nonautomated retrieval procedures, by contrast, may take considerably longer, perhaps several minutes.

To review the use of this ratio, let's consider an example of an organization that has the following retrieval data:

Number of records requested = 150

Total time required to obtain records = 100 minutes

These data would have been obtained by recording the time to locate *each* record and then adding the time required for all 150 records. Through work sampling, not all requests need be recorded; but assume the 150 represent requests over several weeks, selected randomly. The calculations would then be:

$$\frac{100 \text{ min.}}{150} = .667 \text{ (or } 66.7\%) \times 60^* = 40 \text{ seconds (rounded off)}$$

(*In order to express final answers in seconds, multiply by 60 seconds.)

Using the Ratios

Supervisors sometimes express the following concerns about using ratios:

"This (the use of ratios) makes sense, but how would I ever find time to collect the information needed?" Perhaps an assumption made is that ratios are to be used continuously. However, this is not the case. They should be *selectively* administered and should not represent a major time commitment on the part of records personnel in collecting the required data. The three ratio procedures described—may be conducted as infrequently as once a month, or even once a quarter.

Logs or records charts can be used to collect data, and employees can participate by quickly and simply recording needed data. Records supervisors can summarize results with little time and effort and review them against predetermined standards. Good results can become the basis for positive rewards for employees, and unsatisfactory results can signal a review of procedures in order to make operations more efficient.

EVALUATING TIME USE

More and more, the topic of time use is becoming a concern in trying to improve productivity. Since information processing activities require a large amount of each employee's day, obtaining better time use can produce tangible results. This section of the chapter presents a brief overview of the principles underlying time management and gives some suggestions on improving the use of time.

The Nature of Time Management

Using time effectively is a complex but important goal. Few people claim to have enough worktime to do all that is expected of them, yet failure to complete some tasks—or complete them on time—can produce major problems for an organization. Thus, time management can be viewed as a resource in that its effective use and control can be of benefit in many ways.

Using time effectively implies several ideas. First, it implies that a person's work activities are planned and coordinated to make the best use of time. Second, it means that timewasters are identified and minimized and that a person's time is spent on productive and worthwhile tasks. Last, it implies that time use is evaluated to see whether improvements can be made.

Two key concepts in time management evolve around the terms "effective" and "efficient." To be effective means to achieve goals, to do productive tasks that are important. Efficiency relates to doing a "job right," using resources (time, effort, money) in the best possible way. In time management, effectiveness should always precede efficiency. This means it is more important to spend time engaged in important tasks than simply to be very busy working on unimportant tasks. Therefore, successful time management should be viewed first by what a person accomplishes and secondly, by how much is accomplished.

Examining Current Time Use

The starting point in the evaluation process is to determine how a person's time is presently used. For this step a form similar to the one shown in Figure 4–4 may be used. Note that this log, in addition to recording work activities and how much time is spent on each one, requires that each activity be evaluated as to its degree of importance. This step is critical in assessing how effectively time is used.

The work log need be maintained only for several days to have enough reliable data upon which to evaluate the activities. Once completed, results can be analyzed and changes proposed. At this point it would be wise to have employees discuss the results with their supervisor so that mutual agreement on the importance of activities can be reached.

A list of nine steps that can be followed in evaluating current time use and planning for future time use is illustrated in Figure 4–5. The first three steps repeat the process described above and shown in Figure 4–4, while the next six steps describe the remaining efforts that can be made to improve time use. Once a good plan is determined and conscientiously used, positive results will be seen.

MY JOB ACTIVITIES

List each activity you perform in carrying out your job responsibilities. Circle the number indicating the importance of each activity in achieving your job objectives (1 = very important). Then, indicate the amount of time you think you devote to each activity during the week.

Activity	Importance	Time Estimate
	1 2 3 4 5	
	1 2 3 4 5	
	1 2 3 4 5	
	1 2 3 4 5	
	1 2 3 4 5	
	1 2 3 4 5	
	1 2 3 4 5	
	1 2 3 4 5	
	1 2 3 4 5	
	1 2 3 4 5	
	1 2 3 4 5	
	1 2 3 4 5	
	1 2 3 4 5	
	1 2 3 4 5	
	1 2 3 4 5	
	1 2 3 4 5	
	1 2 3 4 5	
	1 2 3 4 5	
	1 2 3 4 5	
	1 2 3 4 5	

FIGURE 4–4. My job activities.

First Step:	List all the different things you do. Perhaps the easiest way to do this accurately is to keep a day-to-day record for a week, adding to this list any tasks that you do only occasionally.
Second Step:	Figure the time now spent for each job—the average time under normal circumstances.
Third Step:	Classify all the things you do according to their importance—

1. Those that are essential for you to do every day.
2. Those that are essential at definite, stated intervals.
3. Those that are essential but come up at unpredictable times and take an unpredictable amount of time.
4. Those that are advisable and important if you can find the time to do them.
5. Those that may come up as emergencies.
6. Those that require time in planning and analyzing.

Fourth Step:	Look for duplications of effort and eliminate them. If you apply work-simplification techniques you can streamline your working habits.
Fifth Step:	Study your tasks to determine which of them can be wholly or partly delegated to others. You may have many people who are qualified to do some of the detailed, repetitive jobs that are taking up so much of your time.
Sixth Step:	Adjust your estimate of the time it takes to do the various tasks according to streamlined methods.
Seventh Step:	Make yourself a realistic timetable. Provide time for the essentials first, then for emergencies. Try to leave some unscheduled time that you can devote to important work that formerly was rushed or neglected, or required after-hours work. Try also to leave time for long-range planning and thinking.
Eighth Step:	Make alternate plans for any disturbances to your schedule that may result from emergency situations. Take a good second look at those "emergencies." You may be able to eliminate them completely with better planning and forecasting.
Ninth Step:	Set the plan in motion, reviewing it from time to time to make corrections and revisions.

FIGURE 4—5. How to organize your time.

REVIEW QUESTIONS

1. Why should information processing activities be evaluated?
2. Why is it impractical to evaluate all operations?
3. Why are performance standards necessary? How are they used?
4. What types of work standards may be developed?

5. Why are quality standards harder to develop and use than other types of standards?

6. What are some of the methods by which standards can be determined?

7. Who is primarily responsible for developing and administering work standards?

8. What is a job performance grid? How is it used?

9. How do a production study chart and a work activity log differ?

10. What are some problems that might be experienced when observing an employee's performance? How can these problems be resolved?

11. What is the primary purpose of using each of the following ratios:
    a. Use ratio?
    b. Accuracy ratio?
    c. Efficiency ratio?

12. How frequently should the use of documents be evaluated? Why?

13. Why might the efficiency ratio vary from organization to organization?

14. Which is more important: using time efficiently or using time effectively? Why?

15. What does employee participation contribute to work measurement studies such as those described in this chapter?

LEARNING ACTIVITIES

1. As file clerk for Pacific Merchandising Corporation, Sue Thomas was expected to maintain records for 300 current customers. Part of her responsibilities were to process correspondence for these 300 firms and to prepare monthly business transactions, along with filing correspondence and order forms. Although three other file clerks had similar work loads, Sue felt overworked in comparison with them. She felt her customers were different than those of the other file clerks and required more time. She demanded that her workload be dropped to 200 accounts.

   a. Would you go along with Sue's request? Why or why not?

   b. What would be the effect on the other employees if Sue's customer load were reduced to 200?

   c. What procedures would you use if you wished to verify Sue's statement that she is assigned more work than her fellow employees?

2. As office manager for the Southern Savings and Loan Company located in Plains, Georgia, Ronald Carter believed that an office should use standards to measure its efficiency and effectiveness. For this reason, Ronald installed the following standards in 1981:

(a) Accuracy ratio—should be at least 99 percent during any given period

(b) Efficiency ratio—should be between the range of 45 seconds to 1½ minutes with an average time of 57 seconds

(c) Use ratio—should be between the range of 20 percent to 30 percent

Not only is it important that Ronald's bank show good results, but his bank is also in competition with three other branches located around the Plains area. To be sure that his office was meeting the specified standards, Ronald had all bank employees keep work logs for seven different three-hour periods over a three-month period. The results from three employees are as follows:

	Employee A	Employee B	Employee C
Number of records requested	78	56	180
Number of records filed	260	106	690
Number of records located	76	56	177
Time required to locate all requested records	1 hour 15 minutes	1 hour 3 minutes	2 hours 58 minutes

a. What are the activity, accuracy, and efficiency ratios for these employees?

b. Did each employee meet the standards prescribed by the office manager? Evaluate the performance of each employee.

II

CLASSIFICATION SYSTEMS

Preface

This section consists of five chapters; four of them concern file classification systems: Chapter 5—Alphabetic; Chapter 6—Numeric; Chapter 7—Subject; and Chapter 8—Geographic. Chapter 9 is about equipment and filing supplies. It also contains some terminology explanations. The words *records, information, documents, materials, files,* and *items* are used interchangeably throughout this section to relieve overuse of the word *files.*

Classification systems are orderly arrangements for organizing and keeping information and materials so they can be located when needed. The alternative to an orderly system is disorder or chaos.

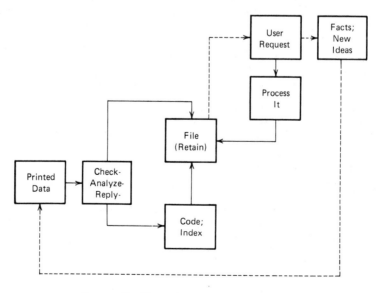

FIGURE A. The information framework.

When planning any type of housing for records, a system of arranging the materials that make up the assortment must be selected. Any files classification system is part of a company's total information framework. (See Figure A.) Systems selected for individual types of records must group materials systematically so that what is contained can be individually or collectively found when needed and thus serve the purpose for which the records were kept.

A records or information retention system (filing system) involves a combination of classifications, hardware, and procedures. The major emphasis in the first four chapters in this section is on classification systems as such. Equipment (hardware), supplies, and procedures are discussed later.

The manner in which materials are classified depends largely on their nature, how they are used, and the technical knowledge of those who design and maintain the systems. Some advantages to a company, agency, or organization that has sound, properly implemented, and well supervised systems are

1. Cohesive "banks" of records and information.
2. Quick access to recorded information because of established systems and procedures.
3. More *useful* records because of the orderly organization and controlled access.
4. Easier movement of materials out of active office space to storage or disposition when their value decreases.
5. Better use of equipment and supplies because of knowledgeable supervision and overall control which we presume to be coordinated.

5

Alphabetic Classification

An alphabetic system is the basis for most classification systems; however, the title "alphabetic system" is used especially to identify name files. That is, in the so-called alphabetic system, materials are classified by business names, individual names, names of government or public agencies or institutions, names of places, locations, or things.

Alphabetic classification is the oldest, most direct, and most widely used classification system. It is a *direct* system because no related index needs to be consulted when locating an item. Its main advantages then are directness and simplicity—as simple as a, b, c.

In spite of today's trend to use number systems because of computer processing, countless types of records are classified alphabetically: business letters, business forms, reports, mailing lists, personnel files, medical records, and legal cases, to name a few. Through the alphabetic system, these materials can be filed individually and collectively so they can be located when needed.

Regardless of the type of records, there must be clearly defined rules to follow for standardization. Order is achieved in an alphabetic filing system by following an *a* to *z* sequence, but rules are needed to standardize the handling of various types of names: for example, titles of government departments, names of institutions, etc.

Names are alphabetized by comparing, letter by letter, such units as last names, first names, initials, and parts of firm or institutional names. A *unit* is each part of a name used in indexing. *Indexing* is selecting the caption under which a record will be filed. Thus the name John Doe (2 units) comes before Mary Doe (2 units) and a file labeled Mary Day (2 units) comes before one labeled John A. Doe (3 units) because when filed, names are transposed as shown:

	1st Unit	2nd Unit	3rd Unit
Mary Day	Day	Mary	
John Doe	Doe	John	
John A. Doe	Doe	John	A.
Mary Doe	Doe	Mary	

Names may, of course, have many more than 3 units. Some people have several middle names; for example, Mary Sue Ann Livingston Day.

At first glance it seems that organizing materials alphabetically by name in an a to z sequence is simple. Mere alphabetic sequence is not the main problem though. There are two basic alphabetic systems worldwide:

(1) letter-by-letter and (2) word-by-word (that is, unit-by-unit). Which system is used does make a difference as shown in the following example.

Letter-by-Letter	Word-by-Word
1. Clearance Hardware Store	1. Clear Falls, Idaho
2. Clear Falls, Idaho	2. Clearance Hardware Store
3. Clearlake Produce, Inc.	3. Clearlake P. T. A. Assn.
4. Clearlake P. T. A. Assn.	4. Clearlake Produce, Inc.

In the United States, the letter-by-letter method is used in dictionaries and encyclopedias, but the word-by-word (unit-by-unit) method is used for name files. Whereas the letter-by-letter method is very straightforward, problems arise with long company, government, and institutional names. Problems also arise in the unit-by-unit method when, for example, names are hyphenated, apostrophies are used, names begin with M', Mc, or Mac or when foreign words or abbreviations are used. On the whole, however, the unit-by-unit method is more practical for government and industrial records. Over the decades, filing experts, equipment suppliers, textbook authors, and professional groups such as the Association of Records Managers and

Administrators (ARMA) have developed rules for classification in unit-by-unit systems so that consistency is possible. Unfortunately total agreement about the rules does not exist. There are individual preferences, yet some type of standardization is essential. Records managers, filing supervisors, and office managers need to make decisions about which rules to follow in their companies to establish uniformity.

In this book, we use filing rules endorsed by the Association of Records Managers and Administrators (ARMA). The research on which they are based included textbooks, business and government filing manuals, dictionaries, encyclopedias, phone books, and directories. The fifty-two rules for alphabetic unit-by-unit filing derived in this way are condensed into thirty rules and grouped in this text in four sections as follows:

Name	Number of Rules
I. Individual	7
II. Business	12
III. Institutions	6
IV. Government	5

Exercises and examples given in each of the four sections should be studied carefully because they illustrate the rules.

SECTION I: INDIVIDUAL NAMES (7 RULES)

Rule 1

Transpose names of individuals so that the last name becomes the first indexing unit: last name, first name or initial, and middle name or initial.

	Unit 1	Unit 2	Unit 3
Harold Brown	Brown	Harold	
Harold E. Brown	Brown	Harold	E.
Harold Eddie Brown	Brown	Harold	Eddie

Rule 1a

A surname with a first name but no middle initial precedes the same name with an initial. That is, *nothing comes before something.*

	Unit 1	Unit 2	Unit 3
A. Brower	Brower	A.	
L. R. Brower	Brower	L.	R.
Lisa Ann Brower	Brower	Lisa	Ann
H. Brown	Brown	H.	
Hal Brown	Brown	Hal	
Harold A Brown	Brown	Harold	A.

Rule 1b

When the entire names of two or more individuals are identical, use the name of the city, then the state, then the street name, and finally the numeric order of the house numbers. If house numbers must be used, arrange them in ascending order, from the smallest number to the larger.

	Unit 1	Unit 2	Unit 3	Unit 4	Unit 5	Unit 6
Dawn Ayers, Omaha, Nebr. 1827 Farnam Street	Ayers	Dawn	Omaha	Nebr.	Farnam Street	1827
Dawn Ayers, Omaha, Nebr. 4518 Farnam Street	Ayers	Dawn	Omaha	Nebr.	Farnam Street	4518

Rule 2—Surname Prefixes

A surname prefix is *not* a separate indexing unit. Treat it as part of the name. Such prefixes are De, Du, La, Los, Mac, Mc, San, Van, etc. An exception may be made of M', Mac, and Mc. (Consult your phone book for local practice.) Such names are sometimes filed together as a group at the beginning of the M section. When this is done, be consistent.

			M's, Mc's, and Mac's Grouped	
de Bonneval,	Albert			
DeByle,	Jacqueline		MacNish,	Janie
Larue,	Charles		MacTavish,	Eileen
LaRue,	Walter		McAdam,	Cora
Lefevre,	Iris		M'Diera,	Sara
Macnee,	Tom			
MacNish,	Janie	or	- - - - - - - - - - - - - - - - - - -	
MacTavish,	Eileen		Macnee,	Tom
McAdam,	Cora		Mazure,	Carole
M'Deira,	Sara		Meade,	Sarah
Van Dam,	Bud			
Van der Haas,	Kaye			
Van der Schalie,	Elaine			
Van Liere,	Sharon			

Rule 3—Hyphenated Names

Treat hyphenated last names as one complete unit.

	Unit 1	Unit 2	Unit 3
Hazel Cuyler-Curtis	Cuyler-Curtis	Hazel	
Paul Cuylerton	Cuylerton	Paul	

Rule 4—Unusual Names

When you cannot decide which is the last name, file it as it appears. Oriental names often fall into this category. This type of name may need to be cross-referenced.

	Unit 1	Unit 2	Unit 3	Cross Reference
Ko Ching Shih	Ko	Ching	Shih	Shih, Ko Ching (*See* Ko Ching Shih)
Nhu Diem	Nhu	Diem		Diem, Nhu (*See* Nhu Diem)
Vi-Cheng Liu	Vi-Cheng	Liu		Liu, Vi-Cheng (*See* Vi-Cheng Liu)

Rule 5—Abbreviations

File abbreviations as though spelled in full *when the meaning is known*. Avoid, however, assuming that you know what the abbreviations mean. For example, Billie does not always mean William.

	Unit 1	Unit 2
Geo. Hayden	Hayden	George
Billie Lofton	Lofton	Billie
Bud Lofton	Lofton	Bud
Kate Lorin	Lorin	Kate

Rule 5a

File firm names as used and spelled in full, not by nicknamed versions.

Full Name	Cross Reference to Nickname
American Management Association	AMA
American Medical Association	AMA
Columbia Broadcasting System	CBS

Rule 5b

Treat endings such as Co., Inc., Bros., Ltd. as a filing unit and as though spelled in full.

	Unit 1	Unit 2	Unit 3	Unit 4
General Dynamics, Inc.	General	Dynamics	Incorporated	
General Text Publishers, Ltd.	General	Text	Publishers	Limited
Gibson Bros. Realtors	Gibson	Brothers	Realtors	
Goddard Candies Co.	Goddard	Candies	Company	

Rule 6—Married Women

The legal name of a married woman includes her own first name. If the husband's first name is known, her name *may* be cross-referenced to his; *Mrs.* is put into parentheses at the end of the name. Today, because of women's liberation trends, some women are deciding to keep their own family names, adding the married name to it. For example,

Janice Evans, when married to Jim Fisher could use the name Janice Evans Fisher. Whether the last two units would be hyphenated is a personal preference. If hyphenated, Evans-Fisher would be treated as one unit. If not hyphenated, we would have

	Unit 1	Unit 2	Unit 3	Cross Ref
Janice Evans Fisher	Fisher	Evans	Janice (Mrs.)	Fisher, Jim (Mrs.) *See* Fisher, (Evans) Janice
Mrs. Lois E. Logan	Logan	Lois	E. (Mrs.)	Logan, Dick *See* Logan, Lois E.

Rule 7—Titles

University degrees and titles of distinction such as Captain, Professor, Doctor, Dean, and Reverend, when needed for proper identification (for example, Dr. Walter Peterson, not Mr. Walter Peterson), are written after the name and considered as one filing unit. Otherwise, they should be put into parentheses and disregarded.[1]

	Unit 1	Unit 2	Unit 3
Walter Peterson, M.D.	Peterson	Walter (M.D.)	Dr.
Helen Wilson, CPA	Wilson	Helen (CPA)	

Rule 7a

Titles when followed by one name are filed as written. That is, if only one name is given, then the title becomes the first unit.

	Unit 1	Unit 2	Unit 3
Captain Cook	Captain	Cook	
Prince Philip	Prince	Philip	
Rabbi Goldman	Rabbi	Goldman	
Reverend Goodman	Reverend	Goodman	
Sister Sophie, S.J.	Sister	Sophie (S. J.)	

[1]Some sources disregard titles entirely because they may or may not be used by the individuals themselves. Where they are disregarded and names are otherwise identical, use the city, state, and address as in Rule 1b.

Rule 7b

Titles that give seniority such as Sr., III (Third), and 2nd, are used only when the names to be filed are otherwise identical. Treat them as indexing units at the end of a name.

	Unit 1	Unit 2	Unit 3
Alexander Carlson, Jr.	Carlson	Alexander	Jr.
Alexander Carlson, Sr.	Carlson	Alexander	Sr.
Chester Carson, II	Carson	Chester	II
Chester Carson, III	Carson	Chester	III
Chet Carson, IV	Carson	Chet (IV)	

SECTION II: BUSINESS NAMES (12 RULES)

Rule 1

When a business name contains the name of an individual plus other words, transpose the individual's name.

	Unit 1	Unit 2	Unit 3	Unit 4	Unit 5
Robert Bahr Furniture Stores, Inc.	Bahr	Robert	Furniture	Stores	Inc.
Fred Meyer Studio	Meyer	Fred	Studio		

Exception: When a firm name that includes an individual's name becomes so well known that to reverse it would cause confusion, file the name as it is. If you do this, however, cross-reference.

	Unit 1	Unit 2	Unit 3	Unit 4	Unit 5
Mark Cross and Company	Mark	Cross	(and)	Company	
Marshall Field and Company	Marshall	Field	(and)	Company	
Howard Johnson Restaurants	Howard	Johnson		Restaurants	

Rule 2—Compound Firm Names

In a firm name that contains the full names of two or more individuals, file by the name of the first person given and cross-reference to the others. The order of the second and subsequent names are unimportant when cross-referencing.

	Unit 1	Unit 2	Unit 3	Unit 4		Unit 5	Unit 6	Unit 7	Unit 8
John Tracy, Bruce	Tracy	John	Smythe	Bruce	&	Hanson	Howard	Consultants,	Inc.
Smythe, and Howard Hanson, Consultants, Inc.	Tracy	John	Bruce	Bruce	&	Hanson	Hanson	Consultants,	Inc.
Cross Reference:	Smythe, Bruce (See Tracy, John & Hanson, Howard, Consultants, Inc.)								
	Hanson, Howard (See Tracy, John and Smythe, Bruce, Consultants, Inc.)								

Rule 3—Trade Names

File coined or trade names that may be spelled as either one or two words or with a hyphen as one unit.

	Unit 1	Unit 2	Unit 3
Hi Note Music Suppliers	Hi Note	Music	Suppliers
Hinote Cafe	Hinote	Cafe	
New-Way Cafe	New-Way	Cafe	
Klip-U-Rite Pet Shop	Klip-U-Rite	Pet	Shop
Stop-A-While Restaurant	Stop-A-While	Restaurant	

Rule 4—Hyphenated Firm Names

When proper firm names are hyphenated to form one firm name, treat each name as a separate filing unit.

	Unit 1	Unit 2	Unit 3
Georgia-Pacific, Inc.	Georgia-	Pacific	Inc.
Prentice-Hall, Inc.	Prentice-	Hall	Inc.
Wilkies-Reston Publishers	Wilkies-	Reston	Publishers

Rule 5—Single Letters

When single letters make up a company name, file them as separate units, unless hyphenated.

	Unit 1	Unit 2	Unit 3	Unit 4	Unit 5	Unit 6
ABC School Suppliers, Inc.	A	B	C	School	Suppliers	Inc.
B-W Bakery	B-W	Bakery				
Triple A Accountants, Inc.	Triple	A	Accts.	Inc.		

Rule 5a

Each letter in the name of a radio or television station is filed as a separate unit.

	Unit 1	Unit 2	Unit 3	Unit 4	Unit 5
WJR Radio Station	W	J	R	Radio	Station

Exception: Local situations may change the order of these units. Check your phone directory.

	Unit 1	Unit 2	Unit 3	Unit 4	Unit 5
WJR Radio Station	Radio	Station	W	J	R

Rule 6—Geographic Names

Treat each word in a compound geographical firm name as a separate filing unit unless it is a hyphenated part of a geographical name or when the first part of the name is not an English word such as *San* in San Francisco.

	Unit 1	Unit 2	Unit 3	Unit 4	Unit 5
Cooper Mtn. Retirement Center	Cooper	Mountain	Retirement	Center	
Mt. St. Helens Volcano	Mt.	St.	Helens	Volcano	
New York State Bank	New	York	State	Bank	
St. Peters Resort Retreat	Saint	Peters	Resort	Retreat	
San Francisco Restaurant Assn.	San Francisco	Restaurant	Assn.		
United States Steel Corp	United	States	Steel	Corporation	
Wilkes-Barre Mills	Wilkes-Barre	Mills			

Rule 7—Compass Points

When a firm name contains compass points, treat each as a separate filing unit.[2] Cross reference may be needed for clarification.

---

[2]Many filing textbooks suggest the opposite—that firm names containing compass points be treated as one unit. Whichever practice is adopted should be followed consistently.

	Unit 1	Unit 2	Unit 3	Cross Reference
North Western Railroad	North	Western	Railroad	(*See also* Northwestern)
South Western Publ. Co.	South	Western	Publ. Co.	(*See also* Southwestern)

Rule 8—Articles, Conjunctions, and Prepositions

Put into parentheses and disregard articles, conjunctions, or prepositions such as *and, for, in, of, the, a, an,* that are part of a firm name unless they are a distinctive part of the name.

	Unit 1	Unit 2	Unit 3	Unit 4	Unit 5
Cafe in the Round	Cafe (in the) Round				
New York State Bank	New	York	State	Bank	
St. Peters, a Retreat Resort	St.	Peters (a)	Retreat	Resort	
The Dalles Oregon Community Center	The	Dalles	Oregon	Community	Center
Top of the Mart Hotel	Top (of the) Mart		Hotel		

Exceptions: When a foreign article meaning *an* or *the* is the initial word of a business name, the name is filed as written.

	Unit 1	Unit 2	Unit 3
LaSalle St. Station	LaSalle	Street	Station

Rule 9—Apostrophes

Consider everything up to the apostrophe; disregard the 's.[3]

		File:	
Johnston's			Johnston
Johnstone's			Johnstone
Johnstons'			Johnstons

Rule 9a

Disregard the apostrophe in contractions and file the word as spelled without it.

---

[3]ARMA recommends disregarding the apostrophe and filing the word as written. Thus Johnstone's would be filed as Johnstones. This practice would be consistent with Rule 9a.

	Unit 1	Unit 2	Unit 3	Unit 4
What's My Line Program	Whats	My	Line	Program
Here's How Products Inc.	Heres	How	Products	Inc.

Rule 9b

Disregard accentual (stress), diacritical[4], and foreign-word markings and file the word as spelled without it.

	Unit 1	Unit 2
Olan Osterbaüm	Osterbaum	Olan

Rule 10—Numbers

When numbers are part of a firm name, index as though spelled in full and use as one unit.

	Unit 1	Unit 2	Unit 3
The Eighteen Club	(The) Eighteen	Club	
Heinz Fifty-Seven Varieties	Heinz	Fifty-Seven	Varieties
The Twentieth Century Limited	(The) Twentieth	Century	Limited

Rule 10a

Numbers of three and four digits are read as hundreds, and the number is filed as one unit: 1406 (fourteen hundred six)

	Unit 1	Unit 2	Unit 3
The 1406 Golf Club	(The) 1406	Golf	Club

Rule 10b

Numbers of five or more digits are read as thousands, hundred thousands, or millions and the number is filed as one unit: 25,000 (twenty-

---

[4]A distinguishing mark added to a letter to show pronunciation: ä, à, â, è.

five thousand), 7,000,000 (seven million). If a title contains several inclusive numbers, start with the lowest number.

	Unit 1	Unit 2	Unit 3	Unit 4
18–21 Club, Inc.	Eighteen	Twenty-one	Club	Inc.

Rule 11—Subsidiaries

When a parent company and subsidiaries are involved, file by the name of the parent or holding company but cross reference to the subsidiaries, divisions, or affiliates. *Poor's Register of Directors* and *Moody's Industrial Manual* help clarify interrelations among companies, but the best authority for the main name by which to file is a company's own letterhead or forms such as invoices and purchase orders.

Parent	Subsidiaries
McGraw Edison Company	Thomas A. Edison Industries Toastmaster Division
Prentice-Hall, Inc.	Reston Publishers

Rule 11a

When communications relate to transactions with individuals or particular departments in a firm, file by the name of the firm. Cross-reference to the name of the individual, the department, or the project title if necessary.

	Unit 1	Unit 2	Unit 3
D. C. Buras, Manager Administrative Methods Dept. General Dynamics, Inc.	General	Dynamics	Inc.
	(Cross-reference as necessary.)		

Rule 12—Foreign Firms

When the name of a foreign firm is written in English, file according to the usual rules. But if it is not in English, file exactly as written. If you can translate, cross-reference.

	Unit 1	Unit 2	Unit 3	Unit 4
Guias Scouts de Colombia	Guias	Scouts	de Colombia	
Cross Reference:	(See Scouts, Girls of Colombia SA.)			
	Also see Colombia (South America Girl Scouts)			
Banco Commercio De Investmento S A Sao Paulo Oirti Algree Brazil	Banco	Commercio	De	Investmento
Cross Reference:	(See Brazil, Oirti Algree, Sao Paulo, SA.)			

SECTION III: INSTITUTION NAMES (6 RULES)

Rule 1

File churches, hospitals, colleges, banks, schools, chambers of commerce, and so on under the first distinctive word in the title. If the name does not contain a distinctive word, file under the name of the city or state. The location part of the name is usually the most distinctive unit for colleges, universities, and banks; likewise, the denomination or location may be the most distinctive part of a church name. Banks are usually filed by city name first because state laws restrict them from expanding to other states. In large files, institutions may be grouped under subject guides such as *banks* or *schools*.

University, Bank, or Church	Unit 1	Unit 2	Unit 3	Unit 4
The University of Michigan	Michigan	(The) University (of)		
First National Bank of Monroe	Monroe	First	National	Bank (of)
Saint Luke's Methodist Church	Methodist	Saint	Lukes	Church

Rule 2—Motels, Hotels

When filing hotel and motel names, reverse the name if necessary so that the most significant word comes first. Add location where possible for further identification.

	Unit 1	Unit 2	Unit 3	Unit 4
Hotel Statler	Statler	Hotel	Chicago	
Stage Coach Motel	Stage	Coach	Motel	Detroit

If a hotel is part of a well-known chain and this is not indicated in the name of the hotel, it may be helpful to include the name of the chain.

	Unit 1	Unit 2	Unit 3	Unit 4
Hotel Georgian, Evanston, Ill.	Georgian (Pick Chain)	Hotel	Evanston	Ill.

Rule 3—Different Addresses

Addresses are used as indexing units only when the names are identical. Index the units in this order: city or town, state, street name and direction (when it is given). If all these units are identical, use house or building numbers next. Go from the lowest number to the highest.

Sears, Inc.)	Farmington Road,	13271
Aurora,)		
Colorado)	Murray Road	4209
Stores)		
)	Murray Road	4833
)		
)	Watson St	4866

Rule 4—Public Schools

File public schools under the city of location followed by Education (Board of) and distinctive school names.[5]

	Unit 1	Unit 2	Unit 3	Unit 4	5	6
Aloha High School, Beaverton, Ore.	Beaverton (Ore.)	School	District	Aloha	High	School

Rule 5—Chain Stores, News Media

File newspapers, magazines, and chain stores under their distinctive titles.

---

[5]Actual practices for listing schools vary considerably. Check your phone directory. Several list schools in the classified directory as "Schools—Public, Private & Parochial, Colleges & Universities." Under this heading, all the schools may be listed alphabetically according to the first significant word of the title, or city schools may be grouped under the name of the city.

	Unit 1	Unit 2	Unit 3	Unit 4
Wall Street Journal	Wall	Street	Journal	
Harvard Business Review	Harvard	Business	Review	
New York Times	New	York	Times	
Red and White Stores, Inc.	Red (and)	White	Stores	Inc.

Rule 6—Estates and Guardianships

File estates and guardianships under the names of the principals. Cross reference to the name of the guardian, trustee, or administrator.

	Unit 1	Unit 2	Unit 3
Estate of Nelly Krance	Krance	Nelly (Estate of)	
Cross Reference:	*See* Archer, Robert (Administrator)		

SECTION IV: GOVERNMENT NAMES (5 RULES)

Rule 1

A breakdown should be made under a main heading—for example, United States Government[6]—according to distinctive words in the name of the subsidiary bureau or unit. Words such as department, bureau, division, commission, office or board are indexed but follow the distinctive name.

Unit 1	Unit 2	Unit 3	Unit 4	Unit 5	Unit 6	7
United	States	Govern-ment	Commerce	Department (of)	Weather	Bureau
			Federal	Aviation Agency	Air Carrier Safety Aircraft Engineering Airport Traffic Hdqts. General Aviation Systems Maintenance	
			Labor	Department (of)	Statistics Division	
			Post	Office	Main Office	
			Selective	Service	Local Board	
			Treasury	Department (of)	Internal Revenue Service	

Rule 2—State, County, City

For state or local agencies, file by state, county, or city, following with the distinctive name of the organizational unit. The words state (of), county (of), city (of) and so on are added for clarity and **are** considered as filing units. Words such as Bureau (of), Board (of) and Commission (of) are put into parentheses and are **not** considered in filing.

	Unit 1	Unit 2	Unit 3	Unit 4
State of New Hampshire, Department of Highways	New	Hampshire	State (of)[7]	Highways (Dept. of)
New York, N.Y. Dept. of Finance	New	York	City	Finance (Dept. of)

Rule 3—Military

Armed Forces (Air, Army, Navy . . .) camps and bases are filed under an identifying word in the title within properly identified subdivisions of the main title, which is the *United States Government*.

Units 1–3	Unit 4	Unit 5	Unit 6	Unit 7	Unit 8	Unit 9	Unit 10
United States Government	Air	Force	Department (of)	Civil Portland Wright	Air Air Paterson	Patrol Force Air	Hdqtrs Base Force
	Army	Dept. (of)	Corps (of) Reserves;	Engineers Fort Fort Sears Sharff Vancouver	Crook Knowles Hall Hall Barracks	Trng. Camp Trng Trng	Center Center Center
	Navy	Dept. (of)	Marine Navy Ship	Corps Recruiting Building	Recruiting District Convrsn. (and)	Portland Repair[8]	

[6]To get information about government units you don't know, use *The Library of Congress List of Subject Headings*, Library of Congress, Washington, D.C. 20025. The *World Almanac and Book of Facts* is helpful. Also helpful is the *U.S. Government Organizational Manual*: it gives names of executive departments, committees, branches, and commissions. It is prepared by the Federal Register Division, National Archives and Records Service, General Services Administration, Washington, D.C.

[7]We do not file by the word *of*.

[8]Telephone directories differ somewhat when indexing military references. The rule given here serves as a basic guide, but the phone directory should be checked for local practices.

Rule 4—Commissions, Committees, and Projects

Committees, commissions, and government projects are often referred to by initials. File by the name in full when it is known and cross-reference to the initials.

File: Armed Forces Service Committee Defense Contract Administration Urban Housing Commission	*Cross Reference:* (*See* FHA) (*See* UHC)

Rule 5—Foreign

Foreign governments are filed according to the same logic as that used for the United States. The identifying name of the country comes first.

	Unit 1	Unit 2	Unit 3	Unit 4	Unit 5
Department of the Interior for the Kingdom of Norway	Norway	Interior	Department		
	Cross Reference: See Kingdom of Norway				
Department of Defense for the Republic of Argentina	Argentina	Defense	Dept. (of)		
	Cross Reference: See Republic of Argentina				

ALPHABETICAL FILING PROCEDURES

Classify files by name whenever practical because it is an easy way to organize materials, as the filing rules just presented show. However, to keep filing systems efficient, procedures as well as rules should be standardized. Efficiency in filing systems is furthered by standardizing such activities as (1) collecting materials, (2) conditioning them for filing, (3) inspecting them for codes and release initials, (4) indexing and coding, (5) cross-referencing, (6) sorting, (7) filing, and (8) retrieving. Ideas for these activities and guidelines for implementation are presented in the following material.

Collecting

Each day, collect materials to be filed by batching them at one place at your work station, either in an out-box, a special drawer, or a special location on a nearby shelf or tub file that has major guide divisions that correspond to the actual files. Items to be filed may include folders, letters, forms, and reports. Efficiency depends on how carefully you follow your systematic procedures and how well you train yourself to put items into a to-be-filed batch as you handle them during the day. (See Figure 5–1.) This also relates to how well you train your associates not to hoard papers. Convince them that items are more likely to be found if properly filed.

A General Guideline
Arrange papers into related groupings (folders, cases, or projects) when possible, as this is the easiest way to file and find information.

FIGURE 5–1. Presort items into related groupings. *(Courtesy Avery Label)*

Conditioning for Filing

This preparation for filing may involve removing pins, paper clips, and rubber bands from materials. You may want to staple together papers that go as a unit; for example, an enclosure that came with a letter. The preferred spot for a staple is diagonally across the upper left-hand corner, but eventually an accumulation of these will cause a bulge in the left corner.

Mend or reinforce damaged items with tape. Attach loose clippings or small items (for example, 5"-by-3"-slips or cards) to a regular sheet of paper by stapling or gluing. Stapling is most commonly used.

A General Guideline

Staple papers that belong together so that they do not accidentally become attached to other papers.

If a document to be filed does not have a specific title, give it one that will help you find and recognize it later.

If an item is oversize and cannot be folded (for example, a poster), file it separately in suitable equipment and cross-reference it to the regular file.

A General Guideline

Bulky or odd-sized materials that do not fit easily into a filing system should be cross-referenced and stored in appropriate locations.

Inspecting

Check documents for filing release to be sure you do not file something which is not ready to be filed. The release mark gives authority to file and may appear in one of several different forms: the writer's initials, the word "file" written on the document, or a diagonal line across the sheet. If there is no release mark, check with the originator.

A General Guideline

Check papers for release marks that indicate they are ready to file. Unless this is done, there is no assurance that a paper has been seen and acted on.

Check document attachments to see if they belong. Check also for missing enclosures. Do not file uncashed checks or money orders as attachments.

Indexing and Coding

Some filing authorities differentiate between indexing and coding. Indexing is a mental decision, whereas coding is the physical action of marking. *Indexing* is deciding the name, subject, or caption by which

an item is to be filed. For example, when indexing a letter, you need
to decide whether the item will be indexed by the name of the

1 Writer or signer
2. Company letterhead
3. Person addressed
4. Person or subject discussed in the letter
5. Location

Coding is actually indicating with a checkmark, an underlined
word, or by encircling a word, the indexing caption decided upon.
Since indexing and coding are performed almost simultaneously, they
are considered here as one activity. Documents may be coded in a variety of ways:

Marking in right-hand corner
Underscoring name, subject, title
Circling name, subject, title
Notating in right margin
Stamping with code or subject

A General Guideline

Index document files so material can be found
when needed. Keep index captions short and
clear.

Read a record carefully in order to find the correct indexing caption. Code it clearly and accurately. Sometimes items need to be cross
referenced because correspondence and related documents are filed
under other captions.

Cross Referencing

Some items may be called by several different names, making it hard
to tell where to find them at times. A cross reference is a filing entry
under a name or caption other than the main one; it also indicates
where that file is. Cross referencing is used whenever a record refers
to more than one person, subject, or company. It eliminates guess-
work. When needed, prepare a separate cross-reference form or use a
photocopy or an extra copy, preferably of a distinctive color marked
"Cross Reference." Two types of cross-reference systems are illustrated in Figure 5–2, the item cross-reference sheet and the permanent
cross-reference folder label. Figure 5–3 illustrates a memorandum
coded for filing and cross reference.

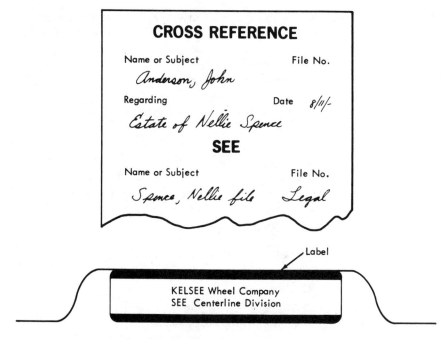

CROSS REFERENCE

Name or Subject   File No.

Anderson, John

Regarding   Date *8/11/-*

Estate of Nellie Spence

SEE

Name or Subject   File No.

Spence, Nellie file   *Legal*

Label

KELSEE Wheel Company
SEE Centerline Division

FIGURE 5—2. Item cross-reference sheet top; a permanent cross-reference (bottom). (*Source: Place, Popham, Fujita,* Fundamental Filing Practice, © 1973. *Reprinted by permission of Prentice-Hall, Inc., Englewood Cliffs, N.J.*)

An individual cross-reference sheet shows

1. The date of the item being cross-referenced.
2. The name or subject of the item.
3. A description of what the item is about.
4. The name or subject under which the original is filed.

File the sheet under the name given at the top of the form. Describe the contents for identification. The main file should be accumulated under the name given after SEE. Cross-reference sheets may be color coded.

A permanent cross reference is a fixed part of a filing system. Identifying data are typed on a label or guide. Such a folder may be moved with files to storage and should be prepared on stock good enough to survive high use.

A General Guideline

Control cross referencing. Restrict it only to situations where it is absolutely necessary.

```
                                                              **  ①  Procedures, Office
    XYZ COMPANY                                               **  ②  Filing

    INTERDEPARTMENTAL

    ━━━━━━━━━━━━━━━━━━━━━━━━━━━━━━━━━━━━━━━━━━━━━━━━━━━━━━━━━

    Date:      July 1, 19__


    To:        All Departments              ④  ┌──────────────────┐
                                               │ File:  a W       │
    From:      Methods Department              ├──────────────────┤
                   **  ③                        │ Refer to:        │
                                               │ Follow-up:       │
                                               └──────────────────┘
    Subject:   Procedure for Company Filing System


    This exhibit represents a copy of a record properly classified and marked
    for filing.  It shows the preferred placement of file designations in the
    upper right corner including the correct method of indicating what cross-
    references should be made.

    You will find the detailed procedures for classifying and marking records
    explained in the Filing Manual (Subparagraph 3.1) which is being sent to
    you under separate cover.


    John Doe
    John Doe
    Manager

                                            Key:

                                            ①  Subject (file designation)
                                            ②  Cross-reference
                                            ③  Cross-reference
                                            ④  Action stamp

                                        **     Underline in red
```

FIGURE 5—3. A memorandum coded for filing and cross reference. (*Source: Place, Pop-ham, Fujita,* Fundamental Filing Practice, © 1973. *Reprinted by permission of Prentice-Hall, Inc., Englewood Cliffs, N.J.*)

Sorting

Sorting is the arrangement of coded papers into a through z sequence before they are put into the files. Sort papers by designated indexing captions.

A General Guideline

Presort papers for filing. This practice saves filing time.

Where papers cannot be filed daily, they at least should be in-
spected, indexed, coded, and put into a sorting tray with guides. (See
Figure 5–4.) Here they should be kept in filing order so that requests
for them before they are filed can be handled easily. If a sorting tray
is not available, use a desk or table top. A routine such as the following saves time:

1. Rough sort documents into alphabetical piles such as A–F, G–L,
   M–R, S–Z.
2. Fine sort each pile. For example, the A–F division should be separated into six piles: A, B, C, D, E, and F.
3. Alphabetize the papers within each pile.
4. Assemble all the documents for actual filing.

A General Guideline

File daily. When filing is not kept up-to-date,
time is wasted looking for papers that are supposed to be in the files.

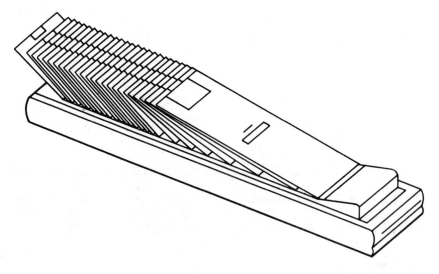

FIGURE 5–4. Sliding racks cut rough-sorting time. *(Courtesy National Archives and
Records Service)*

PARTS OF ALPHABETICAL FILING SYSTEM

Guides, miscellaneous folders, and individual folders are usual parts of an alphabetical file system whether drawer or open-shelf. (See Figure 5–5.)

Guides are signaling devices used in drawer and shelf files to help locate file sections and individual folders. The notation may be either open (A, Ah, Am, Ap) or closed (Aa–Ag, Ah–Al, Am–Ao, Ap–Aq). Open captions are recommended. They are more flexible than closed ones because new alphabetic divisions can be inserted easily.

Individual Folders. Each name with five or more items should have its own folder with the name clearly marked on the tab. (See Figure 5–6.) This is called a caption and may be either handwritten, printed, or typed on a label which is then pasted over the tab. The filing/indexing rules are followed in preparing individual folder captions. Most recent dates come first in the folders.

Individual folders are alphabetized behind related guides. If a file is used often (active), put only six to ten folders behind a guide. When a file is relatively inactive (storage), one guide may be enough for fifteen to twenty-five folders.

Miscellaneous Folders are labeled to correspond to the guide captions. They are used to accumulate items which do not have individual folders. When there are five or six items under the same name, an individual folder should be prepared. In the meantime, pa-

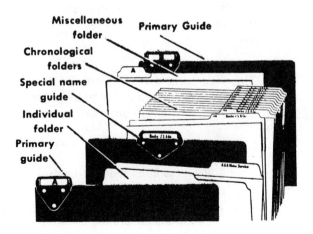

FIGURE 5–5. Typical file arrangement.

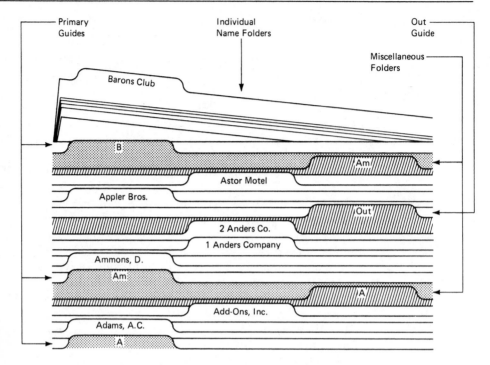

FIGURE 5—6. A correspondence filing system.

pers in miscellaneous folders are alphabetized. When two or more papers relate to the same name, arrange them chronologically with the
most recent date on top. Miscellaneous folders are usually put at
the end of each section, thus also signaling the end of that section of
the file. Uniquely colored tabs in assigned positions may also be used.

Filing

This step is the actual placing of items into open-shelf files or drawer
folders. The procedure for putting items into vertical files is described
in the following; the procedure for open-shelf filing is similar.

1. Put items to be filed on a handy, flat surface near the area in which
   you work.
2. Read the filing code on the item to be filed.
3. Find the right filing storage section.
4. Starting at the front of the section, scan guide and folder tabs until
   you locate the desired folder.
5. Raise the folder and open it. When raising a folder, grasp it in the
   center, not by the tab. Pulling folders by their tabs is hard on the tab
   and may tear the folder.

6. Compare the tab and code to make sure you have the right folder.

7. Put the document into the folder with the heading facing left. If you do not find a folder with the desired name, put the item into the miscellaneous folder for that section. When you do so, check to see if five[9] or more papers have accumulated for that name. If they have, make a separate folder for them.

8. After filing in a section is finished, bring the "follower" at the end of the section up as tightly as possible to help keep all contents upright.

A General Guideline

Use labor-saving devices whenever possible. Work smarter.

The filing procedure is really a subsystem of the total records management system. It is a very important subsystem though because the effectiveness of the entire system depends on the accuracy and efficiency of this subsystem. Flow diagrammed, the steps of the filing subsystem are shown in Figure 5–7.[10]

Some Filing Tips

File records face forward.

Leave one-fifth of a file drawer, or at least 4 inches, for expansion and working space.

"Break" a folder when it contains more than 100 pieces or it is over three-fourths of an inch thick. Make a new folder for the most recent records. Underscore the caption on the old folder in color (red?) so that all new items will be put in the new folder. In addition to the usual alphabetical caption, the first folder might be labeled January 1982–July 1983; the new folder would be labeled August 1983.

Work from the side of a file cabinet rather than from the front. It is easier. However, work directly in front of open-shelf files.

Avoid accidents by opening only one file drawer at a time. Close a drawer as soon as you finish working in it.

Use folders with pockets for swatches, catalogs, or samples; same tab cut as the related folder.

When handling a folder in a drawer, lift it up and rest it part of the way on the side of the drawer. In this way, you can insert papers without losing your place in the file. When you remove a file for quick reference, pull the next file up slightly to mark the place.

In active files, use a guide for every 6–8 folders (1 inch of space); about 20–25 to a drawer.

[9]The number varies a little according to the company and type of files. It is a policy decision.
[10]Figure 5–7 is essentially a manual subsystem. See Chapter 14 for an automated system.

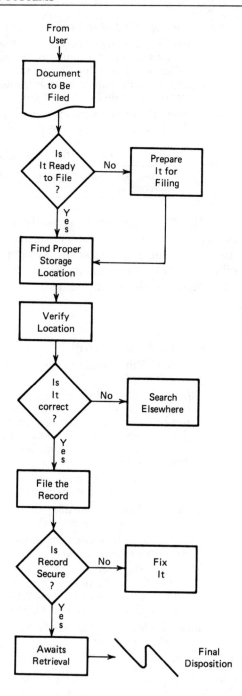

FIGURE 5–7. The filing subsystem.

Retrieving

Throughout the world today there is a new awareness of the value and importance of information. The value of well-processed information as a commodity that facilitates decision making and encourages communication among people is being recognized. More and more attention is being given, therefore, to the processing and handling of paperwork. The tons of paperwork that move through a modern office are of little value unless the information it supplies can be found and used when needed. When a record cannot be found or is found too late, it might as well not have existed. The problem, then, is not just to get records out of the way and stored in safer places than tops of desks or tables. The real issue is, can an item be found when someone wants it?

Today's emphasis is on the fast retrieval of stored information. In fact, one can say that today's managers are more dependent on finding systems than filing systems. Of course, the two systems are interdependent. Items are more likely to be found if they are stored in well-organized systems.

The retrieval procedure is a subsystem of the entire records management system and, as already stated, it is a very important one. It is made up of a series of separate activities as follows:

1. Someone wants and requests some recorded information.
2. The request is received and acted on. A search is made in the location where the record is supposed to be.
3. If the record is found, it is taken out of the file.
4. A charge-out record is created to show where the record was sent and when.
5. The record is sent to the requestor. A due date may be indicated.
6. Ultimately the record is returned to the files.
7. If the record is not located, the requestor is notified.

The retrieval subsystem can be flow diagrammed as shown in Figure 5–8.[11]

Retrieving is finding. A goal of every system is to enable people to find an item when it is needed as quickly as possible. Mis-files and hard-to-locate records are often caused by the following:

1. Filing stations are overcrowded so that there is not enough work space either for efficient filing or finding.
2. Folders are overloaded.

---

[11]Figure 5–8 is essentially a manual retrieval subsystem. For a computer retrieval system, see Chapter 14.

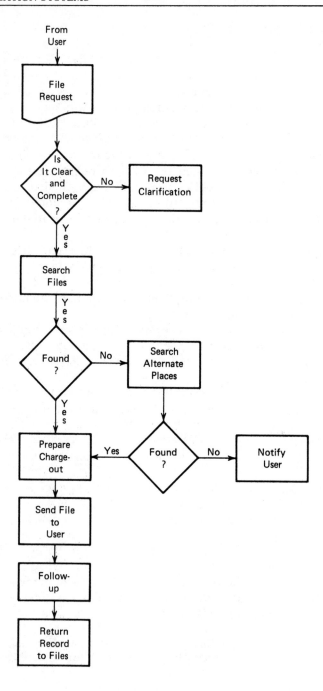

Figure 5—8. The retrieval subsystem.

3. Tabs are frayed, faded, or missing.
4. Paper clips pick up papers and attach them to other records where they do not belong.
5. Papers are not adequately cross-referenced.
6. The paper was filed incorrectly; perhaps it was inserted before or after the folder so that it is between folders.
7. The paper was incorrectly indexed and coded.
8. An untrained person used the files.

The following suggestions may help you find a misfiled record.

1. If only one document is lost, chances are that it is in the wrong folder. Check the folder in front and in back of the folder in which it should be.
2. Look in the sorter.
3. Look under other likely indexing units.
4. If an entire folder is missing, look in
    a. your desk, especially the out-basket
    b. the boss's desk and out-basket
    c. folders with similar names
    d. the transferred files
    e. the charge-out file.

REVIEW QUESTIONS

1. Why do we need to standardize filing rules?
2. What are some differences between filing company names and individual names?
3. What are some differences between filing government names and individual names?
4. What did the employee in central files mean when he said, "Cross referencing can be both a boon and a headache"?
5. If your employer asked you to get a letter from Harry Smith from a project file and you could not find it, what would you do? If you eventually found it in the top drawer of your employer's desk, what would you say?
6. Why is a release mark used on documents to be filed?
7. What does "conditioning" items for filing involve?
8. Describe the basic steps in preparing papers for filing.
9. What is the procedure for selecting an indexing caption?
10. Describe five ways to save time and energy in filing.

LEARNING ACTIVITIES

1. Prepare an index card and necessary cross-reference cards for the following names. Then alphabetize them.

   1. McCall Oil Company
   2. Directors' Furniture Store, Inc.
   3. Bowling Green State University
   4. Hansberry's Appliance Parts Co.
   5. Harold Meier & J. Frank World Travel Bureau
   6. Far-away Travel Service
   7. Tracy Caron, IV, Investment Consultant
   8. TV Mart
   9. B & C Radio & TV
  10. KYXI Radio Station
  11. Lake of the Woods Transmission Specialists
  12. Ohio Transmission Warehouse
  13. Mt. Ranier View Motel
  14. Heidelberg-Schlitz Malt Beverages
  15. General Electric Corp., Maytag Division, Lake Oswego
      B & I Appliance Outlet

2. Find the misfiled item(s) in each of the following groups.

Show the correct sequence on an answer sheet, referring to the items by the numbers and letters used below.

(1) a. The Uhde Corporation
    b. George Uhe Company, Inc.
    c. Senor Juan Uhkiv

(2) a. Mascot's Stores
    b. Mascot, Emma
    c. Mask-O-Neg Co.

(3) a. Arima Trading Assn.
    b. Ari-Evan, Matthew
    c. Arimex Importers, Inc.

(4) a. A & B Auto Rental Service
    b. Ab Bender's Binding Corp.
    c. The AB Radio Station

(5) a. A-One Furniture Store
    b. A-1 Sprinkler System
    c. A-1 Answering Service

(6) a. A & P Food Stores
    b. AP Chemicals
    c. A. P. Little Consultants, Inc.

(7) a. The 904 Avenue Club
    b. Fourth Avenue Gift Shop
    c. The 18 Club

(8) a. 1814 Amsterdam Cafe
    b. 1804 Second Ave. Corporation
    c. 18 East 45th Street Club

(9) a. Neoberg Furs
    b. Neo-Art Studio
    c. Neopolitan Opera Company

(10) a. The University of New Mexico
     b. The Union Club
     c. Novelty Gift Shop

3. On an answer sheet, indicate the correct filing sequence for the following names. Indicate the filing rules that apply.

   1. Martin-Clinton Corporation

   2. Ann Arbor Clothing Store

   3. O and N Garage

   4. East Side Auto Parts

   5. O K Auto Service

   6. Paul's Musical Repair Shop

   7. Northwest Pipe & Supply Company

   8. Union Savings Bank of Manchester

   9. National Bank of Ypsilanti

  10. Slaussen Public High School, Albion, Ohio

  11. Fort Crook Training Center

  12. Navy Officer Recruiting

  13. Civil Air Patrol Headquarters

  14. Multnomah County Implement Center

  15. Michigan (State of) Consumer Protection Division

4. Read the following statements and indicate by a C on your answer sheet those items that you consider to be good filing practices. If you do not agree with the item, do not put a letter on the answer sheet after the number of the statement.

   1. When an item to be filed covers more than one subject, name, etc., cross-reference by the subjects and names that are most likely to be used when the item is requested.

   2. Make an extra carbon copy or a photocopy of an item that is to be cross-referenced.

   3. Mark cross-referenced copies to indicate who signed the cross-reference sheet.

   4. When your boss fails to release an item for the files by initialing it, you may do it for him.

   5. Rough sort items in the same sequence as the file tab guides in which the papers are to be placed.

   6. Fasten items together with a staple when you are reasonably certain they will be asked for in that way.

7. Avoid using color coding in filing systems because it gets confusing.

8. When you have oversized or bulky material to file, cross-reference it.

9. It is not necessary to keep your filing up-to-date.

10. Have your boss turn papers over to you to file.

11. It is all right to let anyone who wishes use your files.

12. File copies of form or routine letters do not have to be made.

5. Write the number of the term in the list on the left that fits the description.

1. Unit	1. Marking procedure for correspondence to facilitate filing.
2. Storing	2. Preliminary alphabetizing of papers according to captions.
3. Sorting	3. Mental determination of caption under which correspondence will be filed.
4. Release marks	4. Each part of a name used in alphabetizing.
5. Label	5. Easily accessible filing cabinets for frequently used records.
6. Collecting	6. Titles printed on guide tabs.
7. Individual folder	7. Notations indicating correspondence is ready to be filed.
8. Indexing	8. The first step in preparing correspondence for the file.
9. Finding	9. Should be used to identify a folder.
10. Filing	10. Standard, vertical storage place for files.
11. Drawer	11. Has the basic function of storage and accessibility.
12. Coding	
13. Classifying	
14. Captions	
15. Active files	

6. After each item in the following list, write the number of the file drawer that it goes into.

Example: D. I. Derizinski

Answer: 13

Aa–Al 1	Bar–Bd 5	Caa–Cd 9	Daa–Dn 13	Fi–Fq 17	Haa–Hem 21	Jo–Jz 25	Ku–Kz 29
Am–Aq 2	Bea–Bk 6	Ce–Cn 10	Doa–Dz 14	Fr–Fz 18	Hen–Hol 22	Ka–Kd 26	Laa–Ln 30
Ar–Az 3	Bl–Bq 7	Coa–Coo 11	Ea–Eq 15	Ga–Gq 19	Hom–Hz 23	Kea–Kol 27	Loa–Lz 31
Bas–Baq 4	Bra–Bz 8	Cop–Cz 12	Er–Fh 16	Gra–Gz 20	I–Jn 24	Kom–Kt 28	Maa–Mn 32

A battery of vertical files.

1. Kirby, Donna _____
2. Garlough, Glenn _____
3. Duer, Albrecht _____
4. Beuerle, Reuben _____
5. Cotterman, Mayme _____
6. Friedrich, Caspar _____
7. Antones, Rachel _____
8. Mao, Philip _____
9. Borch, Gerard _____
10. Haythorn, George _____
11. Grimmer, James _____
12. Blaschak, Arlene _____
13. Djeduski, Stanley _____
14. Gauntlett, Edgar _____
15. Hecht, Bonny _____
16. Cebulkey, Sue _____
17. Anttonen, Gwen _____

18. Dworkin, Cal   _____
19. Cloke, Della   _____
20. Lochner, Stefan   _____
21. Felbeck, Tena   _____
22. Isenbrant, Adriaen   _____
23. Cheever, Reva   _____
24. Atkins, Hugh   _____
25. Hoagbin, Naomi   _____
26. di Pietro, Sano   _____
27. Ivany, Dorothy   _____
28. Kishimoto, Ya   _____
29. Fukano, Mao   _____
30. Memling, Ilana   _____
31. Gaede, James   _____
32. Jeserich, Paul   _____
33. Martini, Simone   _____
34. Kirchner, Ennid   _____
35. Courtney, Ashley   _____
36. Feallock, Bette   _____
37. Matsys, Quinten   _____
38. Leestma, Leo   _____
39. McArdle, Lyod   _____
40. Enid, Helen   _____

7. On an answer sheet, write the letter (a, b, c. or d) that identifies the name that should be filed *last* in each of the following series.

1. (a) Mary Jane Johnson
   (b) Mary Johnston
   (c) Marie Jane Johnston
   (d) Marianne Johnson

2. (a) University of Oregon
   (b) U S National Bank of Oregon
   (c) Oregon Hilton Hotel
   (d) Portland (Oregon) Secretarial School

3. (a) Hilton Washington Hotel
   (b) University of Washington
   (c) The National Bank of Washington
   (d) Washington Banking School

4. (a) James MacCrea
   (b) J. B. McCrea
   (c) The Mac Crea Shoe Stores
   (d) Macreal Sporting Goods

5. (a) The 500 Club
   (b) 10-Hour Cleaners
   (c) 4-Points Motel
   (d) The 20th Century Science Foundation

6. (a) Friar Jim's Lunch Room
   (b) Father Jerald
   (c) Father's Motor Hotel
   (d) The Friars Seminary

7. (a) The Northwest Travel Agency
   (b) The North West Airlines
   (c) Great Northern Lumber Company
   (d) Eileen North (Mrs. Wesley)

8. (a) Arizona Holiday Motor Hotel
   (b) Arnold Plumbing Company
   (c) Arnold's Petroleum Service
   (d) Arnold's Ski Shop

9. (a) Emily Beeson O'Neal
   (b) Eunice O'Neal (Mrs. Edward)
   (c) ONEAL's Body Shop
   (d) E. E. O'Neil

10. (a) Sara Sutherland (Mrs. Stanley)
    (b) S C M Corporation
    (c) Sutton Electrostatic Dry Copier
    (d) Copyright Service

11. (a) Safe-Way Crown Cleaning
    (b) S. A. Waring
    (c) School of Custom Dress Design
    (d) The Seeing-Eye School of Seattle

12. (a) Prince Phillip
    (b) Rose Festival Queen
    (c) General George Mitchell
    (d) Bishop John Keaning

13. (a) USSR
    (b) USA
    (c) Dominion of Canada
    (d) Republic of France

14. (a) Arizona State University at Tempe
    (b) The State University of Arizona
    (c) Austin Peay State College
    (d) Pasadena School of the Sacred Heart

15. (a) California School of Fine Arts
    (b) California State College at Long Beach
    (c) California Maritime Academy
    (d) University of California, Medical Center

16. (a) Donald C. Underwood, II
    (b) D. C. Underwood, III
    (c) D. Underwood, Jr.
    (d) D. Carl Underwood, Sr.

17. (a) Hahnemann Medical Center
    (b) Hampden-Sydney College
    (c) Hampden-Sydney Community College
    (d) Adolph D. Hamilton Medical Center

18. (a) New Jersey Women's College
    (b) Mt. St. Joseph Teachers College
    (c) Misericordia Community College
    (d) Mary Washington College at Lexington

19. (a) University of North Dakota
    (b) Northern Illinois University
    (c) Northern School of Mines
    (d) The City University of New York

20. (a) United Church Training School
    (b) Military Academy at West Point, New York
    (c) United States Naval Postgraduate School
    (d) United University

6

Numeric Systems

Numeric indexing systems are used more and more because computers handle numbers more efficiently than alphabetic characters. Before computer technology took over, numeric systems were used sparingly. They were considered as *indirect* systems because the alphabet is the basic classification system in manual filing, and when items were classified by number, a relative alphabetic index usually had to be consulted to get the number. That is, numeric files were also referenced by a name, subject, or location. Nevertheless, numeric systems were used for certain types of records (checks, inventories, parts, invoices, hospital cases, to name a few). Today though, practically all computer "files" are number based.

COMPUTER INFORMATION

Any type of record can be converted to a numeric system. Computer systems analysts say that any piece of information can be represented by a number and every number can be represented by a hole on a punched card or as a magnetic spot. Because computer systems are numeric, large companies with computer centers are converting more and more alphabetic files to numeric systems for computer processing. After all, when computers are used, information can be retrieved at the flick of a switch, information can be sent to a variety of locations via terminal connections, and memory banks of millions of characters can be addressed and searched with the speed of light.

NUMERIC SYSTEMS

There are many different types of numeric systems: chronological, sequential, significant (codes), decimal-numeric, and even alphanumeric. They can be cards or folders, open-shelf or drawer. They can be straight numeric, also called direct numeric because the contents are referenced first by number since the guide labels are numeric. Special coded systems such as Soundex may combine letters with numbers but are basically numeric systems.

Numeric files may be combined with name files (numeric name system) with numeric primary guides and alphabetic folders backed up by numbers so that individual folders show both a number and name. (See Figure 6–1.)

When named files are also numbered, it is helpful if correspondents remember to include the number when writing, otherwise it has to be looked up in the relative index.

Sets of date guides or folders (1, 2 . . . 12 months or 1, 2 . . .31 days) may be inserted into an alphabetical system to incorporate a tickler subsystem. Charge-out slips, although they give the name of the user, are filed by date with the oldest dates at the front of the file. All tickler files are chronological.

Samples of various types of numeric systems are described in this chapter as follows:

Serial	Chronological/Tickler
Coded Numeric	Alpha-Numeric
Block Codes	Terminal Digit
Soundex	Middle Digit

In numeric systems, each document has a number. Some business records are traditionally handled by number: checks, order forms, inventory parts, catalog items, invoices, contracts, licenses, to name a few. In government, numbers are used in social security, compensation files, licenses, etc.

ADVANTAGES OF NUMERIC FILING

Numeric systems have several advantages. They help to batch records within categories. Batching is especially useful in medical, dental, research, and insurance records which tend to cluster into case histories. For example, when a company works with funded research, all relevant material can be marked with the numbers assigned to the projects so they can be properly identified.

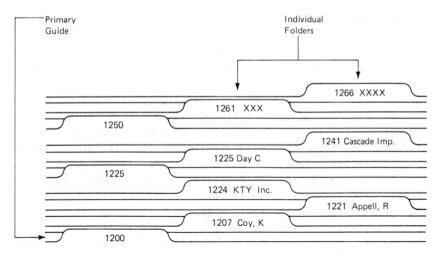

FIGURE 6–1. Combined numeric-name system.

Numeric files are also easy to expand; alphabetical files are limited to 26 letters. As a case expands, new phases or sub-contracts can be added to the main number without disturbing the sequence. For example, if the main case is No. 679, it can be expanded as follows: 679.1 or 679.100.

Misfiled folders are easy to detect. They are obviously out of place. Numbers that are out of sequence are recognized more easily than letters; for example, *7* is immediately detected as out of sequence in 5, 6, 8, 7, 9, but *n* is not so quickly spotted as being out of sequence in k, l, n, m, o, p. . . .

Confidential Information

A numeric system is useful for filing confidential information because there is a certain amount of secrecy to it. The identity of the records to which numbers are assigned is known only to those who understand the system. Unauthorized persons cannot find a file as easily as when an alphabetical system is used. This confidentiality feature is used by Swiss banks where accounts are identified by number, thus protecting customer identity. However, when names in an alphabetic correspondence system are assigned numbers, a double filing system actually results (alpha-numeric—name and number). This double system may be useful in certain types of records; for example, files where an alphabetical back-up system provides an alternative way to locate records. On the whole, the numeric system is impractical for correspondence files.

TYPES OF NUMERIC SYSTEMS

Basically there are two types of numbering systems: (1) serial or consecutive: 1, 2, 3, 4 . . . and (2) coded or significant: 43.8–01:80.

Serial Numeric Systems

The simplest numeric system involves numbering items consecutively in ascending order. This is called the *serial numeric system.*

The serial numeric system is a straightforward method; missing numbers can be noticed easily, thus all numbers can be traced and accounted for. The identity of each number is relatively uncomplicated; it is merely a number in a series:

754, 755, 756, 757, 759, 760, 761, 764, 765 (Missing: 758, 762, 763)

When the serial number system is used for items that are not prenumbered, numbers may be assigned. For example, when a patient is admitted to a medical center, the next available accession number is assigned. The record is then filed by number and cross-referenced to the name. Or, when new automobiles come off a production line, each is assigned the next available "serial" number. That number is then used throughout the system to represent that particular car in transaction records, shipping records, correspondence with dealers, and so on.

Coded Numeric Filing Systems

Some companies do not like straight serial numbering systems because the numbers are nonsignificant. Such numbers, they say, do not tell anything about the item. For example, a straight sequential product number does not tell anything about the size, capacity, model, or function. *Code numbers* on the other hand can do this when certain meaningful letters or key numbers are inserted.

Code numbers may be derived from the item to be filed. Both letters and numbers can be used. Codes are sometimes called *mnemonic systems* because the numbers take on meaning. For example, states use mnemonics in license number systems. The first digit may indicate cities in order of their size, and the second indicate the county. Hence, a Nebraska car license No. 1-4-830 could decode as Omaha (largest city in Nebraska, therefore No. 1), and Douglas County (one of the counties in the area covered by Omaha and identified as No. 4). There are, of course, many other ways of coding license numbers. Social security and zip code numbers are other examples of mnemonic or significant numbering systems. For example, the original United States Zip Code system is a 5-digit number that relates to areas of the country. The first three digits stand for either a particular Section or a metropolitan city. The last two digits of these first three identify post offices in the sectionalized center of the city or Section. The last two digits stand for a delivery area served by the city post office, its branches and stations—

> 73118:   731 Sectionalized Center
>   18 Delivery area in that section

In business, a code could be based on location, function within the organization such as accounting, marketing or production; the originator of the document; and the purpose of the document. For example, a large lumber products industry like Georgia-Pacific, Inc. which has subsidiaries all over the North American continent might code home-office records as follows

> 5 represents southeastern forests
> 18 represents plywood production
> 118 represents tax data for 10-year timber stands
> 11 represents documents *originated* in the home office

Therefore, a document numbered 5-18-118-11 would be identified as relating to taxes on 10-year stands in the southeastern section of the United States being used or marked for use as plywood. The document originated in the home office and related records are probably there also. If not, they can be identified as belonging to the topic by being assigned 5 for southeastern forests, 18 for plywood production, and/or 118 for tax data: 5-18-118.

Block Codes

A *block code* is a simple modification of a straight sequential numbering system. That is, blocks of numbers may be set aside for items that have a common characteristic. For example, Nos. 1–25 might be set aside for accounting forms in a company, Nos. 26–50 for all advertising department forms, 51–57 for administrative forms, and so on. Such numbers soon become identified with the departments to which they have been issued so that, at a glance, when you see Form 30-AG-14, you know it relates to advertising. It has become, therefore, a significant number.

Soundex Code

The conventional Soundex system for manual files converts a name to a 4-character code: one alphabetic character and three numbers, L821. The conversion rules are as follows:

1. Always retain the initial letter of each name.
2. Drop out A, E, I, O, U, Y, W, and H.
3. Assign the following numbers to the remaining similar sounding sets of letters:

$$1 = B, F, P, V$$
$$2 = C, G, J, K, Q, S, X, Z$$
$$3 = D, T$$
$$4 = L$$
$$5 = M, N$$
$$6 = R$$

Example: Pétérsén = P362

4. Special situations:
   a. If there are insufficient letters, fill out with zeros: Stráy = S360
   b. Drop out the second letter in a pair: Túnńéy = T500
   c. Drop out adjacent equivalent letters: Tráckśét = T623
   d. Drop out adjacent equivalents of the first letter: Llámár = L560

The objective of many coding situations is to condense the content of the words and titles by substituting numbers or letters. In Soundex, the substitution is for phonetics. Most shorthand writing systems are phonetic, substituting graphic symbols such as circles, curved lines, dots, or straight lines for sounds, thus reducing the bulk of material that has to be written.

The Soundex system or modifications of it are especially helpful when names that sound alike are spelled differently: for example, Nickels, Nickeles, Nickollas, etc. In such instances, two things can be done: (1) names may be grouped under one common spelling and cross-referenced or, (2) names may be filed by phonetic spelling (Soundex) rather than unit by unit and letter by letter.

When a system is large and contains many similar sounding words or foreign or unusual names with difficult spellings, a phonetic system may be helpful. The authors have seen this system used effectively as a back-up to an alphabetic name file of over a hundred thousand accumulated medical histories.

TERMINAL- OR MIDDLE-DIGIT FILING

A problem with serial numeric filing is that, over time, numbers assigned may run into six and seven digits. Furthermore, as records are retired to storage, gaps appear in the numbering system, and records become unevenly distributed throughout the system. The larger a serial file system, the harder it is to file items accurately because human beings do not handle six- and seven-digit numbers comfortably. It is easy to transpose them. To make matters worse, the most recent additions with the longest numbers are probably on the most active files.

Terminal-digit filing was developed to overcome the problems of serial numeric filling in large systems. It is a space-saving and work-spreading system. The basic difference between regular numeric files and terminal-digit is that, with the latter, the numbers are read from left to right; they are read in reverse. That is, instead of filing in strict numeric sequence, the numbers are read backwards and items are filed by the last digits of the number. For example, a mortgage file bearing the number 377343 would be thought of and filed as follows:

$$\underset{\text{tertiary}}{37} \quad \underset{\text{secondary}}{73} \quad \underset{\text{primary}}{43} \quad \text{or} \quad \underset{\text{secondary}}{377} \quad \underset{\text{primary}}{343}$$

For convenience in reading, the numbers are broken into primary and secondary groupings in sets of twos or threes. In the file itself, guides with numbered tabs separate folders into easy-to-find groups whether open-shelf or drawer files are used. Primary guides are numbered from 00 to 99 when numbers are divided into groups of two figures. Between these primary guides are sets of numbered secondary guides. To find mortgage file 37 73 43, you go first to section 43, then to the secondary guide 73. Here the folder would be filed according to its tertiary number 37.

Gaps in Numerical Sequences

Consideration should be given to the terminal-digit system when records filed numerically are likely, as they age, to develop gaps in their numerical sequence. For example, assume that we have sequentially numbered insurance files which, as policies terminate and are removed from the files, leave gaps. In order to use these space gaps, it is necessary periodically to back-shift folders through all the cabinets or shelves of the system. Since this can involve very large quantities of files, it can be a mountainous and time-consuming chore. An outstanding advantage of the terminal-digit system is that no file area becomes more crowded or more empty than another. An equally important benefit is the elimination of back-shifting.

The terminal-digit system should be used whenever 10,000 or more cases or 25,000 or more cards with numbers of five or more digits are involved.

Distribution of Responsibility

To distribute responsibility for areas of work in large systems, the primary numbers from 00 to 99 can be apportioned by groups among personnel so that each is responsible for a separate section of the files. (See Figure 6–2.) This makes it possible to fix responsibility and to keep a record of returns and requests. A color guidance system may also be incorporated with the terminal-digit method as a further aid to accuracy and efficiency.

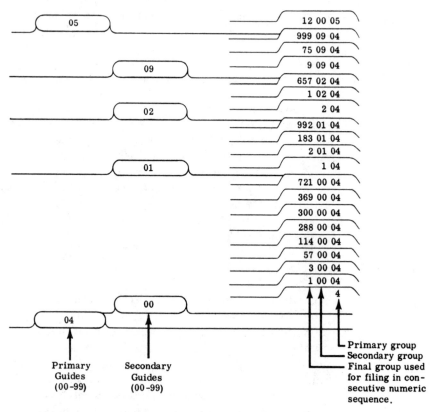

FIGURE 6–2. A terminal-digit file. (*Source: Place, Popham, Fujita,* Fundamental Filing Practice, © 1973. *Reprinted by permission of Prentice-Hall, Inc., Englewood Cliffs, N.J.*)

Let us look at another example of terminal-digit filing. Suppose three documents are numbered 769047, 769447, and 769947 respectively and that the system divides the numbers into sets of threes. Under the terminal-digit system, these items will be filed in different parts of the files because the first would be filed under 047, the second under 447, and the third under 947.

769   047
769   447
769   947

secondary   primary

Middle-Digit System

The middle-digit system is a variation of the terminal-digit system. (See Figure 6–3.) In it, numbers are separated into 2- or 3-digit groups, but the middle group is treated as the primary guide group:

6465402: 646-54-02   646   54   02

secondary   primary   tertiary

In a middle-digit system, the three above documents (769047, 769447, and 769947) would still appear in the same sequence even if a 2-digit grouping is used:

76   90   47
76   94   47
76   99   47

secondary   primary   tertiary

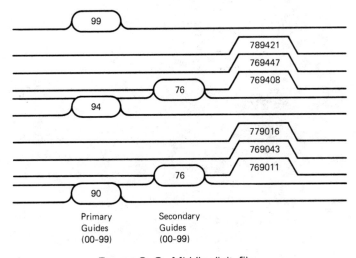

FIGURE 6–3. Middle-digit file.

Why use middle-digit instead of terminal-digit filing? People are naturally creative and as with most things, they get ideas for changes with experience and develop personal preferences. It is no surprise, therefore, that there has been experimentation with the basic terminal-digit concept. Advocates of the middle-digit system claim that it is more accurate than the terminal-digit system, spreads records more evenly and is easier to convert from a straight numerical system.

Small offices, unless they are branch offices, ordinarily do not use terminal-digit systems. Yet, since insurance and manufacturing companies often do, one should understand at least the rationale of the system. Open-shelf files are recommended for large terminal-digit systems. Figure 6–4 shows equipment that might be used for a system that combines hanging folders with rotary, motorized equipment to move the tiers of files.

Date Files

Date filing is useful for grouping documents by day, month, and year. Date files (also known as chronological files) are used for follow-up or tickler systems and have a mnemonic feature because they "tickle" the memory as to the date that an item needs attention.

FIGURE 6–4. A motorized filing system. *(Courtesy White Power Files, Inc.)*

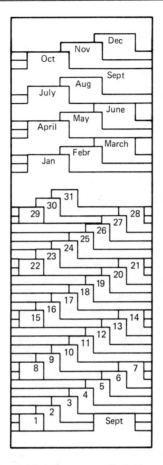

FIGURE 6—5. A "turn-around" tickler card file.

Card-File Tickler

A tickler file may also be a card file on which notations may be made on the cards themselves or memos may be dropped loosely behind the numbered (date) cards. Colored clip-on tabs may be used to signal special action. The entire system may be kept in a file box in a desk drawer or near the phone. Tickler systems, no matter what the type, are important supplemental filing systems and memory aids.

A tickler file can be incorporated into almost any filing system. For example, when used for out-file slips, it reminds one when an item should be returned to the central file. When used with a direct-name alphabetic correspondence file, it calls attention to follow-up actions that should be taken. You can accumulate in follow-up folders in a separate tickler system extra copies of letters or documents to be activated at a given time.

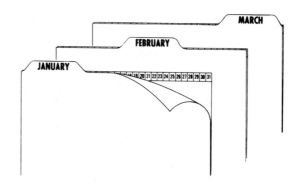

FIGURE 6—6. A date-tickler file. *(Courtesy Shaw Walker Co.)*

Tickler Folders

Physically, a tickler file can be merely a calendar or a series of thirty-one guides or folders numbered consecutively and kept separate from the main file for quick access.

Sets of date guides can, of course, be inserted in a correspondence filing system. The set can be a series of twelve (for the months) or four folders with tab labels 1–8, 9–16, 17–23, and 24–31 (for the days). A folder tickler may include special celluloid-edged folders with movable signals. (See Figure 6–7.)

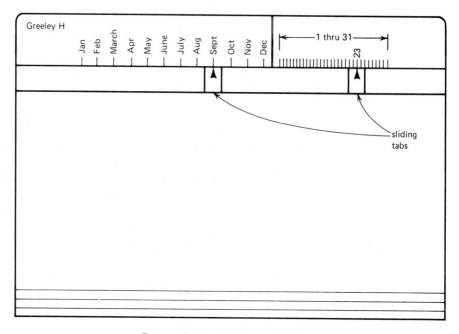

FIGURE 6—7. A follow-up folder.

ALPHA-NUMERIC FILING SYSTEMS

In those instances where for some reason or other name folders are assigned numbers, the file's primary guide captions should be numbers. Folder labels may show both the name and the number. Such dual labeling might be helpful in medical records. (See Figure 6–8.)

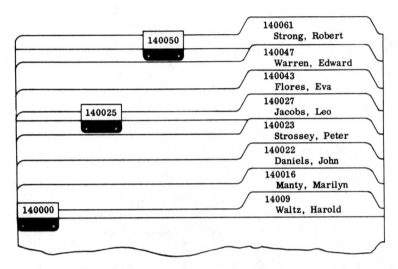

FIGURE 6–8. A numeric-name file. (*Source: Place, Popham, Fujita,* Fundamental Filing Practice, © 1973. *Reprinted by permission of Prentice-Hall, Inc., Englewood Cliffs, N.J.*)

Miscellaneous Folders

Although a numeric system does not use miscellaneous folders, in an alpha-numeric system, miscellaneous folders are positioned similarly to the way they are in alphabetical correspondence files. There should be one miscellaneous folder for each primary guide; when there are five or so papers for a number, an individual folder should be made. Folders numbered to correspond to the guides are clustered behind them in numeric suquence. Primary guides may be numbered in the hundreds or thousands, and the secondary guides, in tens or hundreds. (See Figure 6–9.)

Guide and folder tabs may be straight line or staggered arrangements. One guide is recommended for every five to ten folders. Serial numbering systems can be expanded through the decimal or alpha-numeric systems described in Chapter 7, Subject Classification Systems.

	Primary Guides	Secondary Guides
Hundreds	100	110,120,130,140,150,160,170,180,190
	200	210,220, etc.
	300	310,320, etc.
Thousands	4000	4100,4200,4300,4400,4500,4600,4700,4800, 4900
	5000	5100,5200,5300, etc.
	6000	6100,6200,6300, etc.

FIGURE 6–9. Numeric guides.

Relative Index

Because even the most remarkable memory cannot remember numbers assigned to a variety of records, some type of related index, filed alphabetically by name or subject, is generally used as a back-up for a numeric system. That is, behind every numeric system, there is some type of alphabetized reference index which gives names or subjects that may be sought in the numbered file. A card file is often used for the related index. Index cards are natural annotation collectors, make cross referencing easy, and provide a flexible list of names, addresses, or subjects. A card index is easy to update and manipulate; however, the index may also be kept in a book (an accession book), in a loose-leaf folder, or if not too long, it may be typed on a single sheet of stationery and posted on the side of a file or desk.

Because the related index must be consulted before an item can be located in a numeric system, numeric filing systems are considered to be *indirect*. If for instance, you want the file for the Robin Anderson Estate, in a numeric system, you refer first to the related index to find the number under which the estate documents are filed. Assume, for example, that you work in a law office and a new case (Client Harold J. Harney) is assigned number 81522. The next week, a document for the Harney case comes to the files. We find the number previously assigned to this client by consulting the relative index. The index card should give the name and address of the client and the case number. Other useful information may be included, as shown in Figure 6–10.

Accession Book

An adjunct to a serial numeric system may be an accession book that can also serve as a relative index. For example, in the relatively small

Name: *Harvey, Harold J*	File Number:
Address: 406 Evans Ave / Columbus, Ohio	*81 522*
Acct. Opened: *1/7*	Related File Nos: *10520* *72 461*
Subject: *Pension Plan Laws* See: *Ohio Statute 43-LP-06* *Mich. " 94-PLS-61.8*	*No court action*

FIGURE 6–10. Related index card. (*Source: Place, Popham, Fujita,* Fundamental Filing Practice, © 1973. *Reprinted by permission of Prentice-Hall, Inc., Englewood Cliffs, N.J.*)

professional office of an M.D., dentist, or lawyer, where an average of seven new cases are recorded a week, it seems easier for an office assistant (who may be a registered nurse or a para-legal assistant) to record new clients in an accession book sequentially as they come in.

An accession book shows the next number available for assignment and reduces the chance of making the mistake of assigning the same number to two different cases. It may later be used as a back-up reference to find the number or name of a lost file. An accession book can, of course, become cumbersome to reference as a business grows. (See Figure 6–11.)

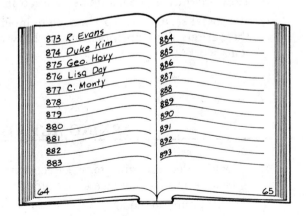

FIGURE 6–11. Accession book.

REVIEW QUESTIONS

1. What is a numeric filing system? Give an example.
2. What are the advantages of numeric filing systems? What are the disadvantages?
3. What is a serial numeric filing system?
4. Describe a situation where a serial numeric system might be used.
5. What is a coded numeric system?
6. Describe a situation where a coded numeric filing system might be used.
7. What are the advantages of a serial numeric filing system? What are the disadvantages?
8. What are the advantages of a coded numeric filing system? What are the disadvantages?
9. Why are numeric systems sometimes used with alphabetical name systems?
10. Why does a numeric filing system need a "related" file? Give an example.
11. What is terminal-digit filing? Give an example of how it works.
12. What is an advantage of terminal-digit filing? What is a disadvantage?
13. What is a tickler system?
14. Describe a type of tickler file a secretary might keep.
15. Give three examples of mnemonic code systems you encounter in your daily life.
16. How are miscellaneous items handled in numeric filing systems?
17. If a social security and a zip code number are mnemonic, what do the various digit positions mean? How do these mnemonic systems work?

LEARNING ACTIVITIES

1. Define the following terms. Record the definitions neatly; use each term in a sentence about office work.
    1. Mnemonic codes
    2. Nonsignificant numbers

   3. Relative index

   4. Serial numbering

   5. Consecutive numbering

   6. Sequence

   7. Ordered numbering

   8. Significant numbers

   9. Terminal-digit numbering

   10. Tickler files

2. Arrange the following numbers for terminal-digit filing.

   1. 531,603

   2. 54,484

   3. 224,083

   4. 843,278

   5. 83,678

   6. 313,639

   7. 152,809

   8. 353,834

PROJECTS

Project 1. Follow-up

Purpose:

This project aims to:

1. help you develop judgment in estimating follow-up time;
2. give you experience with a follow-up file.

Instructions:

Assume that you work for the president of Central Community College and the items listed below are on your desk to be marked for the tickler file.

1. Prepare an appropriate answer sheet.
2. Indicate the appropriate follow-up date for each by checking in the proper column.

		3–7 days	2–3 weeks	Other (Explain)
a.	Notes for an article for the yearbook.		✓	✓
b.	A letter from a prospective teacher.	✓		
c.	A committee report. The next meeting is the week after next.	✓		
d.	Notes for a special lecture to be given in four weeks.			
e.	An announcement about a student-faculty meeting to be held in ten days.			
f.	A letter from a professional group asking for a conference as soon as possible.			
g.	A note about arranging a meeting in three weeks for a visiting instructor.			
h.	A note about a conference with the head of the Physical Education Department to examine some departmental enrollment data.			
i.	A report from a professional association with material in it to be reproduced for use in a large seminar scheduled for the last week of the semester—ten weeks from now.			
j.	A schedule of information about a workshop being planned by your department. The workshop will be held in four weeks.			
k.	Information for the next faculty meeting.			
l.	A reminder to the teachers about ordering new library material for next years courses.			
m.	A note about talking with department heads about changes in course descriptions for the next college catalogue.			
n.	A note reminding the dean about a speaking engagement in six weeks.			

Project 2. Terminal Digits

This project aims to

1. help you better understand the concept of terminal-digit filing.
2. give you experience working with a numeric system.
3. give you experience working on a multiphased project.
4. help you, once again, to review rules for alphabetizing names.

This project uses the forty names that were alphabetized in Learning Activity 6, Chapter 5.

Assign the following customer subscription numbers to the alphabetized list and convert the numbered items to a terminal-digit system. List the names in the order they appear when filed by the terminal-digit system, thus showing how the arrangement differs from the alphabetical list prepared in Chapter 5.

Customer Subscription Numbers

1. 59565	11. 50490	21. 41340	31. 86436
2. 74617	12. 24899	22. 85252	32. 80402
3. 92043	13. 60192	23. 82759	33. 63183
4. 50279	14. 24910	24. 98383	34. 20035
5. 80184	15. 57466	25. 79051	35. 39500
6. 57755	16. 44700	26. 73978	36. 93613
7. 64595	17. 72615	27. 21090	37. 27342
8. 77534	18. 88396	28. 94088	38. 81281
9. 73988	19. 86480	29. 78666	39. 49428
10. 30381	20. 99682	30. 48283	40. 41729

7

Subject Classification Systems

This chapter considers classification systems in which subject titles are given to items that are then arranged alphabetically or in some order adapted to meet the needs of the situation. The yellow pages of a telephone directory are an example of subject filing. A telephone book is also a good example of how to back up an alphabetic name file with a subject index, to re-enforce the one with the other. Can you imagine trying to find the name and telephone number of a television repairman in your neighborhood, of a pet hospital, or of a used car dealer without the yellow pages? You couldn't do it in the white pages unless you knew the names of individuals in these businesses.

Libraries also back up a name file (by author) with a subject file. They further support the classifications with a decimal, alphanumeric system, thus simplifying the storing of items on the shelves (in the stacks) where they are arranged by number. For example, look in the subject card file under *Records Management* and get authors' names and book titles. Next check the author name files and get the reference number for the book you want. Then locate the book by number on the open shelves. The appropriate numbers are lettered at the bottom of the back binding of each book.

Advantages and Disadvantages

A chief advantage of classifying materials by subject is that it provides alternate titles for similar items, for example: employment, applications, or job descriptions. In this way subject classification identifies families of related topics. It is, therefore, a way to cluster related doc-

uments and information around a main title, and is useful in countless situations: the sciences, research and historical eras in archival
collections, to name a few.

Subject systems are also especially useful in small offices with
limited files. Topics coordinated with individual name files are easy
to find and maintain. They make the filing system more flexible.

The main disadvantage with subject classification systems is that
they can get involved, especially when subject headings are not easy
to pinpoint. This may lead to confusion in coding, cross-referencing,
and problems in developing relative indexes.

Businesses use subject filing for such reasons as the following:

1. To organize information that can be called for by subject as well as
   by individual names, thus providing an alternate way to index
   materials.

2. To expand and back up individual name correspondence files, thus
   making them more flexible.

3. To group together in one place papers about a single topic such as
   Insurance or *Meetings.*

4. To organize records that fall into several classifications or subdivisions of a main heading. (See Encyclopedic Arrangements on page
   145.)

Practical Applications

There is no one best way to organize the records of a company into
an orderly system of references for all users. Yet it is important to organize materials for maximum use—so we do our best. Known systems of classification are adapted and integrated to meet various types
of needs. For example, as a simple business correspondence file
grows, it usually becomes desirable to insert topics or descriptors[1]
such as *applications, tax records,* or *speaking engagements,* thus expanding the capability and usefulness of the file. For example, a document may involve a topic as well as names of one or more individuals or the name of an organization. A letter exists from Mr. Charles
E. Gregg, President of D. C. Lloyd and Company; he is also chairman
of the local Red Feather Drive. Although the letter is on the Lloyd
Company letterhead, it is about the Red Feather Drive. This letter

---

[1]A descriptor is a broad subject heading that stands for an idea or concept. It is chosen
as a *name* by which to call for stored materials by a particular group of users. A descriptor is an identification label; for example: Conservation, Contracts, Energy, Expenses,
Insurance, or Loans. It is selected as an overall name for groups of items. In this chapter,
words used as synonyms for descriptor are *title, subject, heading, topic,* and *caption.*

should be indexed and filed by both individual names (Gregg, Charles E.; Lloyd, D. C. and Company) and subject (Red Feather Drive; Charity Funds).

Appropriate Descriptors

Experience shows that when searching for an item, there is an overwhelming tendency to use names first, then topics. That is, when calling for files, users tend to associate names of people (or dates) with projects and activities rather than subject descriptors because it is easier to be specific and recall a name or date than a descriptor. In some instances, users even refer to geographical locations before they use subjects. They recall proper names, approximate time periods, or locations more readily than subjects, unless the subject is simple and well-known to them through frequent use.

Mr. Gregg's letter, then, may be indexed as Gregg, Charles or it can be filed by subject and cross-referenced to his name. The combined name and subject systems give a two-way reference. If the user does not remember Gregg's name, the records can be searched by subject. But by which subject? Which descriptor should be chosen: *Red Feather Drive; Drive, Community; Community Activities; Charity Funds; Contributions;* or *Fund Raising?* This situation illustrates one of the main problems of subject filing—the problem of choosing an appropriate, easy-to-use descriptor. Subject titles are not always easily apparent.

The problem of choosing appropriate descriptors for subject files grows in proportion to the number of users involved. Everyone has his/her favorite words and unique vocabulary. A descriptor that is easy for one person to recall may not come easily to another. Then too, nearly everything has at least two names. For example, consider a simple word like *Room.* Some alternates for this word are space, area, booth, chamber, cubical, apartment, capacity, range, scope, and lodging place.

The task of creating the descriptor for a subject file is often assigned to those who maintain the files, a secretary or an office assistant. Some topics are easy to decide upon; for example, *Applications.* This subject comes readily to mind when one wants to collect, in one folder, correspondence with people looking for jobs in the company and who have written letters or sent application forms. Most subjects, however, are not so easy to create. Some organizations have a very exact procedure to follow in originating and using descriptors. A manager or committee of records users decides on appropriate descriptors and then uses them on a company-wide basis.

SUBJECT CLASSIFICATIONS

A first consideration when designing a subject classification system is to determine the exact nature and quantity of the records. Study how they are called for, handled and used. Study what is to be filed including the size of items and characteristics, such as tapes or computer printouts. Are we looking at a few documents to be inserted in a private office name file kept by one person, or at a series of topics about activities in a professional organization like a local chapter of the Association of Records Managers and Administrators (ARMA) or the American Management Association (AMA)? Are we looking at a collection of books, samples, clippings, or reports about a funded research project on which five or more persons are working; or at a subject system in law, medicine, or accounting where prefabricated[2] subject classifications are available and where there may be cross-referencing to classifications as in pharmacy or biochemistry? In these latter instances, experienced and knowledgeable people are needed to set up the system. Special consultants may be employed. Books on the body of work being classified help to locate appropriate headings. For example, if the file being developed is on nursing homes, a geriatrics book in your local library would be useful.

Creating Descriptors

Whatever the situation, subject descriptors are needed and someone has to create them. In a relatively simple business system, where the subject file may be a spin-off or back-up for private or departmental files, an administrative assistant might take the lead in creating them. After the assistant confers with and reaches at least partial agreement with those who use the records, the descriptors, mutually conceived and at least tentatively agreed upon, should be tried out for a definite time (two or three months) to see how they work. Usually a limit of fifteen to twenty major subjects should be selected. The other classifications should be subdivisions.

---

[2]Prefabricated subject lists are available in such areas as accounting, medicine, agriculture, etc. They have been prepared by experts in these areas (sometimes endorsed by their national professional associations) and can be adapted to individual situations. Some sources for prefabricated classification systems are *Accounting* (American Institute of Certified Public Accountants); *Business* (Harvard Classification for Business Literature (H. W. Wilson Company, publisher); *General* (Subject Headings for the Information File, H. W. Wilson, 950 University Avenue, Bronx, New York 10452). A trained librarian can help you find sources for subject lists in your special interest areas.

If topics are hard to recall, cumbersome, or vague, they should be revised. For example, suppose it was decided to cluster correspondence and documents about company automobile insurance in back of the descriptor *Company Cars*.[3] As time passes, however, nearly everyone who calls for the materials asks for *Automobile Insurance*. Further study shows that the file contents are indeed mostly about car insurance. It is decided, therefore, to re-label the file. Let us assume that there is already a main heading in the files for *Insurance* behind which we have six folders labeled *Fire, Health, Home, Life, Personal,* and *Theft*. Why not label another folder *Automobile* and position it accordingly? We found that the first descriptor (Company Cars) was not a good choice. We tried it, but found it did not work well, so we change it.

It may take a year to get a satisfactory set of descriptors for a file and some titles may be changed several times. It is advisable to make changes only at stated intervals and not continuously. Changes should be made only by an authorized person even though several persons are involved in the decisions. Centralizing authority and responsibility controls and stabilizes the file.

CROSS REFERENCES

Some cross referencing is essential, but keep it under control. When several "names" are involved in a document or a project, cross referencing is necessary.

Procedure

Figure 7–1 shows the procedure for classifying and marking (including cross references) records for filing and is part of a records management manual of XYZ Company. It shows the recommended place on a document for writing the subject designation and the cross references that should be made. A copy of the item itself is often used for the cross reference because with modern technology, copies are easy to make. Or a cross-reference sheet or back-up card file can be made (see Figures 8–5 and 8–6) depending on the situation and on individual preferences.

---

[3]Whenever possible, descriptors should not be longer than three significant words.

```
                                              **  ①  Procedures, Office
XYZ COMPANY                                   **  ②  Filing

INTERDEPARTMENTAL
━━━━━━━━━━━━━━━━━━━━━━━━━━━━━━━━━━━━━━━━━━━

Date:     July 1, 19__

To:       All Departments            ④  ┌─────────────────┐
                                         │ File: a W       │
From:     Methods Department             ├─────────────────┤
       ** ③                              │ Refer to:       │
                                         ├─────────────────┤
                                         │ Follow-up:      │
                                         └─────────────────┘
Subject:  Procedure for Company Filing System
```

This exhibit represents a copy of a record properly classified and marked
for filing. It shows the preferred placement of file designations in the
upper right corner including the correct method of indicating what cross-
references should be made.

You will find the detailed procedures for classifying and marking records
explained in the Filing Manual (Subparagraph 3.1) which is being sent to
you under separate cover.

John Doe
John Doe
Manager

                                    Key:

                                    ① Subject (file designation)
                                    ② Cross-reference
                                    ③ Cross-reference
                                    ④ Action stamp
                                    **   Underline in red

FIGURE 7—1. A memorandum coded for subject filing and cross reference. (*Source:
Place, Popham, Fujita*, Fundamental Filing Practice, © 1973. *Reprinted
by permission of Prentice-Hall, Inc., Englewood Cliffs, N.J.)*

Examples

In any classification system, some cross referencing is helpful; indeed, essential. The following examples from the yellow pages of a
telephone directory illustrate subject cross referencing:

Academies
See *Schools*
Accident Insurance
See *Insurance*

Accountants—Public
Acetylene Welding
See *Welding*

"See" References

When cross referencing, there are two types of *"See"* References: (1) *See* . . . as used above and (2) *See also*. A *See* reference merely directs the user from one title to another. A *See also* reference directs one to additional material or closely related subjects; for example: *Recliners* (*See also* patio/yard furniture). It is a good idea not to be too liberal with *See also* references.

Separate Subject Files

As more subject descriptors enter a correspondence file, it may be useful to set them up as a separate file. This might be especially desirable when keeping personal files that include activities not directly related to the company's business. For example, suppose someone in the company has a farm as a hobby, raising breed horses and cattle. Assume that quite a few clippings, pictures, and literature about prize-winning horses and cattle have been amassed and now infiltrate the business correspondence files. Such material would surely be more useful and retrievable if kept separately. Removal would unclutter the correspondence files.

REQUIREMENTS FOR A GOOD SUBJECT CLASSIFICATION SYSTEM

When a large subject file is set up in business, say in a CPA firm, a prefabricated classification list (see page 140) may be used with adaptations to meet the local situation. Regardless of how it is developed, the first criterion of a good subject file is—can you find what you want when you want it? Some requirements for a good subject classification system are:

1. Subjects chosen should be short and to the point. Descriptors of over three significant words should be avoided. A long subject may indicate a need for a series of subdivisions back of a *general* primary heading.

2. Subjects should be specific; no more than fifteen to twenty primary ones should be selected. Broad subjects such as *Meetings* or *Memos* do not work well. They require subdivisions. For example, the general descriptor *Meetings* might need such subdivisions as *Board, Finance, Personnel, Management*.

3. Subjects should be capable of only one interpretation.

4. Subjects should be mutually exclusive. They should not overlap; for example, avoid such descriptors as *Budgets* and *Financial Reports* in the same file. If used in the same system, they would overlap in content even though they were located in different parts of the file.

5. The designer of a subject classification system should use the language of those who request and use the files. This means teamwork, patience, and compromise with those involved.

TYPES OF SUBJECT FILES

Except for numeric and alpha-numeric subject files which will be discussed later, subject files may be organized in one of two ways: (1) dictionary arrangement, or (2) encyclopedic arrangement.

Dictionary Arrangement

The dictionary arrangement is the straight alphabetical sequencing of subjects regardless of whether they are primary descriptors or subdivisions. This is the method dictionaries use; there is no attempt to group related material or indicate primary and secondary status. Each word is of equal importance with every other, and its relation to other subjects is disregarded unless cross referencing is used. Additions are made by merely inserting an item in its alphabetic order. An example of straight alphabetic subject sequencing (dictionary arrangement) is

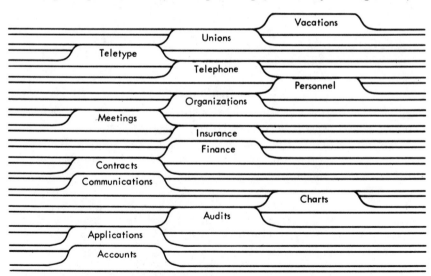

FIGURE 7–2. Dictionary arrangement of subject files. (*Source: Place, Popham, Fujita, Fundamental Filing Practice,* © 1973. *Reprinted by permission of Prentice-Hall, Inc., Englewood Cliffs, N.J.)*

shown in Figure 7–2. This system is suitable for a small subject file, probably no larger than one drawer.

Encyclopedic Arrangement

Some subject areas are so large they must be broken down into various aspects of the total, or there would be a lot of overlap among descriptors. In the encyclopedic arrangement, subclassifications are grouped and alphabetized under primary descriptors. Encyclopedias use this method, hence its name. In the encyclopedic system, folders would be arranged as shown in Figure 7–3.

This type of system works well when more than three or four drawers of materials are involved. When the system is larger, an alphanumeric or decimal classification is recommended in order to control the expansion of the subject "families." This is especially important when the classification is computerized because digital computers process numbers faster than words.

SUBJECT-NUMERIC SYSTEMS

There are three types of subject-numeric systems: (1) simple numeric, (2) decimal-numeric, and (3) alpha-numeric. In simple numeric, numbers are added to subject descriptors; some people find it easier to work with numbers.

Decimal- and alpha-numeric systems facilitate the *expansion* of divisions of primary headings. The need for secondary headings usu-

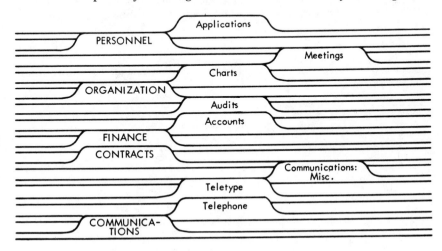

FIGURE 7–3. Encyclopedic arrangement of subject files. (Miscellaneous folders are not recommended in subject files.) (*Source: Place, Popham, Fujita,* Fundamental Filing Practice, © 1973. *Reprinted by permission of Prentice-Hall, Inc., Englewood Cliffs, N.J.*)

ally develops over time, as a business or project grows. For example, if the primary descriptor is *Insurance*, secondary headings eventually become necessary (Accident, Group, Property, Special). Assume that *Insurance* is heading 9. The secondary headings would then be numbered as follows to show their relation to the primary head, No. 9.

> 9. Insurance
>   9.1 Accident
>   9.2 Group
>   9.3 Property
>   9.4 Special

Some people even prefer to use a decimal numeric system when outlining, rather than the traditional but more cumbersome Roman numerals (I, II, III . . .) followed by upper case (A, B . . .), Arabic numerals (1, 2 . . .) and lower case letters (a, b . . .)

> I. XYZ Corporation
>   A. Finance
>   9. Insurance
>   a. Accident
>   b. Group
>   c. Property
>   d. Special

The following examples illustrate how easy it is to expand decimal-numeric systems, adding subheadings as needed.

Expansible Alpha and Numeric Classification Systems

Simple Numeric (Traditional Outlining)	Decimal-Numeric	Alpha-Numeric
I. Audits	1. Audits	10. Audits
A. Banks	10.1 Banks	10.A Banks
1. Commercial	10.11 Commercial	10.A–1 Commercial
2. Federal	10.12 Federal	10.A–2 Federal
3. State	10.13 State	10.A–3 State
B. Government Agencies	20.1 Government Agencies	10.B Government Agencies
1. Energy	20.11 Energy	10.B–1 Energy
a. Dams	20.111 Dams	10.B–1a Dams
b. Nuclear	20.112 Nuclear	10.B–1b Nuclear
c. Other	20.113 Other	10.B–1c Other
C. Private Organizations	30.1 Private Organizations	10.C Private Organizations
1. Business	30.11 Business	10.C–1 Business
2. Fraternal	30.12 Fraternal	10.C–2 Fraternal
3. Religious	30.13 Religious	10.C–3 Religious
4. Social	30.14 Social	10.C–4 Social

Duplex-Numeric

The duplex-numeric system is often confused with the decimal-numeric, but there is a technical difference. The above example is the decimal-numeric, not the duplex-numeric. Both systems are the same basic idea of expansion, but in the duplex-numeric, auxiliary numbers are separated from the parent by a hyphen instead of a decimal, and letters are sometimes *interspersed*. Some users prefer to alternate letters with numbers (200–1, 200–1a, 200–1a–1, etc.) because this permits more in depth or a greater range of classifications within a major area than does the straight decimal-numeric. The duplex-numeric is a hybrid or an admixture of the decimal-numeric and the alpha-numeric systems.

Alpha-Numeric

Hundreds of combinations are possible when alphabetic letters and numbers are combined, especially when decimals are used. An alpha-numeric system provides for large and involved subject systems, with many subclassifications. The following example is of an administrative system in a power company. Notice the use of "Miscellaneous" in this system even though it is not recommended for subject systems. There are also numerous cross-referencing possibilities.

Administrative Systems

ASI Accounting
- 00 Miscellaneous (EPC Supervisors)
- 01 General Accounting Letters of Instruction (Backcharge)
- 02 Class of Accounts (Functional Accounting Manual)
- 03 Cash Flow Forecasts (Includes manila folders: Credits to Uncommitted Costs to 0.N.07779; Cash Flow Forecasts and Analyses, originals; Back-up Info for Cash Flow)
- 04 Cost Estimates (If related to a spec, put in spec contract file)
- 05 Cost Reports (Major)
  - .0 Miscellaneous
  - .1 IBM Reports by G Number
    - .01 G81017, Project Cost Report Summary
    - .02 G51017, Cost Report, Procurement Construction and Service Contracts Summary
    - .03 G30085, Trojan Departmental Costs

.2   Other Cost Reports
  .01   Trojan Construction Line Items
  .02   Construction Trust Fund Account
  .03   Cost for Construction Expenditures and Construction Expenditure Report for Board of Directors monthly ASP report meeting
06   Cost Reports, Lorkus Construction Suspension
07   Insurance
  .0   Miscellaneous
  .1   E. N. A. I. P.
  .2   Colter & McPhierson
08   Taxes/Bonding
09   Claims: Injuries, Damages
10   Budget
11   Furniture, Equipment, Vehicles
  .0   Miscellaneous (Services)
  .1   Furniture and Equipment
  .2   Vehicles (Trailers and Cars)
  .3   Safety and First Aid
  .4   Xerox (Project Administrative Section)
12   Payment Schedules (If related to a spec, put in spec contract file.)
13   ATR Quarterly Reports[4]

Dewey-Decimal System

Over the years, as libraries grew and more and more publications were accumulated in them, librarians have grappled with the task of developing a subject system that would cover the total listing of literature and that could be used uniformly in libraries throughout the country. One of the most famous library classification systems was developed in 1876 by Melvil Dewey. The oldest of the bibliographic schemes, it is still in use although not as much as originally. (Few libraries now use the classification system.)

The Dewey-Decimal system is a modified duplex-numeric system; and is a process of classification for putting library books into related *subject* groupings that correspond to main subjects of books. The system has nine main classes with an extra one for General Works (a sort of miscellaneous).

The Dewey-Decimal main headings with some exemplary subdivisions of the 500 category follows.

[4]Courtesy of Richard Baranovich, President, Portland, Ore. ARMA, 1979–1980.

000 General Works	531 Mechanics
100 Philosophy	531.1 Machines
200 Religion	531.11 Lever and Balance
300 Sociology	531.12 Wheel and Axle
400 Philology (Language)	531.13 Cord
500 Pure Science[5]	531.14 Pulley
510 Mathematics	600 Useful Arts (Technology)
520 Astronomy	700 Fine Arts
530 Physics	800 Literature
	900 History

Extensions, additions, and subdivisions are indicated by digits to the right of the decimal point. A limit of a 6-digit notation is recommended.

An interesting feature of the Dewey-Decimal system is the tendency to give numbers within it mnemonic significance. For example, the digit 5 is used in portions of the system to refer to Italy; thus 450 identifies Italian language and 850, Italian literature. Under languages, a 3 stands for dictionaries, 4 for synonyms, 5 for grammar, etc. A book of Italian synonyms would be 454. Librarians trained in the Dewey-Decimal system learn to deduce information about a book merely by looking at the call number.[6]

The following example is of a book classified by the Dewey-Decimal system:

Arco Civil Service Test Tutor	651.5
by David R. Turner	Tur

Library of Congress Classification

In 1958, a Dewey system editorial office was established in Washington, D. C. under the administration of the Library of Congress to co-ordinate expansions, but since few libraries use the classification scheme today, a new one, known as the Library of Congress classification, was developed. The Library of Congress classification uses the best features of the Dewey and other subject classification plans. Its main categories are as follows:

---

[5]The 500 classification is amplified somewhat to show how decimal expansion works in the Dewey Decimal System.

[6]Joseph Becker and Robert M. Hayes, *Information Storage and Retrieval* New York: John Wiley & Sons, Inc., 1963, p. 32.

A. General Works, Polygraphy

B. Philosophy and Religion

C. History, Auxiliary Sciences

D. History and Topography
   (excluding America)

E–F. America

G. Geography, Anthropology

H. Social Science, Economics,
   Sociology

J. Political Science

K. Law

L. Education

M. Music

N. Fine Arts

P. Language and Literature

Q. Science

R. Medicine

S. Agriculture, Plant and
   Animal Industry

T. Technology

U. Military Science

V. Naval Science

Z. Bibliography and Library
   Science

The notation scheme used is alpha-numeric but the letters I, O, W, X, and Y are not used.

Since the Library of Congress (Washington, D.C.) is responsible for the continuing development of the LC classification, it distributes at low cost (through the U. S. Government Printing Office) copies of in-depth classifications with related indexes.[7] In this way libraries with special subject needs may subscribe only to those classes which apply to their particular interests.[8]

To ensure consistency in classifying library materials, The American Library Association adopted American Library Association Rules (and procedures) based on the Library of Congress classifications.[9] The "call number" derived according to this procedure identifies author name, subject, and book title. This number is recorded on all library catalog cards and serves as a publication's permanent *address*. That is, before a book is actually placed on the library shelves, its call number is printed conspicuously on its spine to ensure that it will be returned to its place on the shelves. For example, Fred Hoyle's *Encounter with the Future* is marked 901.9 H85.

The Dewey Decimal and the Library of Congress classification systems are among the two most widely used alpha-numeric subject classification systems in the United States.

---

[7]The Library of Congress also prepares and sells catalog cards for most American books. The cards provide full bibliographic information, including suggested subject headings plus Dewey and/or Library of Congress call numbers.

[8]Op. cit. p. 33

[9]U. S. Library of Congress, *Rules for Descriptive Cataloging* in the Library of Congress; and *Classification Schedules*, Washington, D.C., U. S. Government Printing Office. (*Classification Schedules* are updated in periodic editions.)

RELATIVE INDEX

Subject files, like numeric ones, need a relative index; otherwise the exact wording of descriptors may be forgotten. It is said that an index to a book is the *key* to its contents; a pointer to the location where an item can be found. In subject classification systems, the relative index (the key or pointer) may be kept in a handbook, in a folder, or on cards (see Figure 7–4) depending on its length and the working preferences of those involved. For card files, manufacturers have such standard sizes available as $3'' \times 5''$, $4'' \times 6''$, and $5'' \times 8''$.

The relative index is any alphabetical listing of main topics, subdivisions, and "See also . . ." words or synonyms. It can be compared to a city map because it covers the *whole* area. Locate the descriptor you want on this map, and it will lead you to the location in the subject file. It also helps when adding new topics so they can be classified in relation to the total system with a minimum of overlap.

A relative index also serves as a cross reference. This function of the index can be enhanced by adding alternate descriptors in parentheses for general topics; for example, *Pollution* (Air Alerts, Smog, Environmental Control). In this same way, the searcher may learn that *Air Conditioning* is also found under *Real Estate*, that *Bonuses* may be found under *Personnel—Pay and Allowances*, and that *Employee Agreements* about inventions are filed under *Patents and Royalties*.

No new file should be given a title until the index has been checked thoroughly. It is also a good idea to check a dictionary of synonyms so that possible alternate titles can be found and cross-referenced. Wherever there is doubt or a problem concerning the identification of a title, a note should be made on the index card.

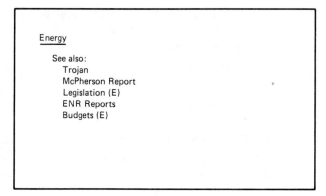

FIGURE 7—4. Relative index card for a subject classification.

REVIEW QUESTIONS

1. What are the advantages of subject files? Disadvantages? When should they be used?

2. What is the procedure for choosing classifications for a subject file?

3. What is a descriptor; a classification?

4. What is the difference between a subject file and a relative index?

5. When only a few items are called for by subject, how do you provide for them in a regular correspondence file?

6. When would you shift from a straight alphabetic subject file to the encyclopedic style?

7. Describe steps you would take in developing a subject file for personal materials relating to space travel and maintained by an engineer in your office.

8. What are the advantages of decimal-numeric or alpha-numeric systems as used in subject files?

9. Give an example of cross referencing in a subject file.

10. You are working in a chemical central file. A researcher calls attention to a new term that has come into use and asks that a new classification for it be added. What steps should be taken before doing this?

LEARNING ACTIVITIES

1. Use the relative index on the left to code the twenty-five papers described on the right.

   After coding these items, you have probably found some descriptors you would like to change. Write at least three new descriptors for the index.

	Relative Index	_code them_	Papers
10.1	Administration		A. Program for annual
10.11	Branch Office	_20.11_	National Records
10.12	Projects Completed		Management Association convention
10.13	Projects in Process		
20.1	Associations		B. Receipt for typewriter repairs
20.11	Conventions		C. List of local colleges
20.12	Meetings		offering data processing courses

(cont'd. on next page)

30.1	Educational Institutions	
30.11	Colleges	
30.12	Universities	
40.1	Equipment	
40.11	Chairs	
40.111	Posture	
40.12	Desks	
40.121	Modular	
40.122	Secretarial	
40.13	Filing Cabinets	
40.131	Card Size	
40.132	Correspondence Size	
40.133	Legal Size	
40.14	Machines	
40.141	Adding	
40.142	Bookkeeping	
40.143	Computer	
40.144	Typewriters	
50.1	Government Contracts	
60.1	Manufacturing	
60.11	Factory	
60.111	Employees	
60.112	Maintenance of Equipment	
60.113	Raw Materials	
60.114	Rent	
60.12	Production Schedules	
60.13	Production Statistics	
70.1	Office Maintenance	
70.11	Heat	
70.12	Light	
70.13	Rent	
70.14	Supplies	
70.141	Stationery	
70.1411	Envelopes	
70.1412	Paper	
70.1413	Carbon	
70.1414	Letterheads	
70.1415	Second Sheets	
70.142	Ribbons	
80.1	Transportation	
80.11	Express	
80.12	Freight	
90.1	Water Rights for Factory	

D. Receipt for office rent

E. Ream of letterhead paper

F. Plan for new factory lighting

G. Union grievance report on treatment of two factory timekeepers

H. Brochure describing posture chairs

I. Directions for operating computer

J. Measurements of space occupied by legal files

K. Change in working hours for factory employees

L. Contract for jungle boots for soldiers

M. Schedule of freight rates

N. Progress report from subcontractor on Job 54

O. New supply of manila envelopes

P. New procedure about sending bulk mail to all divisions of the corporation

Q. Inventory of typewriters

R. Analysis of costs of air conditioning computer room

S. Bill for pads to be placed under all typewriters

T. Report on number of shoes produced three years ago

U. Foreman's evaluation of workers' performance

V. Announcement of seminar of American Management Association on Reduction of Inventory

W. Bills of lading for goods shipped by freight

X. Standards to be followed in buying new typewriters

Y. Inventory of adding machines

2.   *A Subject File Coordinated with a Correspondence File*

Assume that you work in the central files of D. C. Lloyd & Company, Denver, Colorado. Lloyd manufactures a variety of appliances such as amplifiers and microswitches for electronic equipment. The company's main offices and factory are in Denver; a few dealers are scattered around the country, a representative "office" is located in Boston, and plans for a branch in Canada are under consideration.

The company follows a routine procedure of filing correspondence in two separate files: alphabetic by names of individuals and alphabetic by subject. An extra copy (photocopy duplicating process) is made of all correspondence, both incoming and outgoing, for the subject file. Although some in the company regard this as a cumbersome system, the company's president has requested the subject classification back-up file for all correspondence because he thinks it facilitates a more thorough handling and better control of the many different types of items covered by the correspondence.

The twenty-eight letters you are to process for the back-up subject file consist of both incoming and outgoing correspondence.

> Read each letter and copy the number (see lower right-hand corner of each letter) on the relative index after the subject under which you think it should be filed.

Relative Index for Learning Activity 2.

1. *Branch Plants*
   a. Canada
   b. United States

2. *Data Processing*

3. *Development*
   a. Exhibits
   b. Facilities
   c. Produce (See Research)
   d. Research (See Product)
   e. Program

4. *Federal Reports*

5. *Finance*
   a. Accounts Receivable
   b. Accounts Payable
   c. Budgets
   d. Credit (general)
   e. Insurance
   f. Investments

6. *Miscellaneous*

7. *Office*

8. Orders
   a. Back Orders (See Delays)
   b. Delays (See Back Orders)
   c. Credit Information

9. *Personnel*
   a. Applications
   b. Appreciation (See Congratulations)
   c. Condolences
   d. Congratulations (See Appreciation)
   e. Education
   f. Health
   g. Policies

10. *Red Feather Drive*
11. *Security*
12. *Service*
    a. Complaints
    b. Customer
    c. Order Adjustments
    d. Production
    e. Shipments

C A R B O N C O P Y

February 14, 19__

Mr. Keenan Doyle
359 South 40th #3
Aurora, Colorado

Dear Mr. Doyle

We have carefully reviewed your resume for participation in our Accelerated Management Training Program. Your educational background and interest in manufacturing have been important factors in our consideration.

In evaluating the total group of candidates, however, I find that we are not going to be able to offer you a position at this time. With your qualifications, I am sure you have a number of employment alternatives. I certainly wish you every success in the job you select.

Thank you for your interest in our Company.

Sincerely yours

Personnel Director

HOC:rh

1

UNITED STATES NATIONAL BANK OF COLORADO

MAIN BRANCH

8600 ARCADIA AVENUE
P.O. BOX 281
DENVER, COLORADO 80201

February 17, 19__

Mr. Vernon Pellatt
Finance Director
D. C. Lloyd and Company
934 West Van Buren Street
Denver, Colorado 80201

Dear Mr. Pellatt

This is in response to your recent inquiry concerning Signal Appliances, Inc., 2733 South Frontier Drive, Boulder, Colorado. Neighboring bankers contacted on your behalf tell us that the subject has been their customer since 1948, apparently maintaining throughout this time a deposit balance averaging in high four- and five-figure proportions. Credit, secured by accounts receivable, has extended to a high of a medium five-figure amount. A low five-figure amount is currently outstanding. Financial summaries of this company are not available to the bankers.

All banking relations with the company have reportedly been handled in a satisfactory way. Our information tells us that the company is an established one with a history of profitable operations. The bankers hold the subject responsible for normal business commitments.

We trust the foregoing information offered in the usual confidence will be of assistance.

Very truly yours

Wesley Addis

Wesley Addis
Assistant Cashier

wa/e

2

(*Source: Place, Popham, Fujita, Fundamental Filing Practice, © 1973. Reprinted by permission of Prentice-Hall, Inc., Englewood Cliffs, N.J.*)

February 23, 19__

Mr. L. B. Williams
Parker, Smith, and Aiken, Inc.
Investment Securities
1652 Blocker Building
Denver, Colorado 80201

Dear Mr. Williams

After our telephone conversation yesterday, I talked with our President, Mr. Channing Gregory, and he feels that the brokerage for the sale and replacement of securities could be placed with your firm for a stated period, say one or two years, but not in perpetuity.

Our securities are handled primarily through my department and change from day to day. To pass all our security transactions through your organization might be awkward and difficult. We find no objection, however, to your suggestion that you inform us as to stock purchases that in your judgment merit consideration.

I suggest that you prepare an agreement for the services you propose and submit it to us for consideration. As I stated over the telephone, I am not sure our set-up is such that we can advantageously use the services of your company. However, we will be glad to review your proposal and to cooperate with you, if possible.

Sincerely yours

Vernon Pellatt
Director, Finance and Investments

vp/rs

3

February 27, 19__

Mr. C. A. Price
Riley Manufacturing Company
Wilkes Barre, Pa.

Dear Mr. Price

This refers to your telephone call telling us that Order No. 14229, shipped the latter part of January, has not yet reached you. Apparently this shipment has gone astray. We are, naturally, sorry for the inconvenience this is causing you. We are putting out a tracer immediately.

In the meantime, we are air mailing a duplicate order that should reach you in a couple days.

Thank you for telephoning about the matter. We pride ourselves on giving good customer service, and it is only when customers keep us informed as you have that we can take remedial action. We assume that the air shipment will come through all right, but should you not receive it by the early part of next week, let us know.

Yours truly

H. T. Harris
Sales Department

HTH:ef

4

VANCOUVER TRUST COMPANY
571 Water Street
Vancouver 3, B.C.
Canada

268-1054

March 3, 19__

Mr. Channing E. Gregory
President, D. C. Lloyd & Company
934 West VanBuren Street
Denver, Colorado 80201

Dear Mr. Gregory

As I told you when we talked on the telephone this morning, Mr. Lee Yetke (Canadian Pacific) and Mr. Stuart Chapman (Manufacturers National Bank) have agreed to serve on the advisory board to consider the advisability of locating a branch plant and/or a warehouse of Lloyd's in this area. They are both well qualified.

I telephoned them after I talked with you to see about a meeting next week and March 14 is a likely date. We can meet in my office at 9 that morning. I have also asked Larry Whitehead, a realtor, to meet with us as he handles industrial sites. After lunch, we can go out with him and look over several pieces of land he has in mind.

Will you bring a company lawyer or should I ask one of our lawyers to sit in during the morning discussion? Unless you have some special reason for not doing so, I advise using a Canadian lawyer for obvious reasons.

We are glad to have been invited to work as your Canadian representative in this matter. We are also glad to know that Lloyd Company is considering expanding into Canada. Where will you stay while in Canada? Can our travel department help make reservations for you? How many will be in your party?

Cordially yours

Horton Canfield
Horton Canfield
Executive Vice President

HC/dh

5

March 5, 19__

Reservations
Imperial Hotel
Vancouver B. C., Canada

Gentlemen

Please reserve 2 rooms, adjoining if possible, for the nights of March 13 and 14. Mr. Channing E. Gregory, President of our company, will occupy one, and two of our other men (Mr. Vernon Pellatt and Mr. Kenneth Service) will share the other; twin beds please.

Their flight arrives in Vancouver at 3:07 p.m. March 13 so they should be checking in around 4:00.

Please confirm the reservation.

Yours truly

(Miss) Maryanne Butterfield
Secretary to Channing E. Gregory, President

mb

6

Place, Popham, Fujita

March 5, 19__

Mr. Horton Canfield
Executive Vice President
Vancouver Trust Company
571 Water Street
Vancouver 3, B. C., Canada

Dear Mr. Canfield

Mr. Gregory is out of the city today but asked me to write informing
you that he will be in Vancouver March 13, arriving on Canadian
Pacific Flight 607, 3:07 p.m. Accompanying him are Messrs. Kenneth
Service (Engineering) and Vernon Pellatt (Finance).

I have made reservations for them at the Imperial Hotel.

Yours truly

(Miss) Maryanne Butterfield
Secretary to Channing E. Gregory

mb

7

March 8, 19__

Mr. Ralph Wolfram, Contractor
Frontier Building
Juneau, Alaska

Dear Mr. Wolfram

Your letter and the 45-amp amplifier that you returned have been received. We have sent them to our engineering department so that the
amplifier can be tested. Your letter says it "blew" the works.
Previous laboratory tests of these amplifiers show they can stand
twice the load actually recommended for them. Only an excessive overload or a faulty part could have caused the damage you describe. We
will check exhaustively for both.

Since the tests may take up to four weeks, we will be unable to give
you a specific report until that time.

Yours very truly

Peter Hall, Manager
Services Department

PH/ad

8

ARMANDO de AMBRIEX
ENGINEER AND CONSULTANT
Praça deBriel, P 3a
Rio de Janeiro, Brasil   TELEFONE: 20-06-81

March 10, 19__

Accounting Department
D. C. Lloyd & Company
West VanBuren Street
Denver, Colorado

Dear Sirs

Recently I ordered some equipment from you and it arrived last week
safely. I have instructed my bank to send you a cashier's check in
the amount of $300 American dollars drawn to your honor.

I would appreciate it if, when you receive this check, you advise me
at once. Sometimes we have delays and complications in transmitting
monies to distant places. If this happens with the above cashier's
check, I would want to know as soon as possible so that I can start
tracing procedures and authorize a new document.

I am pleased with the equipment I received from your company.

Yours with regards

Sr Armando de Ambriex
Engineering Consultant

9

March 12, 19__

U. S. Department of Labor
Office of Labor Management
  and Welfare Pension Reports
Washington, D. C. 20210

Dear Sirs

Enclosed is a copy of our Employee Savings Plan Annual Report Form
for the contract year ending last December 31, file number WP 91-40-
57. This report covers our Employee Savings Plan for salaried employees with three years service.

Should there be questions relating to the report, please contact us.
If you need further information, let us know.

Yours truly

Personnel Department

HQC:rh

Enclosure

10

March 16, 19___

C A R B O N   C O P Y

Mr. Horton Canfield
Executive Vice President
Vancouver Trust Company
571 Water Street
Vancouver 3, B. C., Canada

Dear Horton

I have discussed with my executive committee various aspects of our
proposed plant in Vancouver. We discussed costs and financing, time
schedule, building restrictions, and economic growth factors. I
showed them pictures of the various building sites Mr. Whitehead
showed us, and they were unanimous in preferring the acreage off Highway 495 because of shipping connections.

The next logical step, it seems to us, is to have our production people
and architect develop a prospective building plan so that we can focus
in on real costs. With the continued rise in labor and building material costs, it may be that some additional financing will be needed
beyond the figures we discussed. I personally think we are being a
bit optimistic, and that our original estimate is too low. In any
event, we will plan to amortize the loan in the same period of time as
originally discussed.

What is the ceiling your bank will advance us? If we must go beyond
it, do you think Mr. Chapman's bank will be willing to get into the
picture?

Can you give us names and addresses of 3 building contractors so that
as soon as our architect has drawn plans and prepared the specifications, we can submit them to the contractors for competitive bids?

I also discussed with my executive committee the matter of paying your
company a flat fee for its services in this matter rather than basing
it on the amount of the loan or on the total amount of our final investment. They agreed that this would be the most logical way to
handle it. We will pay in three installments: the first as soon as the
building plans are firm and all permits and legal documents are in
order; the second, at the completion of the structure; and the third
·3 months after the plant is opened. Let us know if this arrangement is
not satisfactory.

Sincerely yours

Channing E. Gregory
President

CEG:mb

11

VANCOUVER TRUST COMPANY   268-1054
571 Water Street
Vancouver 3, B.C.
Canada

March 19, 19___

Mr. Channing E. Gregory
President, D. C. Lloyd & Company
934 West VanBuren Street
Denver, Colorado 80201

Dear Channing

This replies to your letter of March 16. I think your choice of acreage is a good one.

I have discussed with other people here at the bank the possibility of
your needing more money, and at present it doesn't look as if a larger
loan than the one we anticipate will be a problem—within limits, of
course. We should probably leave it at that, Channing, until your
architect draws up specifications so that we can get a stronger cost
picture.

Within a few days, we will send you the names of three contractors
we've worked with before. Insurance terms and a penalty clause
should be in the contract papers when bids are submitted.

The flat fee terms you describe are acceptable.

Cordially yours

Horton

Horton Canfield
Executive Vice President

12

ROBERTS, BESCH, CONDON, ADAIR, INC.
ATTORNEYS-AT-LAW

COMSTOCK BUILDING, N.E.
AIKEN, NORTH CAROLINA

March 22, 19___

Mr. Channing E. Gregory
President
D. C. Lloyd & Company
934 West VanBuren Street
Denver, Colorado 80201

Dear Channing

On behalf of the partners of Roberts, Besch, Condon, Adair, I want to
thank you for your thoughtful expression of sympathy on the death of
our senior partner, Mr. Daniel K. Roberts.

Our firm has suffered a great loss. He was one of the founders of
this organization and until just a few days before his death, continued to be a strong and respected voice in it. We hope to carry
on in the fine example and tradition which he established for us.

Sincerely yours

Dennis

T. Dennis Besch
Partner

tdb:lc

13

D. C. LLOYD & COMPANY MEMO

To: All Department Heads	Subject: Dennison copiers
From: Geo. Vaughn, Administrative Services	Date: March 25, 19___

May I have your cooperation, please, on an important office service
item? Costs incurred in using the Dennison copiers that are available throughout the Company are extremely high and increasing every
month. The time has come to examine how this equipment is being used
by each department and to control its abuse.

Several departments are going to channel all copy work through a secretary. One is going to log-in all the work done on the copiers.

We feel that some type of control is desirable in order to cut down
on unnecessary copying.

14

April 8, 19__

Mr. Oha Wakun
Director, Department of Commerce
State of Hawaii
Division of Securities
Honolulu, Hawaii

Dear Oha

Thank you for your nice telephone call in answer to my appeal for new ideas about handling credit procedures. It was certainly a pleasure to talk with you; I enjoyed our conversation.

You may recall that I was interested in the fact that banks in Hawaii are apparently unwilling (or prohibited by law; you weren't sure) from giving out credit information. As I indicated to you, I have been wondering what approach to take here at Lloyd's to open up avenues to obtain the information we need more quickly. I am not yet satisfied that the best way to solve our dilemma is through Dun and Bradstreet.

You may remember that we talked of a possible "Code of Ethics" among manufacturers for the exchange of credit information. Adherence to such a code, if it could be established, would enable manufacturers with similar types of customers to exchange information with confidence. I believe the National Retail Credit Association, which is comprised of retail credit grantors throughout the country, has a code of ethics for the exchange of credit information. Such a system should work particularly well if computerized.

As any person engaged in credit work well knows, unless you can get accurate and adequate information about a potential customer fast, it is impossible to make a sound credit decision. I'm sure everyone knows the tremendous importance of accurate credit information and the impact it has on the well-being of a company. If we could establish a good credit system among manufacturers such as they have in other "industries," we would be able to help each other all over the world. For example, suppose a business in Italy placed an order for $3,000 or more with us. As the situation now stands, we have to contact someone in Italy (usually a bank) and hope they'll take time to give us the information we need and that when and if it comes, it will be accurate. Obtaining credit information about foreign customers is particularly difficult because they don't seem to realize that we do hold such information in the strictest confidence.

Oha, I sincerely appreciate your ideas and help in this matter. It was a pleasure to talk with you. I send best wishes to you and yours.

Sincerely yours

Vernon Pellatt
Director, Finance and Investments

15

April 8, 19__

Simpson and McGregor Publishing Company
Wayne Building, Suite 17
Tuscaloosa, Alabama

Gentlemen

Please send us an examination copy of your new book by M. Iris Greene, In-House Development Programs. Bill the company, not Mr. Cutler. Thank you.

Yours truly

Helen Gettis (Mrs.)
Secretary to Harry G. Cutler
Director of Personnel

hg

16

April 8, 19__

Mr. Shannon Grillo
Vice President and Manager
Credit Department
First National Bank of Denver
Denver, Colorado

Dear Mr. Grillo

I want to thank you for the pleasant and helpful visit I had with you in your office yesterday. I appreciated the opportunity to talk with you because you have such a wealth of experience and knowledge in the credit field.

After talking with you, I am convinced the best approach to solving our problem is to revise the credit procedure we are now using. For one thing, it takes us too long to establish a new customer's credit and no doubt we lose business as a result. You discussed some of these things so convincingly that I've decided to present some of the points you made at the next meeting of our executive committee.

I wonder if, at your convenience, you would give me a letter supporting the need to speed-up the credit-check procedure and explain how some of your ideas work and save time. I would appreciate your permission to use the letter with our executive committee, if necessary.

Sincerely yours

Vernon Pellatt
Director, Finance and Investments

VP:i

17

April 10, 19__

Mr. Ralph Wolfram, Contractor
Frontier Building
Juneau, Alaska

Dear Mr. Wolfram

The 45-amp amplifier that you returned last month has been carefully and extensively checked in our laboratory. We found nothing defective.

As stated in our March letter, this equipment will stand twice the load we actually recommend for it so the situation in which it defaulted for you must have been a case of excessive overload.

We are returning the amplifier to you today believing that it is in perfect condition and that it should serve you well, if properly used.

Yours very truly

Peter Hall, Manager
Services Department

PH/ad

18

Place, Popham, Fujita

SIMPSON AND McGREAGOR PUBLISHERS, INC.

17 WAYNE BUILDING
TUSCALOOSA, ALABAMA

AREA CODE 205
262-8471

April 11, 19__

Mrs. Helen Gettis
Secretary to Mr. Harry G. Cutler
Director of Personnel
D. C. Lloyd & Company
934 West VanBuren Street
Denver, Colorado 80201

Dear Mrs. Gettis

We have sent you a complimentary copy of M. Iris Greene's new book,
IN-HOUSE DEVELOPMENT PROGRAMS. As soon as Mr. Cutler has examined
it, write us what he thinks about the book, whether he plans to use
it, and how he will use it.

We will not reprint any part of your evaluation without first clear-
ing it with you. We are asking for Mr. Cutler's opinion because we
have just newly launched into this area of publication—training—
and want to get as much feed-back from customers as possible.

Thank you for helping us.

Cordially yours

I. K. Benson

I. K. Benson
Industrial Text Division

IKB:p

19

A & D RAILWAY

ADOLF & DOUGLAS ARNOLD, PROPRIETORS

MAIN TERMINAL: 46 COTTAGE STREET, SHARON, MASSACHUSETTS 02067

STATION MASTER PHONE: 617-784-6993

April 16, 197_

D. C. Lloyd & Company
934 West VanBuren St.
Denver, Colorado

Gentlemen

Copies of the No. 6229A special freight shipment schedules that you
asked for in your letter of April 8 will be sent to you within the
next day or so.

We hope they are clear and that we may have the pleasure of being of
further service to you.

Very truly yours

Don Morrison

Don Morrison
Supervisor, Freight Shipping Division

DM/jtb

20

ALUMNI OFFSET, INC., LITHOGRAPHERS

175 Varick Street, New York, N.Y. 10014
Telephone: 924-1150

April 17, 19_

Mr. Peter Hall, Manager
Services Division
D.C. Lloyd and Company
West VanBuren
Denver, Colorado 80201

Dear Mr. Hall

I will be in Denver May 12 and 13 and can be available to discuss
with you the publication of the brochures about which you wrote our
Chicago office last week.

Could you suggest a convenient time? I do not know yet what interview schedule our Denver office has arranged for me, but will work
in whatever time you suggest. Perhaps you should, if possible, suggest an alternate time.

I am looking forward to meeting you.

Sincerely yours

H. J. Donahue

Harry J. Donahue
Sales Representative

hjd:r

21

C A R B O N   C O P Y

April 18, 19__

Mr. Ron Johnson
Production Manager
Skagway and Sons, Inc.
Minneapolis, Minn.

Dear Mr. Johnson

Since receiving your letter of April 9, we have scoured our records
and warehouse looking for a reference to the material you say arrived
defective and which you returned. Our suggestion is that you send a
tracer out after this shipment. In the meantime, we do not feel we
can issue a refund until we see the returned merchandise.

We regret this delay and can only hope that you see our point of view.

Yours very truly

Jordon W. Gardner
Sales

JWG:h

22

Place, Popham, Fujita

STANDISH ENGINEERING ASSOCIATES, INC.

Suite 17, Marshall Building
Austin, Texas 78703

AREA CODE 512
581-0663

April 19, 19__

Mr. Don Slatter
Data Processing
D. C. Lloyd & Company
934 West VanBuren Street
Denver, Colorado 80201

Dear Don

I'm writing to congratulate you upon being awarded the Distinguished
Service Award for outstanding contributions in the Computer Association of America. It is a tribute to you, an honor to your company,
and recognition of your many activities in CAA.

Congratulations on an outstanding career in data processing.

Yours sincerely

Dan

Dan Sears
2nd Vice President
Computer Assn. of America

23

D. C. LLOYD & COMPANY MEMO

To: All Department Heads   Subject: Administrative Manual

From: George Vaughn, Ad. Services   Date: April 21, 197_

Recently the firm of Place and Fujita, Records Management Consultants,
proposed that they provide a consulting service in assisting the D. C.
Lloyd Company in establishing a records management program. A pre-
sentation covering a variety of functional disciplines, including
files management, retention scheduling, inactive records storage, forms
management, and the development of an administrative manual, will be
made to our management staff.

Arrangements have been made to discuss this proposal with Place and
Fujita in Conference Room 2 at 10:00 a.m. on Wednesday, April 28.

President Smith has requested that all department heads attend this
meeting.

24

A F C CORPORATION

REFRACTORIES FOR INDUSTRY

April 22, 19_

Mr. Ken Service
Manager, Engineering Division
D. C. Lloyd Co.
934 West Vanburen Street
Denver, Colorado 80201

Dear Sir

I noticed in one of your bulletins that you have started some new
product developments that you expect to complete in a year. You
may know that the AFC Corporation has, for years, helped companies
such as yours facilitate new product programs.

I have asked our Colorado representative to call on you to explain
our services. We hope you will find time to talk with him.

Yours very truly

J. Dan Edwards

J. Dan Edwards
Executive Vice President

hz

25

WESLEY ARCHER & SONS

242-2345
AREA CODE 304

MANUFACTURERS OF INDUSTRIAL SUPPLIES
PENOBSCOB INDUSTRIAL PLACE
HUNTINGTON, WEST VIRGINIA

May 19, 19__

Mr. Arthur Bailey, Jr.
Plant Production
D. C. Lloyd and Company
VanBuren Street
Denver, Colorado

Dear Sir

I met a representative of yours at a Manufacturers Association regional
meeting, and I described to him some equipment that we need in one of
our new plants. By the way, your man was Harry Fisinger. I believe
he is with your Engineering Division.

I have checked the catalog and price list he gave me and the amplifier
parts are listed as Aa3a, Parts 6a, 14d, and 1-01b. I would like six
of each. We will appreciate prompt shipment.

Yours truly

Larry Erickston

Larry Erickston
Plant Production

le-aj

26

Place, Popham, Fujita

May 28, 19__

Research Department
D. C. Lloyd & Company
934 West VanBuren Street
Denver, Colorado 80201

Gentlemen

I work in the engineering design division at Denton Corporation, and
while at a regional engineering meeting in Mobile last week, heard
of some unique research your company is doing on switching circuitry.

Can you send me a copy of your findings please.

Yours truly

E. Hughes.

Eugena Hughes (Mrs)
Research Associate

27

June 12, 19__

Mr. Peter Hall
Services Division, Lloyd & Co.
934 VanBuren Street
Denver, Colorado

Dear Sir

I am writing with reference to some equipment we purchased from your
firm about a year ago. Your advertisements guaranteed complete satisfaction. I'm sorry to report, however, that our experience with
the equipment has not been satisfactory.

We installed the deluxe model AA3 amplifier and related control panel
with the extra sets of micro-switches tied in from remote stations.
The sound effects have been noisy from the very beginning and the
low-to-medium dial settings do not adjust properly. Your service representative out of Boston was up twice to check the unit. In spite
of his servicing, the installation does not operate satisfactorily.

Since we installed the unit in the home of an important and much
respected citizen, and he has an expensive and extensive recording
system connected to it, we are embarrassed about the trouble he has
had with it. I think the public-relations effect of this situation
is important enough for you either to send us a complete replacement
of your equipment (which will be tricky, at this point, to install)
and/or send us one of your servicemen who knows more about the equipment than the man from Boston appears to know.

Yours truly

Ken Towers

Ken Towers
Building Contractor

28

Place, Popham, Fujita

162

8

Geographic Classification Systems and Card Files

Materials in geographic systems are arranged alphabetically according to location; they bring together items by cities, states, or countries. This method of classification is especially suited for certain types of organizations (utilities, mail-order companies, publishers and government departments or agencies) and records such as sales, market research, travel agencies, or major corporations with many branch offices. If the geographic locations of the records do not extend beyond the United States, the arrangement follows this order: state, county, city and subdivisions of towns or cities. A company with international records would follow this order: country, province or district, city, name of company, individual, or subject.

When the operations of an organization extend throughout the world, the *primary* guides should be names of countries, arranged alphabetically. For example, documents related to trade activities handled by Harold Ashworth, an agent in Sydney, Australia, would be classified as follows:

Primary Guide: Australia
Secondary Guide: Sydney
Tertiary Guide: New South Wales (Province)
Individual Name Guide: Ashworth, Harold

163

ADVANTAGES AND DISADVANTAGES

Geographic systems have some distinct advantages and important applications. They have a distinct advantage for businesses that classify information by cities, states, counties, or countries. With geographic classification it is possible to check, analyze, and control information organized on this basis. For example, knowledge that geographic files produce about market trends in certain parts of the country may be more valuable to a company from an overall sales promotion point of view than individual names of customers who bought X or Y products.

Another advantage of geographic systems, especially when visible equipment or computerized printouts are used, is the speed of information retrieval. That is, geographic trends cluster and can be seen at a glance.

A minor disadvangage of the system is in classifying and coding documents, especially if one is weak in geography. For example, there are some dozen cities named *Aurora* in the United States. It might be easy to code an item for Aurora, *Calif.* instead of Aurora, *Colo.*

A more significant disadvantage inherent in geographic systems (where records are ultimately alphabetized) is that the true relationship or juxtaposition of locations is not shown. For example, whereas Oregon and California are neighboring states, they fall, when alphabetized, into quite different sections of a geographic file. Another example is the cities of Washington, D. C. and Arlington, Virginia. Whereas these two communities are close geographically, when alphabetized they fall into different sections, especially when alphabetized by city. That is, the location of records in a geographic file has no relation to their geographic juxtaposition. To some extent, though, this disadvantage can be overcome by using the decimal-numeric scheme or the map & tack system which is explained later in this chapter.

Juxtapositions can be shown by assigning a number to each state in relation to its location on a map, with cities coded in relation to states. Thus the state of Washington could be assigned the decimal digit 30; Oregon, 40; California, 50, etc. See Figure 8–1 which illustrates how states can be coded. With this numbering system, even though state and/or city names are listed alphabetically, geographic juxtaposition relationships are still apparent; for example—

Alabama	290
Arkansas	210
Arizona	90

FIGURE 8—1. Coding geographic locations.

Alaska	10
California	50
Florida	390

In this way, cities, counties, and their subdivisions may also be related numerically to their states; for example—

Illinois	260:	Aurora	260.1
		Chicago	260.2
		Decatur	260.3
		Peoria	260.4
		Rock Island	260.5
		Springfield	260.6

A similar system could be used to classify counties, cities, regions, or states. The system can be modified to meet situations whenever it is desirable to show juxtapositions. To some extent, this concept is the one used in the United States Postal Zip Code system, where the numbers assigned are identified mnemonically with specific parts of the country. (See Figure 8–2.)

The 5-digit zip code identifies areas in the United States in order to simplify mail distribution. When creating the system, the United

FIGURE 8–2. National zip code areas.

States was divided into ten geographic areas which were numbered from 0 to 9. The first three digits of the 5-digit number stand for the national area and a sectional post office distribution center. The last two identify associated post offices served by the sectional center; that is, a delivery area.

Example: 43451

<u>4</u>	<u>34</u>	<u>51</u>
National	Sectional	Post
Area	Center	Office

On the whole, geographic classification is simple. Given a *map*[1] of the area to be covered, there is no problem about chosing descriptors as there is in subject systems or of referring to rules as there is when indexing individual name files. A map may act as a relative index.

---

[1] A gazetteer or atlas covering the area might also be used. Webster's Geographic Dictionary or Lippincott's Gazetteer are good worldwide references although a librarian may be able to help find a map that is better suited for a specific local situation.

MAPS AS RELATIVE INDEXES

When filing any type of records geographically, a map should be available for reference and clarification. The procedure used for the 1980 Census illustrates the use of maps when working with records identified only by location, not by name. Each address register and related records that were assigned to a census enumerator were accompanied by a map of the area to be worked by that enumerator. In this way, the several hundred residences in each register who had not mailed in their census record forms and had to be visited personally by enumerators could be easily located. Enumerators plotted each day's itinerary and grouped their records by *streets* (a type of geographic classification), then consulted the map for juxtapositions. Hence, a day's itinerary might group records and schedule visits to addresses on Farmington, Allen, and Walker Streets, three streets adjacent geographically but not alphabetically. When used in this way, a map not only shows juxtapositions of various cities, counties, or areas but helps to arrange related records for appropriate geographic filing. It can be used as a reference when classifying and coding the records; it makes filing and retrieval easier; and it may help to locate misfiled or lost documents. In this regard, a map acts as sort of organizer or relative index.

Of course, snags may occur in geographic filing depending on the area being covered, the function of the records being filed, and the size of the system. Locally a district may be incorporated into a city and lose previous identity, or a street name may be changed. For example, what was Wayne Road, may, as a result of a new shopping mall or a highway development, become part of Route No. 5 or an expressway exit ramp, and so the original name, Wayne Road, is lost.

As corporations in the United States trade more and more in world markets, geographic classifications pose special problems for them too. Countries change their names; for example, Ceylon is now called Sri Lanka and Rhodesia is Zimbabwe. Here again, carefully dated maps may act as a useful reference. Where a company's records reflect international trade, as more and more do (i.e., the foreign car market), a file of dated maps can become an important reference.

GEOGRAPHIC FILING PROCEDURE

Accuracy in filing depends on good work procedures in addition to well-designed systems. The following are steps for preparing material for geographic files:

1. *Inspect.* Has the item been released for filing?

2. *Code.* Circle the indexing units: Location, name, or address. Underline the primary unit. It may help to number units in their indexing order; i.e., Location (1), Name or address (2).

3. *Cross Reference.* Cross reference to subjects, individual names, or alternate locations. Cross referencing in geographic systems is important because United States citizens often change geographic locations, and a cross reference may be the only means of locating a file.

A copy of a document can be an effective cross reference. Extra copies are easy to make with modern copying equipment. Whether you make a copy or prepare a cross reference sheet (see Figures 8–3 and 8–4) is a matter of preference and judgment. If most of the cross referencing in the system seems to be between individual name and geographic folders, it may be helpful to make a back-up card index by names and cross reference on the cards. For example, if there is considerable cross referencing to the chain store Payless, Inc., list on the card the locations of stores and key individuals with which your company corresponds. (See Figure 8–5.)

Back-up card files also help to accumulate related items because they may contain not only names and old plus current addresses of individuals or companies, but subject topics, dates, or bits of information about individuals or programs. For example, see Figure 8–6.

4. *Sort.* Rough sort first by primary guides; then fine sort by subcategories until all classifications in the system have been used; that is, secondary, tertiary, and individual name guides.

If a geographic system contains many individual name folders, it is still advisable to rough sort first by the *primary* guides—names of countries, states, or cities.

5. *File.* After locating the proper folder for an item, lift it from the drawer and insert the new document at the front of the folder, face forward, most recent date on top.

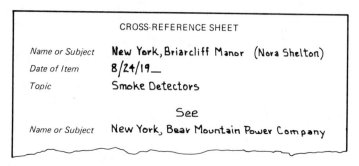

FIGURE 8–3. Cross-reference for geographic file.

Bear Mountain Power Company
Poughkeepsie, NY 10018

August 14, 19__

Mr. Norman Baker
Sales Representative
Baker Appliances 2
Briarcliff Manor, New York

File: NY, Bear Mt. Power
Cross-ref: NY. Briarcliff Manor
(Nora Shelton)

Dear Norm

Nora Shelton of 1706 Main St., Briarcliff Manor, writes that she is not satisfied with the way one of our smoke detectors works. She bought it from you and wants to return it to us. She wants a full refund plus installation costs.

Since the Hear-Easy detector is our best seller and we rarely get complaints about it, may we hear from you about the situation as soon as possible.

Sincerely yours

Ken Barton, Sales Manager
Bear Mountain Power Co. 1

FIGURE 8–4. A letter coded for geographic filing.

PAYLESS, Inc.

See also: *Portland*
J. R. Hestor, Area Manager
Allen Kline, Sales Representative

Salem
Helen Corbet, Regional Manager
Kirk McClure, Promotions

FIGURE 8–5. Cross-reference card.

ASHWORTH, Harry
   1659 Croden Lane
   Sydney, Austrailia

SEE: AUSTRALIA, (New South Wales)

Note--Became agent 10/80; age, 36; visited
United States plant training center 8/18-23/80.
Main attribute: very personable and knows many
people in his province.

FIGURE 8—6. Cross-reference card.

Merging Classifications

Special subject folders, chronological expansion inserts by date or month, and individual name folders of correspondence or other documents can be merged into a geographic file. That is, the system can be a combination of folders labeled for subjects, individual names, and geographic locations. Even numbers can be added. Such a combination is particularly possible in a multipurpose file in a private office. When this type of file evolves, folder tabs for each category should be either color coded or assigned a special cut and position. For example, with a 5-cut tab, the first position (5–1) could be assigned to geographic primary guides, the next (5–2) to secondary guides, the third (5–3) to *Miscellaneous* and *Out* folder tabs and the last two (5–4 and 5–5) to individual name folders.

Figure 8–7 geographic file with individual name folders illustrates this concept. A center tab (3–2 position[2]) is used for primary geographic guides (state) and position 3–1 for a secondary guide (city). A fifth-cut tab is used for an alphabetic tab (5–1) and for corresponding folder tabs (5–3). Individual folder tabs (3–3) are at the right and are also given a code number.

Back of the main guides (5–1) in Figure 8–8 (geographic and individual name folders) we have miscellaneous folders (5–2), special dividers (5–3), individual folder alphabetic guides (5–4), *Out* tabs (5–5) and individual folder tabs (3–3).

---

[2]These numbers refer to a tab size and position. The first number is tab size; the second position: 3–2 = a 3-cut tab size, in the second position.

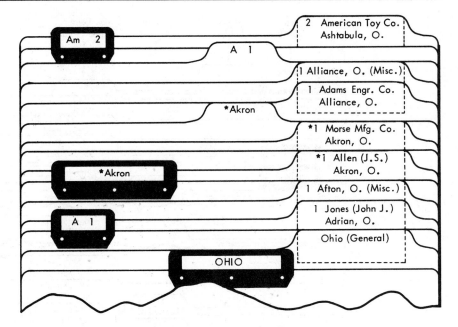

FIGURE 8–7. A geographic file with individual name folders. (*Source: Place, Popham, Fujita*, Fundamental Filing Practice, © 1973. *Reprinted by permission of Prentice-Hall, Inc., Englewood Cliffs, N.J.*)

Many different guide and folder combinations are possible depending on the type of records filed, supplies available, expertise of the system designer, and how the records are used. One important guideline when creating any filing system is, **"keep it as simple as possible."** Do not introduce unnecessary color coding, numbering or special subdivisions. Make everything in the system serve a useful purpose.

Miscellaneous Folders

Miscellaneous folders may be placed behind primary folders in each section. They are used in geographic systems just as in other filing systems. When you have about five pieces of active correspondence or documents relating to one item, make an individual folder.

If the miscellaneous folder is for a state, its contents should be alphabetized in the following order: (1) name of city, (2) individual correspondent, (3) date. If the folder is for a city or county, contents are alphabetized by (1) name of individual correspondent, and (2) date. The most recent date is on top.

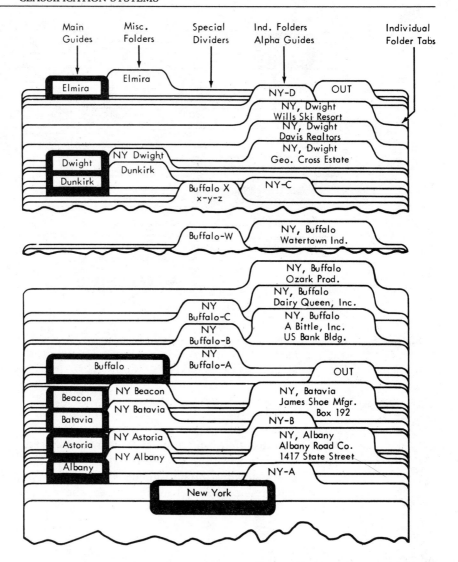

FIGURE 8—8. Geographic and individual name folders.

Charge Outs

If an active folder is removed (miscellaneous folders should never be charged out), insert a charge-out *folder* in which to store new items that come in while the original folder is out. Or, substitute a charge-out *card* for the document removed, with an OUT-tab that protrudes conspicuously. Out guide tabs are usually lined up in one position.

If only one document is taken from a folder, a charge-out *sheet* with a conspicuous tab may be used. Color coding may also be used.

Color Coding

Color coding is a means of instant identification, as illustrated by today's red, amber, and green traffic lights. It can work for you in classification systems of all types. It speeds up recognition, thus saving time; it simplifies identification, aids communication, and prevents overlooking messages or misplaced names. Color is no newcomer to filing systems but use it with judgment. Too many colors—a rainbow effect—boggle the mind.

Map-and-Tack Geographic Systems

To some extent, the so-called map-and-tack system, although in reality a visual display (see Figure 8–9) is an adaptation of color coding. For example, when used in a lumber industry, green tacks or pins with colored heads can be used to spot newly seeded areas on the map; red, a recently burned-over or devastated area; yellow, an area where trees are ready to harvest, etc.

The map-and-tack scheme can be used to identify area emergency calls, the results of an advertising campaign, a special school

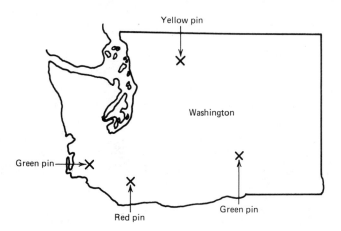

FIGURE 8–9. Color-coded map and tack system.

population, or the distribution of users of special products in area sampling surveys, to name a few examples of applications.

To be meaningful, map-and-tack files must be kept up to date. This is true, of course, for all filing systems. Much time is lost looking for documents and information when files are not maintained. Sometimes backlogged files are the result of poor work habits. Other times they may be the result of a poorly designed or too elaborate system. Records management systems should be tailored to meet the needs of the situation at hand and kept as simple as possible. The map-and-tack system should be used only when its unique characteristics really help data collection and display.

Labels

In geographic systems, it is helpful to have the first line on folder labels or tabs correspond to primary guides. For example, if the primary guide is a *country*, the first unit on the label should be the country's name. (See Figure 8–10.)

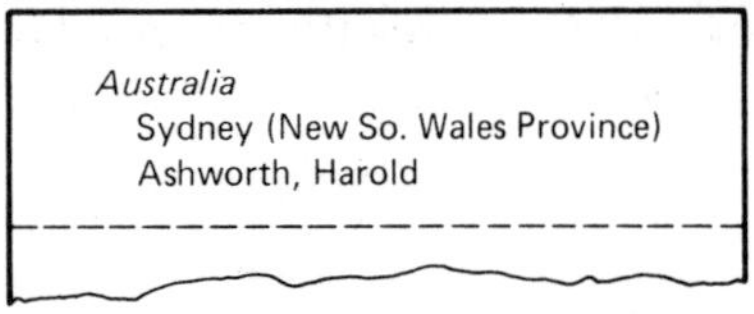

Figure 8–10. Label in a geographical system with country name first.

Folder labels also facilitate permanent cross referencing. For example—

Figure 8–11. Permanent cross-reference label.

CARD FILE SYSTEMS

This chapter and others in this book mention card files as back-ups for filing systems, but there are many other uses for card files.

Card files have an important function in records management. Special equipment has been developed for moving and storing them. Some equipment is motorized. The card systems described in the following material include vertical files, wheel files, and visible files. Computer files are not discussed here.

Advantages

Card files have the following advantages:

1. Each card is a separate, durable unit on which information can be accumulated. It can be taken from a file and handled separately.
2. Cards are easy to keep in sequence. It is easy to add or take them out of a file.
3. Card systems are easy to manipulate. It is easy to add to or take information from them.
4. Cards of the same size are easy to handle in batches.
5. Small batches of cards are easy to move in a work station or office.
6. Standardization of card sizes and equipment permits interchangeability among systems and provides flexibility.

Some type of card system is used by all businesses. Cards are used to accumulate information about customers, transactions, sales territories, products, etc. They may be arranged geographically, numerically, by date, or by subject. They may be stacked on edge or fanned out flat on trays or panels. They may be cross-referenced; tab signal systems are easy to use with them.

Guides

A guide should be used in manual systems for about every twenty-five cards so that individual items can be located quickly. (See Figure 8–12.) Guides are available with alphabetic breakdowns in sets ranging from twenty-three guides to thousands. Standard sets for 60, 100, 150, and 200 dividers are available. (See Appendix Standard Divisions for Alphabetic Guides.)

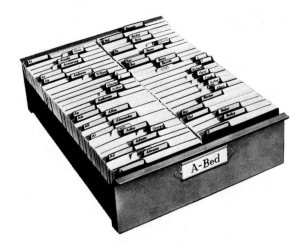

Figure 8–12. Flexindex card file. *(Courtesy Esselte Pendaflex Corp.)*

Sizes and Styles

Cards can be cut to any size, but there are several standard ones: 5″ by 3″, 6″ by 4″ and 8″ by 5″. Traditionally, we write across the breadth of a card, but there is no reason one should not turn cards in order to write lengthwise on them.

Cards can be plain or ruled; tinted or white. Like a form, they can be designed for various situations.

Designing Card Forms

When designing a card form, decide ahead of time how much information will go on it; how it will be ruled (horizontally or vertically), used, and filed; how it will be filled in; and the type of equipment used with it—typewriter, rotary wheel file, etc. When a card form is preprinted, the *variable* data gathered are posted to it. *Constant* (preprinted) data should be arranged on a card form so that the variable data are easy to identify, thus making it easy to post and find items. (See Figure 8–13.)

When card files need to be carried from one work station to another, they may be punched at the bottom and fastened into a drawer with a rod, the same way guides are sometimes fastened into file drawers.

ARMA

AMERICAN RECORDS MANAGEMENT ASSOCIATION 15th NATIONAL CONFERENCE
Century Plaza Hotel, Los Angeles, California

Name: (Mr./Mrs./Miss) ______

Company Name: ______

Address: ______

______

City: ______

State/Prov. ______ Zip ______

ARMA Chapter: ______ Non-Member ☐

My wife is registering: Yes____ No____

If yes, her name is ______

SEMINAR AND TOUR REGISTRATION
Monday, Oct. 12 (See Program)

AM (Write In) ______
PM ______

Tuesday, Oct. 13 (See Program)

AM (Write In) ______
PM ______

Wednesday, Oct. 14 (See Program)

AM (Write In) ______
PM ______

REGISTRATION FEES

FULL CONFERENCE — Members ☐ $ 90.00; Non-Members ☐ $125.00
Fee includes reception, seminars, luncheons, and banquet.
NOTE: $35.00 of non-member registration may be applied toward ARMA membership.
Check here for application. ☐

ONE DAY REGISTRATION ☐ $ 40.00
Fee includes seminars and luncheon on any day of attendance.

BANQUET ☐ $ 15.00

LADIES PROGRAM ☐ $ 30.00
Fee includes: Tour through Universal Studios and Beverly Hills, A Harbor Tour, A special seminar on "Record Keeping in the Home," evening social events, and banquet.

SPECIAL EVENTS AND TOURS
Arrangements will be made for special events scheduled through Thursday, October 15. Please note your preference. The cost is not included in registration fee.

Disneyland ☐ Knott's Berry Farm ☐ Marineland ☐

PAYMENT OF FEES
Make check or money order payable to: 1970 ARMA National Conference and mail to:
Worldway Postal Center
P.O. Box 90550
Los Angeles, California 90009

For additional registration forms, write amount here. ______

Your Pre-Registration Becomes Part of the Earlybird Drawing

FIGURE 8–13. Convention registration: A preprinted card. (*Source: Place, Popham, Fujita,* Fundamental Filing Practice, © 1973. *Reprinted by permission of Prentice-Hall, Inc., Englewood Cliffs, N.J.*)

TYPES OF CARD SYSTEMS

The following types of card systems are described below: (1) vertical, (2) wheel, and (3) visible.

Vertical Card Files

Cards stand upright (on edge) in so-called vertical files, and can be compressed tightly to economize on space. But when new items are posted, the card must be lifted out of the file and put on a flat writing surface; then it must be re-filed. For this reason, *visible* card files are recommended where new items are often added to a card reference file.

Visible Card Files

Visible card files are fanned out with overlapping edges. (See Figure 8–14.) The "overlap" leaves a *visible* margin which is how this system gets its name.

FIGURE 8–14. A visible index panel. *(Courtesy Business & Institutional Furniture Co.)*

Visible cards can be stored in trays, narrow flat drawers, books, or suspended on panels. Regardless of how they are stored, they all have the same advantage of quick access. Important items are written on the bottom visible margin and are visible at all times.

An advantage of visible files is that it is easy to add new items to a card. To do so, just lift the cards ahead of the one on which you want to write. (The cards fit on a trunnion wire, as can be seen on Figure 8–15 and are easy to lift.) The ease of adding new items to visible card files is a timesaver.

Signals

Another advantage of visible files is that they are easy to signal. Tabs can be attached to the visible strip in any position or color. In a subscription file, for instance, a red tab might mean that the subscription is past due or a yellow tab might signal that the subscription is for a school to which copies are mailed in bulk. These color signals can be read at a glance and special items are quickly located in the file.

When designing a visible card, put the indexing captions and signal code areas on the bottom edge where they are visible.

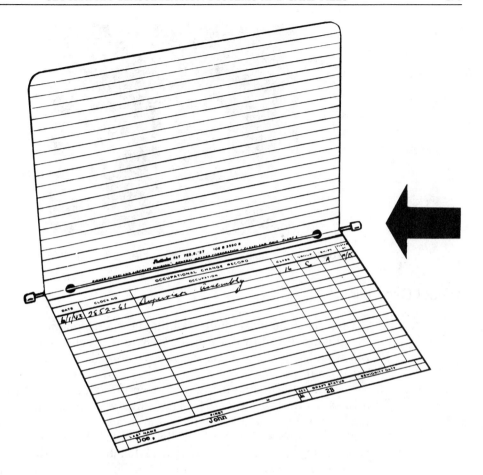

FIGURE 8–15. Visible system card on trunnion wire for easy posting. (*Courtesy Data-vue Products Corp.*)

Mobility

One type of visible file often used for name and address listings or price lists is made up of strips which are fitted into a panel. (See Figure 8–16.) In addition to total visibility when looking at a panel, new strips are easily added without breaking alphabetic or numeric sequence. Merely pull out the strip that is to be removed, or push two strips apart to make space for inserting a new one.

FIGURE 8–16. Visible insertible strip file. (*Courtesy Wilson Jones Co.*)

Wheel Card Files

A card file sometimes found standing near a telephone is a wheel file. (See Figure 8–17.) In it, cards are easy to reference by merely turning the wheel, and new items usually can be added without removing cards from the wheel.

Wheel files come in sizes suitable for cards that hold from 4 to 5 lines up to 8″ by 5″ cards. Large cards are suitable for accumulating case records such as medical summaries, research projects, or investment records. Small wheel files for a few hundred cards may be kept on top of a desk, whereas desk-height wheels that hold thousands of large cards may be housed in a movable tub file and stand within easy reach, as part of a work station.

FIGURE 8–17. A handy reference rotary desk file. (*Courtesy Rolodex Corp.*)

The Unit Concept

The first advantage given for card systems on page 175 is that cards make good *unit* records because each card can be handled separately. A sheet of paper can also be handled separately. Is it, therefore, not also a *unit* record? Perhaps, but the unit concept referred to in card files is that cards lend themselves to accumulating easily accessed files of data. As mentioned in this chapter, they make a good back-up system for geographic files because they facilitate cross referencing and the accumulating of related bits of information. (See Figure 8–18.) Unit card records become "master cards" of accumulated data; they are easy to reference and transport. Therefore, although a sheet of 8.5″×11″ stationery could conceivably become a unit record, the concept is not so naturally applied since sheets, being limp, need to be supported and maintained in folders or binders.

Card *unit* systems, where each card is an easily accessed unit, are flexible and adaptable. They have countless applications: source references, personnel records, project data, etc. Except when visible equipment is used, the key caption on a unit card record should be put in the upper left corner because this is an easy spot to see, especially as one thumbs through a tray or fans through a deck of unit cards. (See Figure 8–18.)

WORLD Affairs Council

Room 72, 461 N.E. Yamhill Road
Poughkeepsie, New York

J. M. Baker in charge of programs.
Vickie Strozio, assistant to Baker.

FIGURE 8–18. A reference card. (*Source: Place, Popham, Fujita,* Fundamental Filing Practice, © 1973. *Reprinted by permission of Prentice-Hall, Inc., Englewood Cliffs, N.J.*)

REVIEW QUESTIONS (Geographic Systems)

1. What is geographic filing?

2. What is an advantage of geographic filing? A disadvantage?

3. Describe two situations where a company might use geographic files.

4. Describe a record-keeping system in which one might insert geographic guides into a regular alphabetic correspondence name filing system.

5. What problems do you see in merging geographic guides with regular alphabetic correspondence name folders?

6. How are charge outs handled in geographic filing?

7. What is a map-and-tack geographic file?

8. Describe a situation in which a map-and-tack file should be used.

9. What do you see as a disadvantage of a map-and-tack file? An advantage?

10. What do you do with miscellaneous items in geographic systems?

11. How do you cross reference in geographic systems?

12. When might you use a supplementary card system in geographic filing?

13. How would you sort items for a geographic file?

REVIEW QUESTIONS (Card Systems)

1. Name five advantages of card filing systems.

2. What are the advantages of vertical card files? Disadvantages?

3. What are the advantages of visible files? Disadvantages?

4. What are the advantages of wheel files? Disadvantages?

5. What guidelines should be used when designing a card form?

6. What are constant data on a card form? Variable data?

7. Give three standard sizes of card files.

8. How do you signal special items on vertical cards? On visible cards?

LEARNING ACTIVITIES

Answer each of the following fourteen items with a *yes* or *no*.

Example:

In a geographic file would you file:

Answer

x. Mamie W. Lasonde, Aspen, North Carolina, after Lasons   x.___no___
    Service, Aspon, South Carolina
1. Eisenberg Furs, Pratt City, Oklahoma, before Eisenberg,
    R. L., Piper Lake, Ohio?
2. The Four Ed's Restaurant, Brooklyn, New York, before The
    Four-Forty Grill, Brooklyn, Michigan?
3. Lane-Bender Associates of Scranton, Pennsylvania, before
    Lane Bryant of Scranton, Pennsylvania?
4. Neo-Art Studio, Wheeling, West Virginia, before Neo Clas-
    sical Art Studios, Inc., Wheeling, West Virginia?
5. Kel-Mer Van Corp., West Port, New York after Kelmer's
    Bargain City of West Point, New York?
6. Fiberbilt Sample Case Co., Arlington, Missouri, before Fiber
    Case Novelty Co., Arlington, Massachusetts?
7. National Bank of Detroit (Michigan) before National Bank of
    Butte (Montana)?
8. The Iberia Air Lines of Spain, New York City, before Iber-
    American Distributing Company of New York City?
9. Lady Lyda Corp. of Johnson, Vermont before Lady Lyda Ca-
    pers Cookies, Johnson, Virginia?
10. LaCloche D'Or Cafe, Leeds, Massachusetts, before Mrs.
    D. LaCloche, Lees, Massachusetts?
11. Jacob Rice Glass Company, Eden, Kentucky before J. C.
    Rice, Edan, Kentucky?
12. Paulette Rheem of East Town, New York, after Paula Rhem
    of Easton, New York?
13. N.Y. Philharmonic Symphony Society, New York, before
    N.Y. Phoenix School of Design, New York?
14. Progressive Electronic Contractors Corporation, Uptown,
    New York, before Progressive Electronics Company, Up-
    town, North Carolina?

PROJECTS

Project 1. *Updating Subscriptions*

Figure 8–19 shows map of the United States divided into five areas:
Northwest, Southwest, Central, Northeast, and Southeast.

Prepare forty index cards for subscribers to a professional magazine. Include names and addresses.

Alphabetize the forty cards:

a. Rough sort by state.

b. Fine sort where there are two or more cards for a guide.

FIGURE 8–19. Map of the United States. (*Source: Place, Popham, Fujita*, Fundamental Filing Practice, © 1973. *Reprinted by permission of Prentice-Hall, Inc., Englewood Cliffs, N.J.*)

c. Make a set of guides by pasting "tabs" to additional cards. Insert the individual name-and-address cards behind the guides.

Update the file by writing the following corrections on the appropriate cards:

Changes

a. Change Belle Meachim's subscription (Fairfield, Conn.) to 88 Phillips, Bridgeport, Conn.

b. Change the spelling of Abrons House, Miller, Nebraska, to Abrown House.

Additions

1. George Fink Industries, Satlow Drive, Fort Atkinson, Wisconsin

2. General Offices, Adam's Brush Company, 14 Mullett Drive, Lynwood, California

3. Horological Works, Inc., 15 Castle Building, Richmond, Virginia

4. Kriwow Farms, Inc., Denver, Colo.

5. Highway Transportation Study Headquarters, N.Y. Metropolitan Region, 201 Park Avenue, New York, New York

6. Roland Walton, 731 Amsterdam Avenue, Miami, Florida

7. Robert Rogoff, 691 State Building, Duluth, Minnesota

8. Theo. Quarg, 105 Mill Road, Scranton, Pennsylvania

9. Prepare index cards for the above additions. File them.

10. Print in the names of the states on the map. With a colored pencil, plot the distribution of the subscriptions you have for twenty-three states by placing a dot or x at the appropriate location. (This part of the project simulates working with a map-and-tack file.)

11. Prepare a brief summary statement showing the total number of subscriptions by state and area: Northeast, Central, Northwest, Southwest and Southeast. Give the summary an appropriate title.

Subscribers to QUICK THOUGHTS

1. Mrs. Mario Buccellati, 705 Plaza Street, Black Hills, South Dakota.
2. Dennis Horowitz, 277 First Avenue, New York, New York
3. Vincent Finn and Son, One Madison Street, Cleveland, Ohio
4. Mrs. Lolita Roche Diaze, 17 Sherwood Road, Ypsilanti, Michigan
5. The Culver Fabrics Shop, 4518 So. 69th Street, San Antonio, Texas
6. Henry Csigay, 1543 Marlboro Blvd., Superior, Wisconsin
7. The Eastside Methodist Church, 70–74 Carling Blvd., Minneapolis, Minnesota
8. Barney Cuccioli, 60 Riverside Drive, Freeport, Maine
9. Camp Na-Wa-Kwa, Sheridan Lane, Bangor, Maine
10. Hayes Malcolm, Manhattan Drive, Fort Lauderdale, Florida
11. Michael Malge, Corning Road, Orange, Texas
12. The Maline Associates, Inc., 4633 Tower Building, San Francisco, California
13. The Ponce DeLeon Hotel, Fairfield, Florida
14. Smilow-Thielle Furniture, 1860 Cresset, Chicago, Illinois
15. The United Ignition Corporation, 11352 Chambers Building, Detroit, Michigan
16. The United Nations Mission (Pakistan), 8 East 65th Street, NE, Washington, D.C.
17. United States Academy Motel, Highland Falls Road, Arlington, Virginia
18. Office of the Auditor General, United States Air Force, 641 Washington Street, New York City
19. United States Coast Guard Base, St. George Bay, Long Island, New York
20. Administrative Office, National Aeronautics and Space Administration, Western Division, Olympia, Washington
21. Harkness Naval Base, Floyd Bennett Field, Brooklyn, New York
22. Wright Patterson Air Base, Columbus, Ohio
23. The National Bank of Pueblo, Pueblo, Colorado
24. US Projector Corporation, WOW Building, Des Moines, Iowa
25. J. C. McWade, Hanson Blvd., Albuquerque, New Mexico
26. Miss Belle Meachim, Gold River Drive, Fairfield, Connecticut
27. Mathew McO'Neal, Greview Road, Long Beach, California
28. The In Friendship Cafe, Commerce Building, Philadelphia, Pennsylvania
29. The In-Tag Suppliers, 18285 Archer Building, Dallas, Texas
30. J. G. McOrlly, 4200 East Washington, Butte, Montana
31. McSorels Old Timers Inn, Galesburg, Illinois
32. Al Horswell, 4829 South Blvd., Beverly Hills, California

33. Karl Fink, M.D., 140 Medical Center, Boston Massachusetts
34. Mary Bubniak, Professor of History, University of Nebraska, Lincoln, Nebraska
35. Mrs. Shirley Buchalter, West End Avenue, Beacon Hill, Massachusetts
36. Jack Adams M.D., 14 Hilton Road, Bradford, Pennsylvania
37. The Abrons House, Miller, Nebraska
38. The Academy of American Poets, 1078 Madison Avenue, Shelby, North Carolina
39. Cooper-Bessemer Corporation, General Offices, Scranton, Pennsylvania
40. Geneno Brothers, Realtors, Acme Building, Jacksonville, Florida

Project 2. A Card File for Catalogs

Purpose:

In this project, you are a records buyer in the purchasing department of an airplane manufacturing company. You work with about 300 catalogs of different sizes and thicknesses. About fifteen hundred different items are ordered from the thousands of articles described in them. You decide that a related card system by subject would make it easier for you to work with the catalogs.

This project aims to:

1. give you a systems design problem to think about and solve on your own;
2. give you experience in designing a card file form;
3. give you experience in setting up a card system.

Instructions:

Design a card for quick reference to information the catalogs contain

a. for a vertical card system
b. for a visible card system.

Use a regular catalog for ideas about which items to include on the cards.

9

Equipment and Supplies

Over three thousand companies manufacture and sell filing equipment and supplies. Because the "tools" they manufacture—file station equipment, file cabinets, specially designed shelving, storage and magnetic media containers, folders, guides, etc.—are used in records maintenance systems of all types, records managers must be knowledgeable about them. They must know which systems are best served by file cabinets, open shelves, cartridges, carrousels, or automated equipment. They must decide which vendor to use. Selection of equipment should consider the type of records involved, personal preferences, office decor, budget, reference ratios in both active and inactive areas, storage needs, and special maintenance problems, if any.

There are many different kinds of equipment from which to choose. It is often hard to know which is best for a company's particular needs; which to buy in quantity, and on which to standardize. Standardization simplifies buying, keeps systems uniform and neat, and makes transfer easier among systems throughout a company.

Equipment and supplies discussed in this chapter include drawer files, shelf files, rotary files, and some motorized, suspension, and storage equipment; folders, guides, dividers, tabs, and such miscellaneous items as labels, sorters, and even work stools. The chapter ends with some equipment and supply guidelines, and comments about centralized buying, work station design, and layout trends.

DRAWER FILES

Three types of drawer files are described here: vertical, drop front, and lateral. Each has unique advantages and characteristics which contribute to efficient work methods when filing or retrieving materials or when combined with work stations. For example, the drop front increases storage capacity and the lateral improves accessibility.

Vertical

Vertical files are so called because folders and documents stored in them stand on end, vertically. Vertical files for letter or legal size records come in 2-, 3-, 4-, 5-, and even 6-drawer styles. (See Figure 9–1.) They are 24, 26, or 28 inches long but some, usually the portable ones, are only 18 inches long. A standard 26-inch drawer can hold 3500–5000 sheets plus guides and folders. Drawers vary from 12½ inches wide (letter) to 15½ inches (legal). Most are 10 ⅜ inches deep. A folder is 9 inches high plus a ½-inch tab, so there is a ⅞-inch clearance (10 ⅜ - 9½) at the top of the drawer. Even metal-tabbed guides measure no higher than 10 inches, leaving ⅜ of an inch in the clear.

Applications

Four-drawer files are widely used, but three-drawer files can also be used as counters over which to serve customers. One- and two-drawer files make convenient additions to work stations when used as desk files.

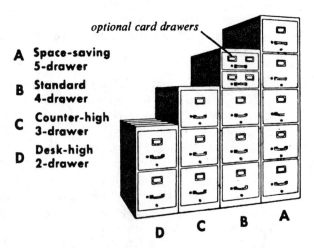

optional card drawers

A **Space-saving 5-drawer**

B **Standard 4-drawer**

C **Counter-high 3-drawer**

D **Desk-high 2-drawer**

D   C   B   A

FIGURE 9–1. 2-, 3-, 4-, 5-drawer vertical files.

Five- and six-drawer files have the advantage of conserving space. By making drawers slightly shallower than the usual 10⅜ inches, a six-drawer cabinet uses the same area as a conventional five-drawer file. Only ¹¹⁄₁₆ of an inch is allowed for tab clearance. Satisfactory in storage areas, five- and six-drawer files are not recommended for active files.

Interchangeable Drawers

Interchangeability of drawers is a feature that influences the selection of drawer files. As contents of files become less active, they should be moved to low-priority locations, and it is easier to move an entire drawer than to unload contents, move them, and reload in a new location. Interchangeable drawers provide flexibility within a records maintenance system network.

Drop Front

A drawer file variation that saves internal space is a drop-front as shown in Figure 9–2. The drop front provides 4 extra inches of interior working space when the front is latched forward. When accumulated, the space saved becomes significant. Two 4-drawer drop-front files save the equivalent of two 18-inch long drawers $(4 \times 4 = 16$ per file $\times 2$ files $= 32$ inches.) Consider how this saving multiplies in a storage area of fifty or more files.

Because drop-front files provide extra work space, it is easier to find and file materials in them. The front area can even be used as a temporary "holding" space while working in the drawer.

Lateral

Instead of pulling out 18 to 28 inches, the drawer of a lateral file pulls out 13 to 16 inches depending on whether it contains standard or legal-size documents. This space-saving feature makes it convenient to use lateral files in aisles or at desks. (See Figure 9–3.) Files opened broadside (laterally) save both aisle and working space. Lateral files for letter or legal size documents come in 2-, 3-, 4-, and 5-drawer styles, 26, 30, or 42 inches wide. Folders can be stored either facing the front of the drawer or the length of the drawer. Modular 2- and 3-drawer lateral units can also be stacked as shown in background of Figure 9–3 to accommodate various types of work stations.

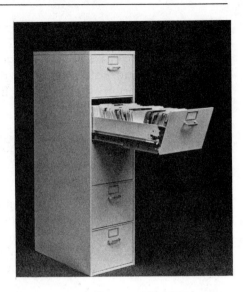

FIGURE 9—2. File with drop front provides extra working space. *(Courtesy The General Fireproofing Co.)*

FIGURE 9—3. Lateral files provide extra working space and are readily accessible. *(Courtesy Esselte Pendaflex Corp.)*

Quality Features

File drawer quality features described below include file strength, suspension construction, and fireproofing; security locks; follow blocks; and mobility.

Strength

Several features distinguish a high quality drawer file: ballbearing drawer suspension rods with steel telescoping slides, insulated walls to withstand heat and provide a degree of fireproofing; and braced inner construction, braced for extra rigidity. When a drawer is full, it weighs sixty to seventy pounds. Loaded drawers handle best when they move on telescoping slides with ball-bearing rollers. Another feature of a good drawer file is a guide rod strung through holes in the bottom of guides, thus holding them securely in place.

Security Locks

Security locks are desirable file drawer features. Gang locks will, in one operation, engage all drawers in a cabinet. Combination locks for single drawers are also available. Figure 9–4 shows a 4-drawer file with a combination lock and a drawer on telescoping slides with insulated walls.

Follow Blocks

Until a file drawer is full, some device is needed to hold contents upright. A common file drawer supplement for this purpose is a follow block or compressor. This device should release easily and slide back and forth on guide rails at the bottom of the drawer, locking into the desired position automatically. (See Figure 9–4.)

Mobility

Readily accessible work materials make jobs easier. Equipment that brings work to the worker saves time and effort. (See Figure 9–5.)

Almost any type of filing equipment can be mobilized by providing wheel bases. In storage areas, high density automated shelving is available that glides along tracks on flanged wheels. One aisle does the job for four or five compacted rows of shelves which can be wheeled apart, with the flick of a button if automated. (See Figure 9–6.) Sometimes access aisles occupy as much as 50 percent of usable space. With mobile systems, manual or automated, much of this space is reclaimed.

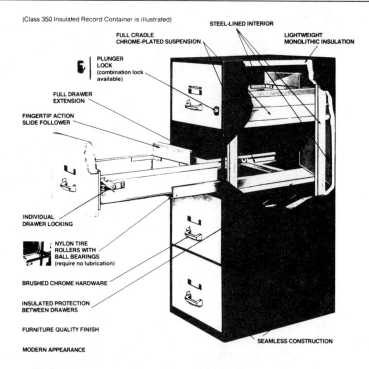

(Class 350 Insulated Record Container is illustrated)

STEEL-LINED INTERIOR

FULL CRADLE
CHROME-PLATED SUSPENSION

LIGHTWEIGHT
MONOLITHIC INSULATION

PLUNGER
LOCK
(combination lock
available)

FULL DRAWER
EXTENSION

FINGERTIP ACTION
SLIDE FOLLOWER

INDIVIDUAL
DRAWER LOCKING

NYLON TIRE
ROLLERS WITH
BALL BEARINGS
(require no lubrication)

BRUSHED CHROME HARDWARE

INSULATED PROTECTION
BETWEEN DRAWERS

FURNITURE QUALITY FINISH

MODERN APPEARANCE

SEAMLESS CONSTRUCTION

FIGURE 9—4. A 4-drawer file cabinet, insulated and reinforced. Telescoping drawer supports and a combination lock. *(Courtesy Diebold, Inc.)*

FIGURE 9—5. Mobile tub file at a work station. *(Courtesy Systems Mfg. Co.)*

FIGURE 9—6. Automated shelving provides movable aisles. *(Courtesy Hill & Knowlton, Inc.)*

Tub and Open Access Rollaways

A flexible piece of equipment is the open access rollaway tub file. This easy-access file is available in standing or sitting heights. It may be used to hang folders, house trays of cards or computer printouts. Some are equipped with moveable shelves or over-file sliding work areas and locking covers (see Figure 9–5). Easily moved from area to area as needed, tub rollaways are flexible additions to various types of work stations. Those containing confidential material can be rolled into a walk-in vault for extra safety.

Open Shelf

Closed cabinets of some type or other will be used for years to come, but open files offer cost, time, and space savings advantages. The shelving may extend to the ceiling and can be used in open office areas to absorb sound. Contents are visible at a glance and are easy to get at. (See Figure 9–7.) Files of documents, magazines, books, binders of cases or research, catalogs, reels of tapes, blueprints, computer printouts, X-rays, and samples can be filed on shelves.

FIGURE 9—7. Open shelf files. *(Courtesy Barry Wright Corp.)*

Possible Problems

Possible problems of open shelf files are:

> lack of confidentiality
> use by unauthorized people
> lack of control in filing operations, hence frequent misfilings.

Dividers

Ordinary folders like those used in drawer files may be transferred to shelf files when proper shelf guides and dividers are used. Shelf dividers (see Figure 9–8) help keep materials upright when hanging folders are not used. The dividers may be portable boxes or metal sheets that hook into the shelf. Portable boxes make handy document containers when located on a readily accessible shelf as part of a work station. When files become inactive, the boxes can be labeled and reversed on the shelf, thus providing their contents relatively dustproof storage.

Rotary

Rotary files are designed to rotate either horizontally or vertically according to the principles of a carousel merry-go-round or a Ferris wheel. (See Figure 9–9.) Basically a vertical rotary file takes up less

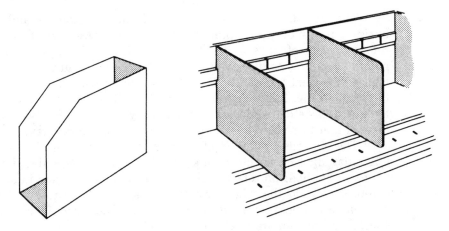

FIGURE 9—8. Portable box and metal dividers for open shelves. (*Source: Place, Popham, Fujita, Fundamental Filing Practice, © 1973. Reprinted by permission of Prentice-Hall, Inc., Englewood Cliffs, N.J.)*

space but more people can, at the same time, access horizontal units. Each tier rotates independently, thus providing work station flexibility. Units with five to eight tiers create multipurpose work stations for printout reports, disk packs, tape reels, binders, folders, and cards. Units have been made up to 16 feet in diameter; diameters vary, of course, depending on record size and capacity requirements. Either motorized or manual operation is available. Units can be custom designed as compatible components to various types of work stations.

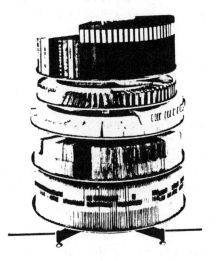

FIGURE 9—9. Tiered rotary file.

Though rotary files hold card records, binders, folders, and other business items, they have other applications too. We have all seen the rotating series of trays in a gift shop showcase which pauses a moment at each tray to display the items on it before it automatically rotates to the next tray. One jeweler uses a motorized vertical tray file for order filling. Small envelopes containing jewelry items are put in the file alphabetically by customer name. When called for, buttons are pushed that turn the wheel automatically to the desired tray.

The elongated rotary track hung with garments has also become a familiar sight in dry cleaning establishments. Spices and dishes are stored in kitchens on rotary shelves; slides may be indexed in a home carousel file. On the whole, rotary files are easily visible and their contents are quickly brought to the worker. They also adapt well to special coding and are easily color coded.

Motorized

The movement of papers being processed is part of the mainstream activity of any business office. One of the factors that determines how efficiently papers are moved in an office is the type of equipment used. Whenever motorized or automatic equipment is available, it should be used, because it saves time and effort in moving and processing paperwork. It may also increase the quality of the work by cutting down the chance for human errors. Employee time is one of the biggest cost factors in business and can be saved with powered equipment. A rule of thumb guideline when comparing automatic with manual equipment costs is that if the motorized equipment pays for itself in two years in cost of employee time saved, it is a good investment.

Special Features and Equipment

Records such as drawings, blueprints, offset mats, stencils, and tapes need special equipment. Special equipment with features designed to handle such materials include hanging files, motorized files, tape files, and storage/security files. A separate chapter is devoted to automated files (Chapter 14) and card files were discussed in Chapter 8, so they are not included here, although some of the equipment discussed relates to them.

Hanging Folders

Hanging folders are suspended from an inner drawer or shelf rack (See Figure 9–10) and eliminate folder sag and slump. They do, however, use extra space because of folder hooks and the frame on which

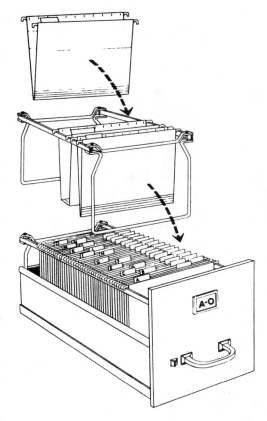

Figure 9–10. Hanging folder racks. *(Courtesy Esselte Pendaflex Corp.)*

they hang. The initial cost of a hanging-folder system is likely to be more than for regular files because of the special equipment. Unless regular folders are put inside hanging folders, it is inconvenient to charge out contents because folders with hooks are awkward to carry in a briefcase or use with other work papers at a desk. Their contents may, of course, be transferred easily to regular folders for out-of-file use. Systems analysis studies can reveal the special record keeping situations where hanging folders are justified.

Tape Files

Tape files have widespread use today, especially as offices continue to adopt some form of electronic data processing. Billions of digits of data and hundreds of computer programs are filed on magnetic tape which must be protected from dust, scratches, and be readily available as needed by computers. Tapes may be stored in equipment similar to that used in regular filing (See Figure 9–11.) but the trend is to

FIGURE 9—11. A tape library. *(Courtesy Hill & Knowlton, Inc.)*

use hanging, self-threading cartridges with wrap-around plastic bands and pressure sensitive labels for easy identification. Canisters, carrying cases, and mailer boxes are available as needed.

Beatrice Widbrew, Tape Library Manager for Bradford Administrative Services since 1978 emphasizes six basic considerations for an efficient tape library.[1]

1. Physical layout; provide quick access and keep a sharp eye on flow of tapes to and from the computers. Plan ahead for expansion.
2. Select and carefully train dependable personnel.
3. Make the best of what is available but plan for the future.
4. Set up procedures that explain how the library handles each phase of its part in the company's total information processing system.
5. Review equipment and systems for security; check off-site backup tapes.
6. Tapes need to be scheduled for regular maintenance. Those held on a long-term basis should be cleaned once a year. Those used daily should be cleaned every twentieth time the tape is used.

Maximum security tapes may be kept in an ordinary safe or in specially designed magnetic media record safes with double-door and

---

[1]Beatrice Widbrew, "Six Steps to an Efficient Tape Library," *Information and Records Management*, April 1980, p. 48.

double-wall construction and with special inner compartments for disks, microfilm, microfiche, and punched cards as well as for magnetic tape. (See Figure 9–12.)

Safes

Often vital or confidential records need added protection in a safe. When selecting such equipment, comparisons should be made among the variety available from different manufacturers. Records managers are usually responsible for researching and then recommending equipment for the maximum protection of highly confidential and vital records.

No claim is made by vault or safe manufacturers that their regular equipment will protect tapes from explosions or other calamities. During a fire, tapes, disks, or similar magnetic materials stored in a standard insulated vault or safe could be damaged or destroyed by high temperatures and humidity. Regular safe equipment is tested for 150 degrees F or 85 percent relative humidity. (Paper combusts at 350 degrees.) Special safes must be designed for protection beyond this.

Special fire-resistant, free-standing safes with insulation between two steel walls may withstand temperatures up to 1700 degrees

Figure 9–12. Safe-keeping for a variety of electronic data processing media. *(Courtesy Diebold, Inc.)*

or can fall through a destroyed floor without bursting. They are equipped with various types of locks; key, time clocks, and combinations. Safes can also be built into existing walls and structures. A walk-in space might be needed for mobile tub file overnight storage. Or an inner drawer and shelf configuration can be designed for tapes, reels, disk packs, and microforms as shown in Fig. 9–12. Unique interiors can be custom designed for various needs.

Special Storage Equipment Features

Only special materials are stored in safes; most are stored in inactive or off-site areas in transfer boxes (see Fig. 9–13) and binders on open shelves. The selection of storage boxes, binders, and shelves is affected by how much the contents will be used in storage as well as by the items to be stored. Reinforced, corrugated, fiberboard boxes (12″ × 15″ × 10″) are popular. Most have hand holes for easy carrying; some have front label frames or preprinted label forms. Some have lift-off lids, others a simple tie-down-close top; some are stored in steel framework shelving and pull out with a front handle like a regular file. With the latter equipment, each drawer is operational even when boxes are stacked to the ceiling.

Figure 9–13. Transfer box storage. *(Courtesy Gussco Mfg., Inc.)*

Called transfer boxes or archives containers, storage boxes are letter/legal size but can also be used to hold cards, microfiche, checks, ledgers, and even printouts (although the latter are best stored in binders or suspension folders).

Corrugated cardboard, of which the boxes are made, can be treated to make it water repellent and protect the boxes from either a sprinkler system, rain, or mildew. Some boxes are reinforced with double walls, metal corner braces or steel reinforcement rods and can be stacked on top of each other without the added expense of steel framework shelving. Low-cost, all steel transfer files or used file cabinets can also be used for cancelled checks, tab/index cards, supplies, etc. The combinations that are possible with such equipment are limitless and call on the ingenuity and perceptiveness of the records manager. The final criteria are that material should be organized in order to be easily accessed, protected against the deterioration of time and that equipment should be adapted.

SUPPLIES

Equipment and supplies represent a considerable cost to business; the cost of paper itself has increased sharply. When selecting guides, folders, and related filing supplies, records personnel should consider need, general quality, durability, possible standardization, centralized buying, distribution controls, recycling (if any) and cost. The following describes some specific things to watch for when selecting folders, guides, dividers, tabs and labels, and miscellaneous items such as sorters, stools, and ladders.

Folders

Paper documents should be stored in identified folders, not put loose in a file drawer. Ideally a folder should be thin, stiff, and strong with a hard, smooth surface so that it resists soiling and slides easily in and out of the files. (See Figure 9–14.)

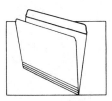

FIGURE 9–14. Tab-cut, reinforced, scored folder. (*Source: Place, Popham, Fujita, Fundamental Filing Practice*, © 1973. *Reprinted by permission of Prentice-Hall, Inc., Englewood Cliffs, N.J.*)

Composition

Folders are made of manila, kraft, jute, or pressboard. Even plastic folders are available; some are plastic coated for durability. Top-grade folders come in different weights: 8-point (medium weight), 11-point (heavy), and 14-point (extra heavy). Some have special inner pockets or clasps to fasten documents. (See Figure 9–15.)

Expansibility

Folders are scored at the bottom so they can be expanded. Some have only one score, others have several thus providing a flat surface for the bottom of the folder as it fills. Although not ordinarily recommended, folders can expand to thicknesses up to two inches.

Size

The traditional concept of a folder is the letter (8½ × 11 inches) or legal size (8½ × 14 inches) for paper documents. However, new office systems are introducing new types and sizes for nonpaper "documents." For example, word processing folders are designed espe-

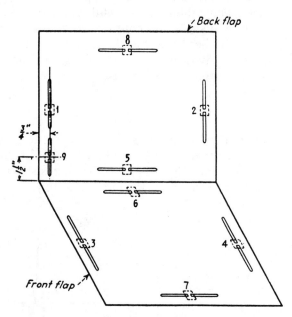

FIGURE 9–15. Location of fasteners in folders. (*Source: Place, Popham, Fujita,* Fundamental Filing Practice, © 1973. *Reprinted by permission of Prentice-Hall, Inc., Englewood Cliffs, N.J.*)

cially to co-file magnetic cards, source documents, and regular hard copy.

Color

Solid-color folders or folders with color coded strips can be adapted to various filing systems: digit, alphabetic, geographic—or given special significance such as confidential, material from the president's office, or a general charge out. (See page 173 for more on color coding.)

Binders

The term *binder* has two general uses: (1) It is a natural development from folders with inner pockets and clasps. That is, it is a suitable pocketed folder with or without a tie-down flap. This type of binder comes in a variety of styles from the familiar single pocket orangish kraft envelope type with tie-down flap, to a multi-pocketed one which sometimes substitutes for a briefcase and is often used in law offices for briefs. (See Figure 9–16a.) (2) The other "binder" compresses papers so that a three- or four-inch thickness of bound documents while firmly compressed still opens easily, lies flat, and stays open when used. A folder with a metal fastener (see Figure 9–16b) is a type of binder. Other types are available and are used to store accumulations of forms or for computer printouts which may be suspended on swivel flanges for easy reference. Bound printouts are less susceptible to the general abuse of loss and scatter incurred by unbound material.

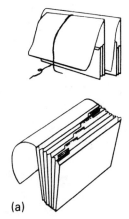

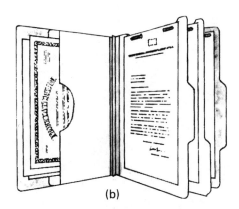

(a)　　　　　　　　　　　　　　　　　　　　　(b)

FIGURE 9–16. (a) An expandible folder with a tie string and pockets; (b) Specially designed word-processing folder. *(Courtesy Gussco Mfg., Inc.)*

Guides

Guides are the signposts of a filing system. They also help to keep folders upright and prevent sagging. A guide must be durable because it takes the strain when files move back and forth as a drawer is opened and closed. (See Figure 9–17—Durable guides: celluloided, angled, metal riveted, and with rod projections.)

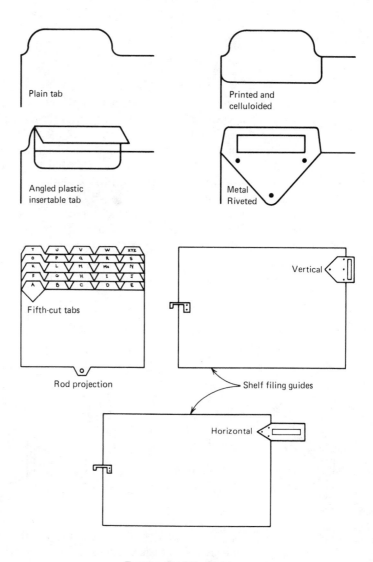

FIGURE 9–17. Guides.

How many guides to a drawer or shelf? Experts recommend one for each 6 to 8 folders in active files. This averages out to about 15 per drawer. Fewer, of course, are needed in inactive files.

Regular

Regular guides are usually stiff pressboard. Thickness is measured in points, one point being 1/1000 of an inch. A 25-point guide is .025 inches thick; a 20-point guide is lighter; a 35-point, heavier.

Hanging

Guides and folders used in hanging files discussed earlier in this chapter are equipped with plastic, metallic, or steel hooked side hangers and are available in the usual letter or legal sizes as well as for special files. For example, self-stick "hang-its" attachments convert a standard diskette jacket to a hanging file pocket strong enough to hold several dozen word-processing diskettes.

Out

Out guides are customarily used over and over again, so they need to be the same durable construction as regular guides. When the guide is ruled across the front (see Figure 9–18), the name and identifying data of the user can be written on the next available line each time the guide is used, thus acting as an on-the-spot follow-up, showing who has the file and the date it was taken. Dropped into a folder as a substitute for a removed document, this type of out guide also needs a prominent tab.

Dividers

In most files, guides act as dividers, but not always. Shelf files use metal dividers that interlock at the back of the shelves or modular box-like units may act as dividers. (See Figure 9–8.) Dividers range from pressboard to plastic and steel and have several functions. For example, drawers may be divided vertically to handle two or three rows of cards or several types of materials. Properly selected, dividers prevent slumping folders and increase file organization.

Tabs

File tabs, in addition to serving as guide posts for finding, may double as handles for moving files back and forth in a file drawer. That is, tabs may be handled a lot and some kind of reinforcement is needed.

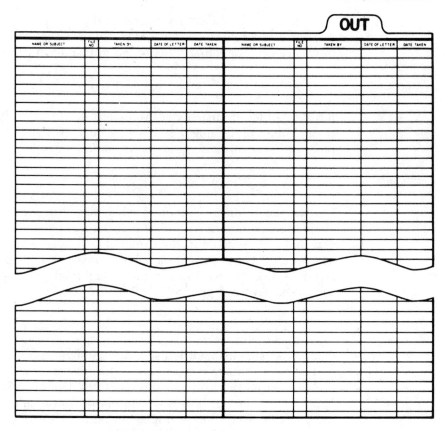

FIGURE 9–18. Out guides ruled for identifying data. (*Source: Place, Popham, Fujita, Fundamental Filing Practice, © 1973. Reprinted by permission of Prentice-Hall, Inc., Englewood Cliffs, N.J.*)

Tabs or guides are metal framed or plastic reinforced or coated. Remember to systematize tab positions; when aligned, they speed up both finding and filing.

Insertable tabs are often used on guides. (See Figure 9–19.) It costs less to change tab inserts than to replace a whole set of solid-tab guides. Sets of preprinted tab inserts are available in countless alphabetic breakdowns based on statistical studies of individual and company names.[2] Pre-printed tab inserts with numbers, geographic locations, common names, dates, etc. are also available. Tabs that hold inserts may be angular, metal edged, or riveted to the guide. (See Figure 9–17.) Riveted tabs are durable. Angular tabs provide maximum visibility.

[2]See Appendix: Standard Divisions for Alphabetic Guides.

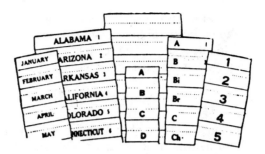

FIGURE 9–19. Tab inserts.

Folder tabs, although not metal edged, may be reinforced with a double thickness although many are a mere single thickness extension of the back of the folder. They are, however, somewhat strengthened by a paste-on label.

Cuts

The width of a guide or folder tab is known as its cut. A fifth-cut tab is 1/5 of the entire width, whether letter or legal size. Most popular cuts are 1/5 and 1/3, although cuts of from 1/7 to full width are regular stock items. The spot where a tab is placed along the top width is known as its position. A 1/5 cut tab can be at any of five positions (see Figure 9–20); a 1/3 cut at any of three. When ordering, specify cut and position; for example, 1/3 cut, 2nd position.

Labels

Hundreds of varieties of labels are available in many sizes, colors, and shapes singly, in sheets, or rolls. Self-adhesive labels are also available. Some labels are plastic coated for greater durability. Labels inserted into plastic holding tabs are best for heavy wear.

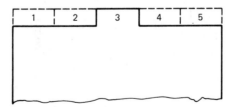

FIGURE 9–20. Tab cuts.

Files are neater when labels are typewritten. Use block form when a label contains several lines. They easily hold up to three lines of identification data. Color may be used advantageously (color coding has already been discussed).

Signals

A signal is a visual aide that can be used to communicate all kinds of information. The advantages of signals in visible filing systems and the ease with which they can be used were described on page 178. Metal and plastic tags snapped into special locations on cards and folders are easy signals to use. Color is, of course, used as a signaling device in all kinds of systems including tickler files. There is plenty of room for creative thinking when developing signal systems in files. (See Figure 9–21.)

Labor-Saving Devices

There is not enough space in this chapter to describe the many labor saving devices available to facilitate the handling of filing and information processing. There is a wide variety and many items illustrate the principle of "work smarter, not harder": work organizers, copy holders, racks, trays, conveyors (some mechanical), transporters, and facsimile devices used to speed the movement of data from one location to another. As a sample of this variety of available equipment, only ladders, stools, and sorters are described here.

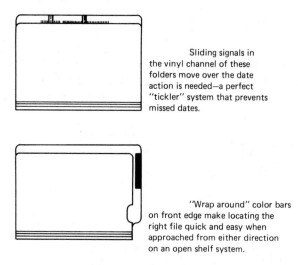

Sliding signals in the vinyl channel of these folders move over the date action is needed—a perfect "tickler" system that prevents missed dates.

"Wrap around" color bars on front edge make locating the right file quick and easy when approached from either direction on an open shelf system.

FIGURE 9–21. Folder signals.

Ladders and Stools

In shelf or storage areas with containers stacked to the ceiling, ladders are important pieces of equipment. Stand-alone ladders that move easily, lock into position, with trussed frames and braces and have handrails as part of a security frame, are safer and easier to use than the old hook-on type. A platform ladder also provides a work area. They are available in assorted sizes. (See Figures 9–22 and 9–23.)

Stools serve two purposes: to sit on while working in files near the floor or to step on for that extra height when reaching for something. Stools with caster-locking devices that stabilize instantly under

FIGURE 9–22. A mobile safety platform ladder. *(Courtesy Business & Industrial Furniture Co.)*

FIGURE 9–23. A stabilized foot stool. *(Courtesy Business & Industrial Furniture Co.)*

weight are recommended. Spring-mounted casters retract under pressure to allow a grip ring at the base to "lock" onto the floor.

Some thought should be given to where items such as ladders and work stools will be stored when not in use.

Sorters

Sorters are work organizers because they facilitate initial batching and coding and reduce refiling time. They put material into the right sequence for an alphabetic or numeric system. Some sorters are round, based on the rotary principle; others are rectangular and slide back and forth on a track. (See Figure 9–24.) Rotating or sliding, they bring the needed slot to the worker. Both types have labeled slots or flaps that hold presorted items until they are taken to the files.

EQUIPMENT ANALYSIS

Throughout office work, well-selected equipment and supplies enable people to work more efficiently. Their selection should be based on information about needs, uses, costs, authoritative opinions and alternatives. Selections should be studied and planned so that they enhance the overall image and service records management projects throughout a company. An analytical problem-solving approach when making selections is helpful and is illustrated in Figure 9–25.

FIGURE 9–24. Sorter. *(Courtesy Tab Products Co.)*

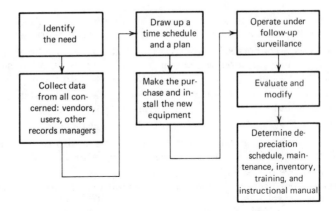

FIGURE 9–25. Analytical problem solving.

Cost and feasibility studies are important and negotiations with vendors should be explored and entered cautiously. Also, when new equipment or supplies introduce changes, care should be taken to make them democratically, working patiently with the people who are affected by the new system and procedures.

The following is a checklist of questions to use before purchasing equipment/supplies.

EQUIPMENT PURCHASING CHECKLIST

1. What is the background of the situation? That is, were the specific needs of people examined who requested the equipment/supplies? What is the primary need? How are the items to be used; by whom and how often? What kinds of records are involved; what volume?

2. Is a participative, team approach being used with those who will use the equipment/supplies preparatory to making the purchase?

3. Who authorized the purchase? Why?

4. Where will items be used—central location or individual departments?

5. What company policies affect the purchase of records management equipment/supplies? Have they been checked for the situation now being considered?

6. Is the contemplated purchase replacing something which is now on hand? If yes, what will be done with these items?

7. Is used equipment to be considered? Can equipment be leased with a purchase option? (Tax benefits, investment credit, and fast write-offs are some of the benefits that accrue when equipment is leased.)

8. What kind of follow-up is regularly made of equipment/supply utilization or when something new is introduced?

(Continued on next page)

9. What different makes and models of equipment are available? Were they compared? Were they demonstrated? Were they checked against original requirements?

10. How were vendors selected? Were several consulted? Did you deal directly with the supplier manufacturer or did you go to a local vendor? What services do local dealers offer? How important is it to establish rapport with them?

11. How do new equipment/supplies affect systems, work stations, methods, work procedures and routines now in use? Has this been studied?

12. How do new purchases affect office space and layout? Has this been studied?

13. What is the price range of the equipment/supplies being considered? Are savings documented on a dollar/cents basis? Which factor is most important—work effectiveness or cost economy?

14. Have other users been consulted? (Consult records managers in other companies, go to equipment/supply shows, and talk with other potential customers while there.)

Ergonomics in the Office

The study of designing work station components so they facilitate productivity and are as compatible as possible with creature comfort is called ergonomics. It is a technology that coordinates physiological factors that make a work space more effective with psychological factors by considering how they relate to productivity, employee physical comfort, and resulting morale. In total, ergonomics considers tools, material, equipment, furniture, methods of work, and organization of work as well as lighting, acoustics, color, interior climate, and spatial layout as they affect workers. It is the science of applying and coordinating factors that contribute to the creation of satisfying and productive work environments. Ergonomics is an area of knowledge in which records managers should be informed because the environment in which they set new equipment and related work stations affects the morale and productivity of people.

Productivity Related to Equipment

When inflation and business recessions occur, "overhead" cost areas such as office work and records management are watched closely. At such times, records managers must look for ways to improve efficiency, productiveness, and service. In the same way that many manufacturers invest large sums in factory equipment to increase production and efficiency, records managers need to provide their function with the best possible equipment/supplies to increase records management production and service. Every aspect of equipment/supplies purchasing and control, work station design, and final results should be analyzed for effectiveness because they are all part of the big picture of overall records management throughout the company.

Productivity can be defined as how much you make on what you use. A mark of professionalism in records management then is to make all resources productive, equipment/supplies as well as techniques and systems. A suggestion for achieving this is to study the flow of paperwork in the company, especially the main office "paperwork" producers (computer and copy centers). How much of what they produce is only partially used; how much goes quickly to inactive files? Look, too, for the most active record areas because they may be the most profitable ones in which to improve production. Question the effectiveness of equipment/supplies used in these areas. Look for simpler and lower cost ways of tooling their operations. Look for equipment/supplies that save work and improve efficiency. For example, an automated file of microfiche can save hundreds of square feet of floor space and may reduce the number of people needed to work the system. Or, replacing a system with color-coded supplies may reduce errors and speed filing/retrieval time at little extra cost. Conveyors that move records, facsimile transmittal devices, and sorters also may improve productivity to and from a file holding station where checking, coding and indexing are in process. Or, hanging file equipment can improve referral to computer printouts.

OFFICE FURNITURE

New ideas about office equipment and furniture utilization have changed the appearance and enhanced the productivity of modern office work stations. Built-in accessories; work organizers; custom-designed, at-hand shelving; new file/desk combinations; rotary files; tack boards; accoustical screens; modular wall systems—all provide combinations of work surfaces, carrels, storage spaces, and privacy (when wanted) as well as area dividers that enhance individual production and the flow of work among work stations. These items are easily adapted to information processing and records keeping personnel. Modular designs and new concepts about work flows allow components to be arranged in a variety of functional stations that offer ample desk space and comfortable access to records and equipment. Some stations are roll-a-rounds or semi-circular; some are back-to-back to make the most of available space. (See Figure 9–26.) Such arrangements make it possible to cluster several work carrels which might be desirable where several employees work together in central files or a computer tape library.

FIGURE 9—26. Coordinated work stations. *(Courtesy Wright Line)*

A new feature in work station design is modularity. Manufacturers are designing carrels with work surfaces, desk/table legs, storage units, and machine stands that are interchangeable and create customized work stations to fit individual needs. For example, a microfilm work station may consist of a surface for a viewer, have built-in or adjacent storage for microforms, rotary files for film cartridges, tiertape filing units, and specially fitted drawers. These components can be arranged to meet individual preferences, which is especially convenient for left-handed employees.

CENTRALIZED BUYING

Centralized buying is the practice of having one department, usually purchasing, buy needed materials, machinery and equipment for a company. The "buyers" become specialists and savings from quantity buying result. Rarely, however, does a company practice 100 percent centralized buying. Department heads are usually allowed a certain range of discretionary buying, say $50 to $100, for emergencies or special needs. Also, the purchase of some special materials such as file supplies and equipment may be entrusted to the specialist in the area—the records manager, for example, who in turn sets standards and does centralized buying for the function throughout the company. It is about this type of centralized buying—filing equipment and supplies—to which the following refers, for it seems appropriate that after devoting a chapter to filing equipment and supplies, some thought should be given to their purchase.

To save time and money through centralized buying and control, equipment/supply selection guidelines should be established. These should explain how centralized buying and distribution work throughout the company and something about comparative shopping procedures, uniform depreciation schedules, and utility studies. Carefully selected equipment/supplies by a capable records manager cut costs and improve records management service throughout a company.

It is not easy for a company to tie the hands of department heads in purchasing items to under a hundred dollars since most of them need authority to buy day-to-day supplies or emergency items. Therefore, most companies allow a few hundred dollars to department heads for discretionary buying. Where this is the situation, department heads may buy special folders or filing equipment individually, not through central purchasing. This type of buying is hard to control and when it gets out of hand, may reflect a communications breakdown between general service functions such as records management and individual department heads. That is, the amount of discretionary buying done in records equipment/supplies may depend on the rapport between central purchasing and department heads.

Independent buying of filing equipment and supplies should not be encouraged, nor should it be completely discouraged because of individual judgment among company department heads, their motivation and their morale. On the whole, however, there is little question that centralized purchasing is more efficient than letting each department do its own purchasing. When records managers are responsible for centralized buying of equipment and supplies, much thought should be given to communication with those in the company who are likely to buy equipment/supplies on their own. Even when a policy, backed by authority, supports centralized buying and control, these people may need to be won over, not mandated into it. The participative/consultative approach is useful in situations of this type because through conferences or committees composed of representatives from several departments, mutual problem discussions and joint decision-making sessions are possible.

REVIEW QUESTIONS

1. What are the benefits of standardization when buying filing equipment/supplies?

2. What are the dimensions of a standard vertical file drawer?

3. What is the advantage of three-drawer files? One- and two-drawer files? Five- and six-drawer files?

4. What is the advantage of interchangeable file drawers?

5. What is the advantage of a lateral file drawer?

6. Describe some quality features of drawer files.

7. What does *mobility* mean as used in relation to filing equipment? How is mobility an advantage?

8. Give an example of how a tub open-access rollaway file might be used.

9. What are the advantages of open-shelf filing? The disadvantages?

10. Why must open-shelf guides be side-tabbed?

11. What kind of dividers are used with open-shelf files? In suspension files? Why are they important?

12. What are the advantages of rotary files? Describe an application.

13. How are tape files stored?

14. What are some basic considerations for a tape library?

15. What does one look for when buying a typical storage file box?

16. What factors should be considered when selecting a safe?

17. What factors should be considered when selecting filing supplies?

18. Describe a top-quality file folder.

19. What two types of binders are most often used in filing? How are they used?

20. What are the characteristics of a good file guide?

21. What are the characteristics of an *out* guide?

22. What are the characteristics of good folder tabs? Guide tabs?

23. What are the considerations when selecting sorters, ladders, or stools for filing areas?

24. What are the phases of a problem-solving approach to selecting filing equipment?

25. What are some important questions that should be asked before filing equipment/supplies are purchased?

26. Define records management *productivity*. Give an example.

27. What are the advantages of the centralized buying of filing equipment and supplies?

28. What factors should be considered when buying furniture and equipment for filing work stations?

LEARNING ACTIVITIES

1. Visit a filing installation in your community and describe the following:
   a. Filing equipment used
   b. Type and quality of folders, guides, and binders
   c. File work stations and their equipment

2. Write definitions for the following terms.

   1. Compressor
   2. Divider
   3. Position (1st, 2nd, . .)
   4. Suspension file
   5. Binder

   6. Scoring
   7. Productivity
   8. File Guide
   9. Tape library
   10. Mobility

3. This exercise aims to help you organize for future job use a folder of reference materials about filing equipment/supplies.
   a. Make a list of filing suppliers in your community and check magazines and newspapers for pictures of their advertisements.
   b. Collect materials about a new filing supply or equipment that was not discussed in this chapter. Give a little information about the item.
   c. Prepare an organized index or table of contents for the material you have collected.

III

CONTROL OF INFORMATION AND RECORDS

10

Techniques and Procedures for Controlling Information

Emphasis in this chapter is on control activities and procedures used to receive, process, file and retrieve information. The goal of these control activities is to (1) reduce processing time, (2) minimize costs, (3) provide information to users in an accurate manner and (4) avoid unnecessary handling of information.

PROCESSING AND FILING INFORMATION

Steps that are a part of the processing and filing of information are illustrated in Figure 10–1. Although each step represents a separate set of activities to be performed by records personnel, the nature of the tasks and the time and effort required to complete them vary considerably. Small organizations with few records to process and control can easily and quickly accomplish them—and usually without formal (or written) guidelines on how the processing should occur. In contrast, large organizations will frequently use a written policies and procedures manual that specifies how records are processed. When the volume of records an organization produces and uses is large, and many records personnel are employed, a policies and procedures manual is a useful tool in standardizing operations and coordinating activities.

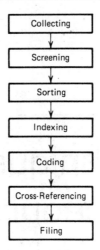

FIGURE 10–1. Processing and filing steps.[1]

Step 1: Collecting Information

Business records can be collected as part of the receipt of mail or preparatory to storage after action on the information is completed. Incoming records should be centrally collected, perhaps either at a mail room or at the work station of one of the records personnel. Clear authority and responsibility for records collection should be assigned to appropriate individuals. In a small firm, one person may be assigned such responsibility while several people may be used in larger organizations. In some cases, large organizations designate one person from each department or office to collect records.

The collection point for receiving information should be centrally located, making it easy and convenient for personnel to use. For incoming mail, a records employee may wish to mark documents with a time stamp indicating the date and time each is received. Such marking creates a permanent record of when information is received, and can help in making sure prompt action, if necessary, is taken.

Step 2: Screening Documents

The screening process involves checking documents to be sure action is completed and the documents are ready for filing. Some means of indicating that action is completed should be marked on the document by the person(s) responsible. This is important since records employees who screen documents may not know if action was com-

---

[1]See also *Guidelines* for processing these steps, Chapter 5, Section: Alphabetical Filing Procedures.

pleted without asking another person or a supervisor—a time-consuming process. Some businesses put a distinctive release mark, such as an initial, signature or stamp, on the document indicating it is ready for filing. (Nonpaper records may put release marks on the document's folder or carrier.) Another technique commonly used when several individuals are involved in taking action or reading the information is to use a routing slip. This device controls the flow of a document throughout an organization and records who has seen it and the action taken. A routing slip, such as the one illustrated in Figure 10–2, can be attached to a document or its carrier and stored with it. In this way, a written record of the routing of the document is obtained.

Step 3: Sorting Records

Sorting is the process of making a preliminary arrangement of materials, before they are filed, for the purpose of minimizing filing time. The arrangement used to sort the documents can either be an alphabetical, numerical, geographical, chronological or subject classification, corresponding to the filing method used.

Sorting can be done in one or more steps depending on the volume of records to be sorted and the filing method used. For example, sorting can be done alphabetically by separating documents into each letter of the alphabet from A to Z. Or, a "rough" sort can be used in which documents are placed into larger categories, such as putting all of the A-B-C's together, the D-E-F's together and so on.

ROUTING SLIP

Name	Dept.	Date Received	Action Taken

FIGURE 10–2. Correspondence routing slip.

A variety of equipment can be obtained to make the sorting process quick and easy. For example, a vertical sorter (shown in Figure 10–3) can be used for alphabetical (as shown), numerical, or subject arrangements. Other sorting devices such as wire racks or expansion folders (see Figure 10–3) also promote efficient sorting.

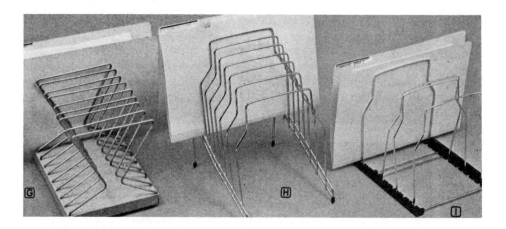

FIGURE 10–3. Sorting equipment. (*Courtesy Smead Manufacturing Co.*)

Step 4: Indexing Documents

After a record has been officially released for filing, it is examined by a records clerk to determine its filing classification. The mental process of deciding where to file a record is *indexing*, although some writers call it *classifying*. The process involves selecting the right name, subject, number, location or date under which to file a document, depending, on the filing method used.

Indexing is important to the accurate processing and storage of information. A mistake here will prompt a mistake in coding—perhaps in cross referencing—and filing the document. The result of incorrect indexing may be a record incorrectly filed; one that either will not be found when needed or retrieved only after an exhaustive search of the files. Therefore, it is important that the indexing of documents be assigned to someone who is trained and familiar with the organization and the filing methods used.

Selecting proper classifications for records requires both common sense and knowledge of filing practices. Selecting the right name to use as an index, for example, requires analyzing how the filing system is organized, how users might call for the document, and how other similar documents have been indexed. Part of this decision-making process is subjective and may be confusing when several people are involved. For this reason, records personnel should develop uniform guidelines and practices, along with discussing and resolving difficulties encountered in the process.

An example illustrates the complicated decisions that may be a part of indexing. Consider trying to index a letter from the "Modern Technology Company, Inc." and signed by "Thomas Adams, President." Furthermore, assume the content of the letter is totally related to a legal matter involving another company, the "T.M.D. Engineering Corporation" and its chief engineer, "Ron D. Book." Given this information, what name would you use as the indexing unit? Would others agree with your decision? Would records users be able to retrieve the document without any difficulty?

Step 5: Coding the Documents

Coding is closely related to indexing; once a document is indexed it should be immediately marked with the proper identifying name, number, location or subject. The physical act of marking the document is *coding*. In most cases the same person indexes and codes simultaneously.

Several techniques may be used to mark the document. Any one of them is satisfactory as long as records personnel are consistent and follow prescribed company policies. The techniques include:

1. Write (or print) the appropriate name, number, subject, location or date on the document. Put this mark in a highly visible location to facilitate retrieval. (Normally the most visible location is the upper right-hand corner of a document.)

2. Stamp the document with the appropriate identifying classification.

3. Circle or underscore the proper name, subject, location or number wherever it appears on the document. (Note: this mark should be large and dark enough to make it highly visible.)

Of course, other techniques may be originated and used to code documents effectively. Like indexing, coding is an important step if records are to be filed correctly and retrieved easily. Coding also makes the refiling of documents easier because uncoded documents would have to be reindexed each time they are taken from the files and subsequently prepared for refiling.

Figures 10–4 and 10–5 illustrate two techniques for coding documents: writing the appropriate classification onto the document and circling the proper classification.

Step 6: Cross Referencing

If a record might be requested by more than one name, subject or other classification, it is necessary to cross-reference. Alphabetic or subject methods necessitate considerable cross referencing. Although cross referencing is sometimes necessary, its use should be limited. Excessive cross referencing requires extra time and filing supplies, uses additional filing space, and can make the retrieval process cumbersome.

The process of cross referencing involves several steps: 1) determining the need for cross referencing, 2) selecting the most appropriate cross-reference classification, 3) coding the document with the cross-reference notation, and 4) establishing a cross-reference record. Figures 10–4 and 10–5 illustrate how records can be coded for cross referencing. In Figure 10–4, the secondary classification "Business Mathematics" is underscored and an "X" placed in the right margin indicating the cross reference. Similarly, Figure 10–5 has the cross reference ("professional organizations") circled and an "X" coded in the left margin.

After coding the document, a records clerk can either prepare a cross-reference record (as shown in Figure 10–6) which is filed as the cross reference, or a copy (carbon or photocopy) of the document can

SOUTH-WESTERN PUBLISHING CO.

INCORPORATED

Telephone 513-271-8811   5101 MADISON ROAD — CINCINNATI, OHIO 45227

October 11, 1979

Mr. David Hyslop
Bowling Green State University
Business Education Department
College of Bus. Administration
Bowling Green, OH 43403

Dear Mr. Hyslop

You have in your possession a copy of BUSINESS MATHEMATICS--A College ✗
Course which is a careful, systematic approach to teaching business
mathematics. You may not be aware that this text is merely the core
of a complete teaching/learning package. In addition to the textbook,
the package includes the Student Supplement, teacher's key, teacher's
edition of the Student Supplement, and achievement tests.

May I suggest you pick up your copy of BUSINESS MATHEMATICS--A
College Course by Gossage and browse through it carefully. For your
convenience, a brief which points out the outstanding features of
this complete teaching/learning system is placed inside the front
cover.

BUSINESS MATHEMATICS—A College Course is a book you should seriously
consider for your classes. It won't let you or your students down.

                    Sincerely yours

                    Larry A. Reynolds, Assistant Manager
                    College/University Department

jaf

Cincinnati • Chicago • Palo Alto, Calif. • Dallas • New Rochelle, N. Y. • Brighton, England

FIGURE 10—4. Coding and cross-referencing a document.

be filed in place of the cross-reference record. Each method is satisfactory; the choice depends on the expense and convenience involved
in either preparing a cross-reference record or making a copy of the
document.

Step 7: Filing the Document

Filing the document is the final step in the process. It too is important
and must be done conscientiously. However, if the preceding six
steps have been done thoroughly and accurately, the physical act of

AMERICAN ASSOCIATION OF UNIVERSITY PROFESSORS
ONE DUPONT CIRCLE · SUITE 500
WASHINGTON, D.C. 20036
Telephone 202—466-8050

WALTER ADAMS, *President*
Michigan State University
BERTRAM H. DAVIS, *General Secretary*
Washington Office

Dear Professor:

The Washington Office of The American Association of University Professors has been informed of your new faculty appointment, and, on behalf of the Association, it is a pleasure to extend to you our congratulations and best wishes for success in your new position.

As you may know, this Association is the nation's largest and most active professional organization in higher education. Established in 1915 to advance the standards and welfare of the academic profession, the AAUP over the years has come to be recognized as the authoritative voice of the profession.

The Association's membership of more than 86,000 is now represented by some 1,300 local college and university chapters in fifty states and by 45 state conferences which facilitate the work of the chapters. Much of our work is described in the enclosed information brochure.

If you have not yet had an opportunity to support the Association's principles and programs through membership in the AAUP, I would like to invite you to become a member at this time. An application form is included in the enclosed brochure. If you are already one of our members, we would appreciate it if you would pass the brochure on to a colleague.

Again, congratulations on your new appointment. We hope to welcome you as a new member of the Association.

Sincerely yours,

Bertram H. Davis

BHD/jb
Enclosure

FIGURE 10–5. Coding and cross-referencing a document.

placing documents into their respective storage locations can be accomplished quickly.

Documents should be filed soon after the other steps in the process have been completed. Accumulating records to be filed is fine if the accumulation period is reasonable—perhaps one or two days. But allowing records to "stack up" and await filing for longer periods can be harmful in several ways. First, if the record is needed while resting among many other records, retrieval may take considerable time. Second, records that are allowed to accumulate rarely are controlled and can easily be lost, damaged, or misplaced. Last, when records employees are faced with filing an overwhelming number of records, they may become careless.

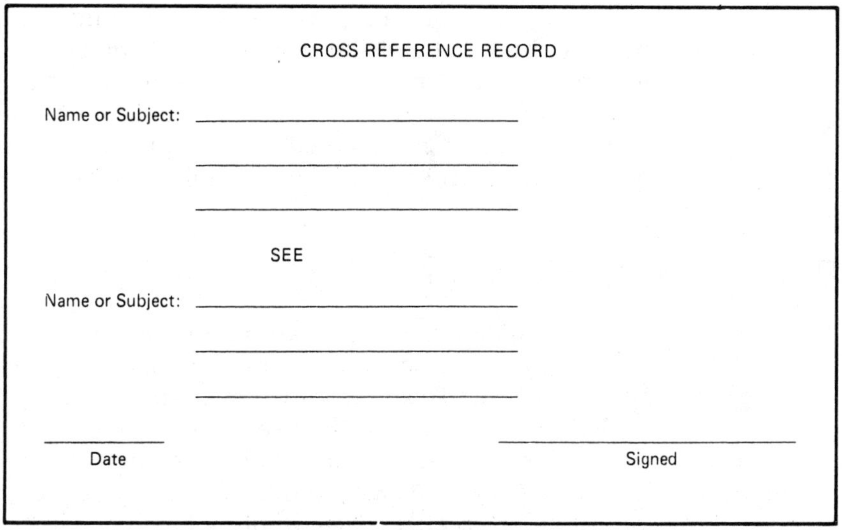

CROSS REFERENCE RECORD

Name or Subject: _____

_____

_____

SEE

Name or Subject: _____

_____

_____

_____   _____
Date   Signed

FIGURE 10—6. Cross-reference record.

RETRIEVAL PROCEDURES

The primary value of retaining records is to have them available for future use. Thus, retrieval procedures are essential elements in being able to deliver the right information to the right person in a timely manner. Perhaps nowhere is control more important than during the retrieval process; and by installing controls, records can be checked out, used and returned with optimum effectiveness and efficiency.

Steps in the retrieval cycle are outlined in Figure 10–7 below:

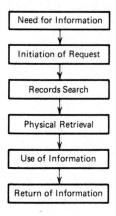

FIGURE 10—7. Retrieval cycle.

²See also cross-reference illustrations, Chapter 5.

Because of the varied ways of retrieving information today, specific activities that constitute these steps vary considerably. With the advent of automated systems, new retrieval procedures have emerged that differ from those used with nonautomated retrieval systems.[3] Procedures described in this section relate primarily to manual retrieval systems, although some of the principles and guidelines given apply to any type of system.

Step 1: Need for Information

Two beginning questions regarding the retrieval of information are: Who will be allowed to obtain the information? How will the information be used? Today, we are very aware that vast amounts of information are available and that we need to limit access to it to authorized individuals. This concern has resulted in federal legislation (Privacy Act of 1976) which limits the use of certain categories of information or records. Organizations are increasingly aware of the need to protect information and control its use. Accordingly, more and more firms are implementing controls in this area, and requiring that only those individuals who have a specified right and need to use certain information be allowed to do so.

Step 2: Initiation of Request

Filed material may be requested verbally (phone or person-to-person) or by a written request. Most requests are informal verbal requests or memos between two employees. This is especially true in a small organization or within a centralized department of a large company.

However, a large organization, because of the volume of records and their use by personnel in many departments or at various geographic locations, may use a requisition form appropriate for controlling documents. A requisition card, similar to the one shown in Figure 10–8, is helpful because it is a written record of the disposition of the requested document. The form is normally completed by the person requesting the information and could include the following items:

1. Identification (name, number, subject, etc.) of material being requested
2. Description of contents of record(s)
3. Date of request
4. Reason for request (Why is record needed? How will it be used?)
5. Date record(s) will be needed
6. Date when material will be returned
7. Name, title or department of person requesting material

[3]See Automated Indexing, Chapter 14.

```
┌─────────────────────────────────────────────────────┐
│                 REQUEST FOR RECORDS                   │
│                                                       │
│   Date of Request _____               │
│                                                       │
│   Name/Subject/Identification of Record(s) Requested: │
│                                                       │
│   _____   │
│                                                       │
│   _____   │
│                                                       │
│   _____   │
│                                                       │
│   Date Records Needed _____   │
│                                                       │
│   Anticipated Date of Return _____   │
│                                                       │
│                 Requested by                          │
│                                                       │
│   Name _____ Department _____ │
│                                                       │
└─────────────────────────────────────────────────────┘
```

FIGURE 10—8. Requisition card.

Once completed, the requisition form (or a copy of it) is retained in the files until the material is returned.

Step 3: Records Search

Obtaining the material requested should be a simple process. A records clerk, or whoever has responsibility for the filed materials, should conduct the search. Allowing other personnel to scan the files and retrieve documents may result in lost or misplaced records. For this reason, many organizations limit the search and retrieval of files to designated personnel. (See Retrieving, Chapter 5.)

Step 4: Physical Retrieval

Once a document has been removed from the files, some record should be made indicating that the record is checked out and who has temporary custody of it. A common way to do this is through an out guide. (See Figure 10–9.) Out guides show who has a record, when it was taken, and what specific item(s) has been removed. This information can be written on the face of the out guide or a requisition card attached to it. Some out guides have special pockets for requisition cards.

Once completed, the out guide can be placed in the files as a substitute for the borrowed record. In some cases, a separate card file may be maintained to indicate what records have been borrowed.

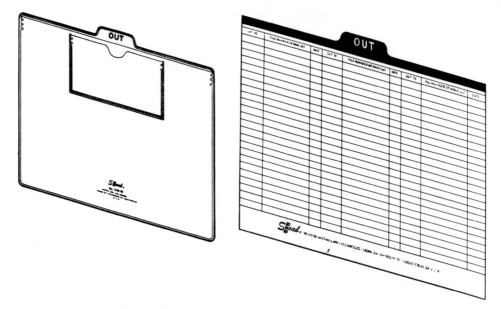

FIGURE 10—9. Out guides. (*Courtesy Smead Manufacturing Co.*)

Step 5: Use of Information

During this step the physical control of the document is in the hands of the borrower. If someone else needs to obtain the document, the out guide or requisition card tells who has it, and this person can be notified directly.

Step 6: Return of Information

In most cases, borrowed records are returned on or before the due date. Once returned, indicate this by removing the out guide or making a notation on the requisition card. However, if records are not returned on time, a files representative should personally notify the borrower or send a follow-up memo. This follow-up reminder should be sent within two or three days after the due date. Waiting longer might result in permanently losing a record or not having it available when someone else requests it.

A follow-up or reminder device often used is a tickler file. (See Chapter 6.) A tickler file helps control the return of records. It is arranged chronologically with each month divided into days, as shown in Figure 10–10. When requisition cards are filed chronologically, records personnel can check this file each day to see what records should be returned.

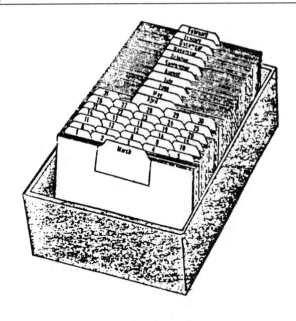

FIGURE 10–10. Tickler file.

IMPROVING INFORMATION PROCESSING EFFICIENCY

The goal of controlling information processing procedures is to ensure that they are being accomplished efficiently and as planned—Efficiency is a key word in an operation and is particularly relevant today as we try to improve the productivity of organizations.

In this chapter, efficiency can be thought of as improvements in the processing, storing, and retrieving of information. Efficiency means that operations are being completed without waste, duplication or unanticipated results, while using resources wisely. In examining efficiency for information processing activities, three areas can be reviewed: work flow, communication networks, and physical layout of the work area.

Work Flow

A major feature of an efficient processing system is that of work flow. To be efficient, work (tasks associated with processing information) should be coordinated and flow in a smooth pattern, without bottlenecks, wasted efforts, or delays. In studying work, flow areas to investigate include:

1. Steps required for processing information or completing a task.
2. Duties and work loads of the people who do the processing.
3. Distance information must travel as it is being processed.
4. Time delays or bottlenecks, if any.
5. Completed tasks and how well they achieve predetermined goals.

Work flow patterns can be studied by listing them as they presently occur and then analyzing them for possible changes or improvements. A form such as the one illustrated in Figure 10–11 can be used for this purpose. Simplifying the steps in the work flow or eliminating unnecessary ones can reduce costs and improve efficiency, especially where tasks are done repeatedly.

Communication Networks

As information is processed, communication channels among employees are formed to facilitate the orderly transfer of information. These channels can be of two types: those designed to process written information and those used for facilitating verbal information. Both can be reviewed for possible improvement. Like work flow, communication networks should be simple, well designed, and efficient. They should minimize the number of people in the chain of communication and ensure that each person's messages are given and received clearly. Possible areas to review in improving communication networks include:

1. The number of people who communicate with each other in order to process information.
2. The physical location of the people in the communication process.
3. The barriers that may exist in obtaining clear, timely and effective communication.

Physical Layout

A popular work design that encourages efficient information processing is known as the work center concept. Under this design, each employee's work area is laid out to produce efficient motions. The work area, including a desk, files, equipment and furniture, is grouped together to permit easy motions and reduce unnecessary activities or movements. An underlying principle is to have as much information as possible that is needed to complete a task within arm's reach.

Chapter 9 discusses a variety of filing equipment that is available to facilitate efficient work methods. Modular furniture such as that shown in Figure 10–12 facilitates the use of filed materials and is flex-

Present Method ☐   Proposed Method ☐

Page ____ of ____

FLOW PROCESS CHART

SUMMARY

	Present	Proposed	Difference
◯ Operations			
⇨ Transportations			
☐ Inspections			
D Delays			
▽ Storages			
Distance Travelled	ft.	ft.	ft.
Time			

JOB _____

_____

Subject Charted _____

Chart Begins _____

Chart Ends _____

Charted By _____ Date _____

DESCRIPTION OF EVENT	Operation / Transpor. / Inspection / Delays / Storage	Quantity	Distance in feet	Time	NOTES
1	◯⇨☐D▽				
2	◯⇨☐D▽				
3	◯⇨☐D▽				
4	◯⇨☐D▽				
5	◯⇨☐D▽				
6	◯⇨☐D▽				
7	◯⇨☐D▽				
8	◯⇨☐D▽				
9	◯⇨☐D▽				
10	◯⇨☐D▽				
11	◯⇨☐D▽				
12	◯⇨☐D▽				
13	◯⇨☐D▽				
14	◯⇨☐D▽				
15	◯⇨☐D▽				
16	◯⇨☐D▽				
17	◯⇨☐D▽				
18	◯⇨☐D▽				
19	◯⇨☐D▽				
20	◯⇨☐D▽				
21	◯⇨☐D▽				
22	◯⇨☐D▽				

FIGURE 10–11. Flow process chart.

FIGURE 10–12. Work center concept. *(Courtesy Conwed Corporation)*

ible in prompting efficient motions when completing a task. The L-shaped or U-shaped work desk is particularly effective since it provides plenty of work space and permits documents to be stored, retrieved, and used with a minimum of motions.

Principles for designing an efficient work center include the following:

1. Desks should permit maximum utilization of surface space and allow for documents being processed to be placed within arm's reach.
2. Filing equipment should be easily accessible and, if possible, allow a worker to retrieve or file documents with a minimum of standing or walking to other locations although some standing and walking are recommended for body circulation and relaxation.
3. The most frequently used documents should be stored closest to the worker, at convenient locations.
4. Furniture, files and related equipment should be arranged to allow flexibility and modification as changes occur in work routines or processing methods.
5. Work groups who perform similar or related duties and need access to the same information should be located near one another.

REVIEW QUESTIONS

1. What are the seven steps in the process of filing records?
2. Under what conditions might an organization benefit from having a policies and procedures manual for controlling records?
3. Why should the collection of records be centrally controlled?

4. When would it be appropriate to mark incoming mail with a time stamp?

5. What activities are completed when records are screened?

6. What is a release mark? How is it used?

7. When might it be appropriate to use a routing slip? What information is recorded on a routing slip?

8. Why does sorting records reduce the time needed for filing them?

9. Define indexing. Why is the indexing step important?

10. What are some of the various ways in which documents can be coded?

11. Where on the document should the coding marks be placed?

12. Under what conditions should a document be cross-referenced? How is a document coded for cross referencing?

13. Why might an organization control who has access to information or business records?

14. In what ways might filed materials be requested for use?

15. Why would a requisition card be used in some organizations? What information is contained on the card?

16. What is the purpose of using out guides?

17. In what way can a tickler file be an effective tool in controlling the return of documents?

18. Why should an organization stress efficiency in their information processing activities?

19. What areas should be reviewed to investigate how efficient work flow is?

20. What are some of the advantages of the work center concept as they relate to improving the efficiency of information processing activities?

LEARNING ACTIVITIES

1. The two file clerks in the office of Dayler Insurance Company have been troubled by the lack of concern among office employees regarding checking out and using records from the central files. Although the clerks have responsibility for the files and for checking out procedures, the employees seem to prefer to retrieve the records themselves. However, this situation has produced several problems:

records are taken and not returned on time

in some cases the returned records have been misfiled

employees borrow a record, but rather than returning it, they lend it to another employee

employees fail to complete and use an out guide when records are removed

If you had responsibility for records control in this office, how would you solve the above problems?

2. Five years ago the Goodwin Construction Company adopted the subject filing method for their documents. During the early days of implementing this new system, the 10 office employees developed a good system for classifying and cross-referencing documents. However, the business has grown considerably and now has developed many subjects under which to file documents. The result of this has been much confusion in determining how to classify the records, along with widespread use of cross referencing.

What suggestions would you give this company to simplify its classifying activities and to reduce excessive uses of cross referencing?

11

Forms Management

Business forms are the most widely used type of business document. Many business transactions involve one or more forms. Forms serve a variety of functions—recording, transmitting or storing information. As pointed out by Maedke, et al.:

> Correspondence and reports may outnumber the business form in executive offices, but in all other offices three out of every four records are business forms. Business forms serve as the chief means of communicating information in a methodical, standardized, and repetitive way.[1]

A form is a means of communication—both within and outside an organization. Forms are used to collect information for internal decisions. They also provide information to outside agencies or organizations. Forms standardize the reporting of information; by their very nature, they structure the type and amount of information that is assembled. Because of this standardization, organizations can use the information to make comparisons and contrasts, or to show such relationships as trends, increases or decreases. The standardization also permits the information from the form to be automatically or electronically processed and stored, thereby reducing labor costs and time.

An important aspect of using forms is to apply principles of managerial control to their creation, use and disposition. By applying these principles, the goals of reduced costs and operating efficiency are more likely to be achieved. When large volumes of forms are used, considerable increases in savings and efficiency are gained. For example, if we save a minute or two in processing a purchase order of

---

[1] Wilmer Maedke, Mary Robek and Gerald Brown, *Information and Records Management* (Beverly Hills, California: Glencoe Press, 1974), p. 233.

which a company uses several hundred daily, the savings per item times the number of forms used yields a significant overall saving. Now expand this thinking and imagine what savings could occur if *all* necessary forms in the company were processed efficiently.

DEFINITION OF BUSINESS FORMS

A form can be defined as a printed paper record upon which information is recorded and subsequently used. It is used repeatedly and may serve a single or multiple purpose. For example, a form may be used for cash receipts (single purpose), or another may be used for purchasing and inventory control (multiple purposes). A form may be short or small—perhaps a post card size; or it may be lengthy, containing several pages.

Some forms are used only for internal purposes and never leave the office. Others supply information to people or organizations outside the office. Some organizations (particularly federal or state agencies) require information which necessitates the use of a form.

There are many examples of forms that we encounter in society. We complete a form to apply for credit, to obtain our cars and drivers' licenses, to charge purchases, to pay income tax, etc. In fact, most transactions within an organization require the completion of forms.

TYPES OF OFFICE FORMS

A common business form found in offices today is a single printed sheet of paper designed by someone in the office. Sometimes guidelines and policies are available for creating forms; but more often, especially in small offices, employees freelance and reproduce them in their own reprographics departments. In other cases, an office may hire a local printer or office supply store to design and produce required copies.

Types of forms which may be used in offices include unit-sets, continuous forms, carbonless forms and MICR and OCR forms.

~ 1. *Unit-Set Forms.* A unit-set form may be used if an office needs several copies of a form. It saves both time and effort since a typist or writer can prepare the copies simultaneously.

Unit-sets are versatile and used for many transactions. Carbon paper may be assembled to make the number of copies desired. Examples of unit-set forms are given in Figure 11–1.

~2. *Continuous Forms.* Continuous forms possess the feature of having all forms attached but are perforated to allow detaching when needed. They are time savers when used with a typewriter or other equipment that permits continuous feeding as the forms are being processed. For example, a store may use continuous form invoices to record customer orders; when one invoice is filled and the sale completed, the next invoice may be moved into position for immediate use. With the increased use of automated office equipment, more continuous forms will be used to increase efficiency. Several examples of continuous forms are given in Figure 11–2.

Continuous forms may be assembled in a variety of ways. Popular ones include the fanfold or the removable side strip as illustrated in Figure 11–2. Since most continuous type forms are used with office equipment, it is suggested that records supervisors consult office suppliers to determine which type best fits their needs.

– 3. *Carbonless Forms.* Perhaps you have already used carbonless forms. Have you ever written on an apparently carbonless form and

FINDLAY, OHIO 45840

Social Security #	/	/	Date

UNION STATIONERY CORP., WOODSIDE, N. Y.

12416

	Name			
	Address			
		DESCRIPTION		**AMOUNT**
By				
Charge				
Credit				

INVOICE

PAYMENT IS DUE UPON RECEIPT OF INVOICE

FIGURE 11–1. Unit-set forms. *(Courtesy Findlay College, Findlay, Ohio)*

FEDERAL EXPRESS

PLEASE COMPLETE ALL INFORMATION IN THE 7 BLOCKS OUTLINED. SEE REVERSE SIDE FOR PREPARATION INSTRUCTIONS.

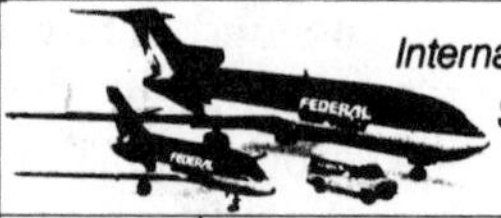

International Service Only

IN BOND

FOR CARRIER'S USE ONLY

O

D

AIRPORT OF DEPARTURE | AIRPORT OF DESTINATION

①

TO (CONSIGNEE NAME) | CARRIER'S USE ONLY

COMPANY

STREET ADDRESS

CITY | PROV/STATE | COUNTRY | POSTAL CODE

CARRIER CODE: **400-**

AIR WAYBILL NO: 0 06493734

②

FROM (YOUR NAME) | YOUR FEC ACCOUNT NUMBER

COMPANY

STREET ADDRESS

CITY | STATE | ZIP

REPORTING CARRIER

NON-NEGOTIABLE AIR WAYBILL SUBJECT TO TERMS & CONDITIONS SET FORTH ON REVERSE OF SHIPPER'S COPY.

③

COMMERCIAL INVOICE FOR CUSTOMS

MUST BE COMPLETED BY SHIPPER FOR LOW VALUE SHIPMENT AS DEFINED BY CUSTOMS IN THE DESTINATION COUNTRY. REFER TO THE INTERNATIONAL SERVICE GUIDE FOR DETAILS.

IMPORTER NAME (IF OTHER THAN CONSIGNEE)

VENDOR NAME (IF OTHER THAN SHIPPER)

COUNTRY OF ORIGIN | COUNTRY OF EXPORT

PLACE AND DATE OF DIRECT SHIPMENT

NO. OF PIECES | UNITS | WEIGHT

COMPLETE DESCRIPTION OF COMMODITY (LIMIT ONE)

COMMERCIAL VALUE | SPECIFY CURRENCY

RESTRICTIONS FOR INTERNATIONAL SERVICE:

1. Only one (1) package per air waybill.
2. Declared value for carriage and commercial value of contents cannot exceed U.S. $5000.00
3. Package dimensions cannot exceed 90" (229cm) in length and girth combined.
4. Restricted articles, Standard Air Service, Courier Pak Tube/Box and Saturday Delivery Services are not available.
5. The maximum weight per package is 55 lbs. (25kg).
6. Packages that have a commercial value of U.S. $400.00 and greater must be accompanied by 1 copy of a U.S. Shipper's Export Declaration and 3 copies of the prescribed Country's Customs Invoice Form.
7. Government Bills of Lading are not acceptable.

ATTENTION: FEDERAL EXPRESS COURIER.

1. ENSURE AIR WAYBILL IS COMPLETED.
2. DETACH COPIES #1 FEC ACCT., #11 SHIPPER, #12 TRACING BEFORE COMPLETING CHECKLIST.
3. IF COMMERCIAL VALUE EXCEEDS US $400, THE FOLLOWING DOCUMENTS MUST BE SECURELY ATTACHED TO THE PACKAGE:
   3 COMPLETED COPIES OF PRESCRIBED COUNTRY'S CUSTOMS INVOICE FORMS.
   1 COMPLETED COPY U.S. SHIPPER EXPORT DECL.
4. PLACE REMAINING AIRBILL COPIES IN POUCH. MARK PACKAGE WITH FULL NAME OF DESTINATION COUNTRY.

SHIPPER'S INSTRUCTIONS

NO. OF PKGS: 1 | TYPE OF SERVICE (SPECIFY) ☐ PRIORITY ONE PACKAGE ☐ COURIER PAK ENVELOPE

④

WEIGHT (SPECIFY) ☐ LB ☐ KG | DECLARED VALUE FOR CARRIAGE NOT TO EXCEED U.S. $5000.00

DATE OF SHIPMENT

⑤

PAYMENT

☐ Bill Shipper ☐ Cash in Advance

☐ Credit Card

☐ Bill Consignee

CHARGES	PREPAID	COLLECT
FREIGHT		
VALUATION CHARGE		
ADVANCE ORIGIN		
DUTY TAX FEES		
ADVANCE DEST.		
TOTAL CHARGES DUE		

DISPOSITION

☐ DELIVER ☐ HOLD FOR PICK-UP TEL NO. ______

IF SHIPMENT IS REFUSED BY CONSIGNEE OR CONSIDERED UNDELIVERABLE BY CARRIER: ☐ RETURN ☐ DISPOSE ☐ ABANDON

⑦

THE SHIPPER AGREES TO THE TERMS AND CONDITIONS OF CONTRACT AS SET FORTH ON THE REVERSE SIDE OF THE SHIPPER COPY OF THIS NON-NEGOTIABLE AIR WAYBILL AND VERIFIES THAT INFORMATION CONTAINED ON THIS AIR WAYBILL TO BE TRUE AND CORRECT. THE WARSAW CONVENTION MAY ALSO BE APPLICABLE TO THE CARRIAGE OF THESE GOODS

X ______ Signature ______ Date

RECEIVED | F.E.C. EMPLOYEE NO. | DATE/TIME

PRINTED IN USA

RC APPROVED 6-3-80-1

FEDERAL EXPRESS ACCOUNTING

FIGURE 11–1 ***(Cont'd.).*** Unit-set forms. *(Courtesy Federal Express)*

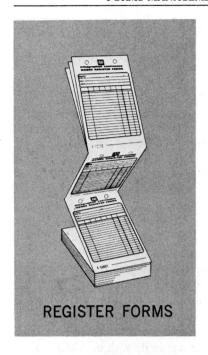

REGISTER FORMS

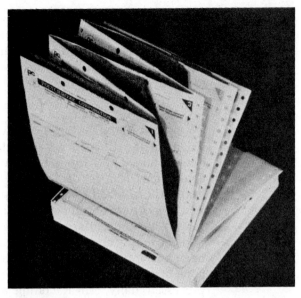

FANFOLD

SPEEDIFLO (Sectional)

FIGURE 11–2. Continuous forms. *(Courtesy Moore Business Forms)*

then observed that your writing was making copies onto other sheets of the form? This is carbonless paper, sometimes referred to as NCR—
—(no carbon required). Such paper is treated chemically so that the pressure of a pen, pencil, or typewriter produces copies. Carbonless forms are easy to use and eliminate the smears often evident with regular carbon forms.

4. *MICR and OCR Forms.* Two types of forms growing in use are Magnetic Ink Character Recognition (MICR) and Optical Character Recognition (OCR) forms because both can be used with automated equipment. That is, data may be read and transferred automatically from OCR or MICR forms to computer storage.

Checks are examples of commonly used MICR forms. (See Figure 11–3.) The coded information on the lower left of the check (check number and account number) is read (sensed) by automated equipment and translated into electrical impulses that are transmitted to a computer for processing. In organizations where such documents are processed daily, MICR coding and automation speed up efficient processing.

OCR forms permit both numeric and alphabetic data to be processed automatically. They have greater versatility than MICR forms since additional coded information such as item descriptions can be transmitted automatically for computer processing. An example of an OCR form is shown in Figure 11–4.

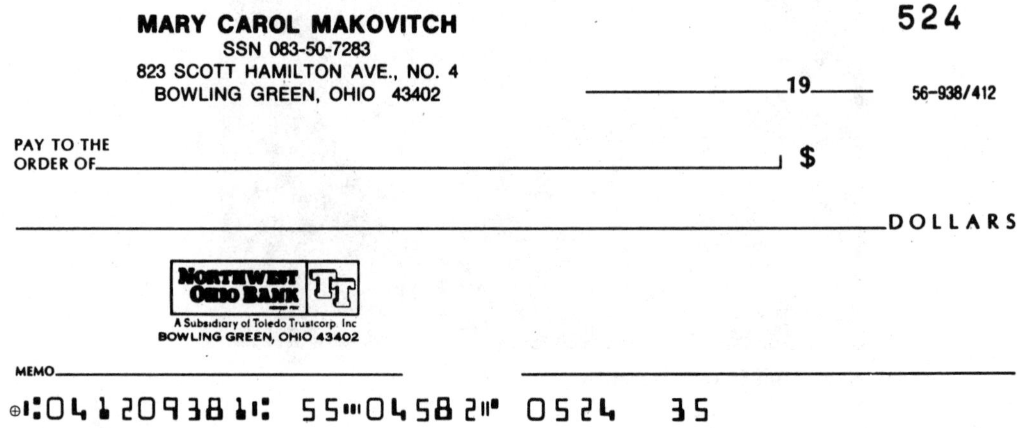

MARY CAROL MAKOVITCH   **524**
SSN 083-50-7283
823 SCOTT HAMILTON AVE., NO. 4
BOWLING GREEN, OHIO 43402   _____19_____   56–938/412

PAY TO THE
ORDER OF_____ $

_____DOLLARS

NORTHWEST OHIO BANK LT
A Subsidiary of Toledo Trustcorp Inc
BOWLING GREEN, OHIO 43402

MEMO_____

⑂I:O4I2O9381I: 55⑂O458 2I⑂ O524   35

FIGURE 11–3. MICR form.

THE LITERARY GUILD 2   49633 7402 016048 7124 03
                                                   0061 1289 0502   1

RETURN THIS FORM WITH YOUR PAYMENT

BILL FOR THIS SHIPMENT ONLY
AMOUNTS INCLUDE SHIPPING AND HANDLING CHARGES

DESCRIPTION	AMOUNT
2 BOOKS ENCLOSED	16.04
PLAN HOME LANDSCAP	
ERRONEOUS ZONES	

MAY 4	AMOUNT NOW DUE ▶	16.04

BILLING DATE

BILLS ARE DUE AND PAYABLE UPON RECEIPT

YOUR ACCOUNT NUMBER
55 079 643536

3175 3095
MRS TYNE E HYSLOP
10811 OAK ST
PORTAGE   OH 43451

11 FOR OFFICE USE ONLY

051-00-R3

FIGURE 11—4. OCR form.

THE NEED FOR FORMS CONTROL

There are several important reasons why forms should be controlled in offices today. First, since processing forms is a major part of typical office work activities, their control affects office efficiency.

The cost of processing forms is substantial. A study of paperwork processing costs in government and industry showed that approximately 84 percent lies in clerical processing operations; about 5 percent is attributed to printing costs; and 11 percent for equipment and file maintenance.[2] An important result of any forms control program can, therefore, be a decrease in office processing costs.

Secondly, an office must decide what information to collect, process and store, and what information *not* to collect. Since forms are the most common way to collect information, records personnel can reduce costs by controlling the volume and type of forms used. In doing this, a records manager should ask such questions as:

---

[2]Benedon, William. *Records Management* (Englewood Cliffs, N.J.: Prentice-Hall, 1969) p. 125.

What purpose does the information on the forms serve?

How does the information help achieve goals?

Who uses the forms?

Is there some other way of obtaining the information without the use of the forms?

Can the forms be reduced or simplified?

For how long should the forms be used and retained?

Lastly, business cannot afford to process and keep unlimited amounts of forms. The organization that creates forms that are never (or hardly) used or retains them for an undetermined time generates unnecessary work and is likely to run out of space. Controls over the generation of paperwork are, therefore, essential in any organization. Forms control is an excellent place to begin such a program.

Principles of Forms Control

A good way to start forms control is to develop a *forms management program* that spells out goals to be achieved. To be successful, the program should be comprehensive and should assign specific responsibility for program phases so that identifiable personnel are held accountable.

A typical forms management program should include the following activities:

Inventory the forms

Review and analyze forms for purpose, use, and efficiency

Consolidate forms to eliminate overlapping and duplication

Eliminate unnecessary and obsolete forms

Coordinate forms with information processing procedures

Control the creation, design and use of forms, reviewing (auditing) these aspects at fixed intervals

Establish standards for uniformity and simplicity of forms

Design forms to facilitate the automated or electronic processing of information

Improve the appearance and functional efficiency of forms

Give better information and service through forms

Once a forms management program is authorized, a logical first step is to inventory all forms used throughout the organization. After that, apply control steps to insure that the above stated objectives are achieved.

Controlling the Creation of Forms

No form should be created unless the need for it can be justified. Someone should specify how each form is used and identify its purpose. The cost of each new form should be estimated before creation is authorized. Some costs to examine include those for

  printing or preparation of forms
  equipment
  storage and distribution
  processing and control
  mailing and postage
  duplication

It is easier—and more efficient—to control forms at their creation than during their use. Too often forms seem to have an endless life and continue to be used long after they are needed. When a new form is created, its life expectancy should be stated. In fact, some records personnel advocate using a "sunset provision" in which a form, once created, has a specified life (for example, two years or five years) after which its use ends. The only way the form can be continued is if after review, it can be shown that it still is justified as serving some purpose.

Whatever technique is used to control the life expectancy of a form, it should define the actual time the form will be used; plus, the form or forms manual (if used) should contain this information. Then, when the life expectancy nears, records personnel can review the need for the form and discontinue it if no longer needed.

Assigning Responsibility for Forms Control

The best way to control forms within an organization is to centralize the control. Without centralized responsibility, each unit or department is free to create its own forms, without regard for duplication or overlapping. With one person assigned responsibility for control, forms are more likely to be coordinated throughout the organization.

In some organizations it is difficult for one person to control forms adequately because of the quantity and variety. Therefore, in large corporations, a committee approach is used. That is, personnel from a variety of organizational units (for example, purchasing, inventory control, personnel, accounting, administrative services, etc.) may comprise a forms control committee. A committee is particularly effective in controlling forms when it represents a wide range of experience and knowledge about organization functions. This does not mean, however, that other personnel should be passive in relation to forms control. *All* levels of management should lend their support if forms control is to be effective.

Controlling Forms Use

After an inventory and classification of forms are made, an annual review (audit) should be conducted to see if they are being used efficiently. A complete forms audit would require examination of all forms in the system, one at a time. Considering that a system may encompass hundreds, or even thousands, of forms, the task of such an audit appears to be prohibitive because of the time involved.

Fortunately, this is not necessary. Sampling can do the job much more quickly, at far less cost, and will provide usable management information which may be employed to orient the forms control program.

With an inventory list as a starting point, the forms control center should survey forms processing procedures and determine their current uses. A questionnaire analysis form, such as given in Figure 11–5, can be used for this purpose. It should be completed by the people primarily responsible for completing and using a form. When these data are analyzed, the forms control manager (or committee) has a basis for recommending needed changes.

DESIGNING OFFICE FORMS

Forms should be designed or redesigned on the basis of a thorough analysis. That is, after a form has been analyzed and found to be necessary, it is designed to meet a specific need. All elements in a form's design should be examined so that the final product will be the best possible.

Not all office or records personnel are likely to be involved in forms design and layout. In a small organization many forms are designed and reproduced within the firm, but in a larger organization, an outside firm may design the forms. However, this does not lessen the need to have someone within the organization decide what information is to be collected, how a form is to be used, and the approximate elements it should possess. This information should be collected by records personnel. No one is in a better position to decide what information should be on the form than the people who will use it.

The following section of this chapter gives guidelines that should be followed when designing forms.

FORMS QUESTIONNAIRE AND ANALYSIS SHEET

FORM TITLE	DEPT	FORM NUMBER
PRIMARY FUNCTION OF FORM		SIZE

HOW WRITTEN?
☐ HANDWRITTEN   ☐ MACHINE   ☐ BOTH   TYPE OF MACHINE

WHEN PREPARED?
☐ DAILY   ☐ WEEKLY   ☐ MONTHLY   OTHER   ANNUAL QUANTITY USED

SOURCE FROM WHICH FORM IS PREPARED

PART NUMBER	PART DISTRIBUTION (Give All Depts. and/or Persons in Order of Usage)	HOW FILED	
		BY ORDER NO., PART NO., ETC.	VISIBLE, FILE, BINDER, ETC.

SPECIAL FORM FEATURES (Design - Construction)

ANALYSIS

POSSIBLE TO COMBINE WITH SOURCE DOCUMENT? WITH SUCCEEDING DOCUMENTS?

STANDARD SIZE? FILING-SIZE?

PROPERLY ARRANGED FOR WRITING MACHINE? FOR HANDWRITING? FOR READING EASE? FOR FILING?

DOES SEQUENCE OF DATA CORRESPOND TO SOURCE DOCUMENT? TO SUCCEEDING RECORDS?

ADDITIONAL PRE-PRINTING NEEDED? (Items, Routing, Instructions for Form Usage)

SUGGESTIONS FROM PERSONNEL USING FORM

SUFFICIENT COPIES FOR PERSONNEL INVOLVED?

PARTS HELD TOGETHER FOR SUBSEQUENT ENTRIES?

Form No. 1241

FIGURE 11–5. Forms questionnaire and analysis sheet.

1. *Title.* Every form should have a title that describes its purpose or tells the type of information the form will contain. For example, if it is used to record equipment purchases for a given time period, a title could read as shown in Figure 11–6.

The title should be at the top of the form in position for quick use and easy filing. A descriptive title helps individuals know the purpose of the form at a glance.

```
┌─────────────────────────────────────┐
│                                     │
│         MAGNUM COMPANY              │
│   RECORD OF EQUIPMENT PURCHASES     │
│       1/1/— through 12/31/—         │
│                                     │
└────────⌣────────────────⌣──────⌣───┘
```

FIGURE 11—6. Form title.

⌐ 2. *Origination Data/Identification Number.* When created, forms should be catalogued and identified. Even though a form has a title denoting its purpose, other origination or identification data are useful.

Numbers may be used to identify a department or function that created and uses a form. A form could be coded as follows:

100—Accounting
200—Production
300—Marketing
400—Inventory Control
500—Administrative Services

Each area could be further subdivided for additional identification. For example, the Accounting Department could have these additional categories:

100—Accounting
   120—Payroll
   140—Taxes
   160—Data Processing
   180—Purchases and Requisitions

Obviously, only a large firm with many different offices or departments would need many subdivisions.

In addition to department identification the subject classification and revision information, if any, could be shown. For example, A1240/1 could identify the department (A for Accounting), the subject classification of the form (1240 for State Income Tax) and the "1" to indicate the first edition of the form. If the same form is later revised, A1240/2 would denote the revision. Or, the coding could include an origination date. This could appear with other identification data and alert records personnel to use the latest revision or to know when the form was revised.

An example of a form showing identification data is given in Figure 11–7. ⌐

```
┌─────────────────────────────────────────────┐
│           NORTHERN PRODUCTS, INC.            │
│                                              │
│                   I1000/2                     │
│                  Rev. 9/80                    │
│                                              │
│                                              │
│         RECORD OF PRODUCT DEFECTS            │
└──────────────────⌒⌒⌒⌒⌒⌒⌒⌒⌒⌒───────────────────┘
```

FIGURE 11–7. Form origination and identification data.

— Some forms are numbered consecutively to facilitate control. For example, purchase orders, payroll checks, sales invoices, etc., would have consecutive coding so managers could monitor the use of these documents.

3. *Instructions.* A long, involved form may need a separate sheet or card for instructions, or the back of the form may be used for this purpose. Whenever possible, instructions should appear immediately before the items to which they apply. If they apply to an entire form (such as instructions on how to complete the form), they should precede the form and may be emphasized by a varying type.

Some possible instructions to be put on the form include:

How each section should be completed—specify where the information should be entered and the type of information requested

The method of filling in the parts of the form—by printing or typing or using a special pen or pencil

The number of copies that should be completed

What to do with the form after completion—where it should be forwarded or how copies may be distributed

4. *Spacing.* If a form is to be used in a typewriter, it should be designed to fit typewriter spacing, both horizontally and vertically. If both typewriter and handwritten fill-ins are involved, provide for double typewriter spacing, at least three lines per inch. If the form is for handwriting only, then additional space may be needed.

5. *Headings and Captions.* Each part of a form should be divided into smaller areas and blocked for easy completion. Within each of the blocked areas, a heading or caption should appear to tell an individual what information is entered there. The heading should be of small type, located not to interfere with the information being entered, and allow sufficient space to complete the section. Further, the heading should be as specific as possible to avoid misinterpretation.

Consider the following examples in Figure 11–8. The first example will capture the individual's complete name and eliminate possible confusion over first, middle or surname. ⌣

Good Heading:

| NAME |
| |
| Last Name   First Name   Middle Name |

Poor Heading:

| NAME |
| |

FIGURE 11–8. Form headings.

▬6. *Grouping and Sequencing.* When items of data are scattered haphazardly on a form, a writer will have problems filling the form; and the reader will have difficulty extracting or interpreting the information. To avoid these problems, group related information and then block off the form to separate the groups. Heavy or double lines can be used to block the separate sections. Figure 11–9 illustrates the use of a heavy line to zone off information.

Items on the form should be placed in a logical sequence and location. Forms should be designed to be completed in a left-to-right, top-to-bottom direction. To avoid confusion on either of these two possibilities, each section may numbered, as in Figure 11–10, a work request form.▬

BOWLING GREEN STATE UNIVERSITY OFFICE OF THE REGISTRAR BOWLING GREEN, OHIO 43403 **4081**

Please print all information plainly.

Print the Name & Address of the person you wish to RECEIVE the Transcript(s)____ TOTAL

	DATE ENTERED B.G.S.U.			LAST QUARTER COMPLETED AT B.G.S.U.	
NAME	MO.	DAY	YR.	QUARTER	YEAR
STREET	SEND IMMEDIATELY	HOLD FOR CURRENT GRADES	HOLD FOR GRADE CHANGE	HOLD FOR NOTIFICATION OF DEGREE
CITY	☐	☐	☐	☐

STATE   ZIP CODE

THIS TRANSCRIPT IS SENT AT THE REQUEST OF:

$1.00 CHARGED FOR EACH TRANSCRIPT.

STUDENT NAME

☐ CASH ☐ CHECK   ENCLOSED. AMOUNT $_____

FIRST   MIDDLE/MAIDEN   LAST

RECEIPTED:

STREET

☐ CHARGE.   AMOUNT OWED $

CITY

DATE SENT

STATE   ZIP CODE

SOC. SEC. NO.   DATE OF REQUEST

Forward Payment to BURSAR!   Use enclosed envelope.

FIGURE 11–9. Registration form. *(Courtesy Bowling Green State University)*

WORK REQUEST (MAINTENANCE MANAGEMENT)

NAVFAC 9-11014/20 (REV. 2-68) S/N-0105-002-7510
Supersedes NAVDOCKS 2351

*(PW Department see Instructions
in NAVFAC MO-321)*

Requestor see Instructions on Reverse Side

PART I—REQUEST (Filled out by Requestor)

1. FROM	2. REQUEST NO.
3. TO	4. DATE OF REQUEST
5. REQUEST FOR ☐ COST ESTIMATE ☐ PERFORMANCE OF WORK	5a. REQUEST WORK START
6. FOR FURTHER INFORMATION CALL	7. SKETCH/PLAN ATTACHED ☐ YES ☐ NO

8. DESCRIPTION OF WORK AND JUSTIFICATION *(Including location, type, size, quantity, etc.)*

9. FUNDS CHARGEABLE	10. SIGNATURE *(Requesting Official)*

PART II—COST ESTIMATE
(Filled out by Maintenance Control Division if estimate requested)

11. TO.	12. ESTIMATE NO.

13. COST ESTIMATE		14. SKETCH/PLAN ATTACHED ☐ YES ☐ NO
a. Labor	$	15.
b. Material	$	☐ APPROVED. PROGRAMMING TO START IN _____
c. Overhead and/or Surcharge	$	☐ APPROVED. BASED ON PRESENT WORKLOAD, THIS JOB CAN BE
d. Equipment Rental/Usage	$	PROGRAMMED TO START IN _____, IF
e. Contingency	$	AUTHORIZED BY 25TH OF _____ AND FUNDS ARE MADE AVAILABLE.
f. TOTAL	$	☐ DISAPPROVED. *(See Reverse Side)*

16. SIGNATURE	17. DATE

PART III—ACTION (Filled out by Requestor)

18. TO:

19. AUTHORIZATION TO PROCEED IS ATTACHED *(Check one if other than PW funds are involved)* ☐ NAVCOMPT 140 ☐ OTHER	20. WORK REQUESTED ☐ HAS BEEN CANCELLED ☐ HAS BEEN DEFERRED ☐ WILL BE PERFORMED BY OTHERS
21. SIGNATURE	22. DATE

(See Part IV on Reverse Side)

FIGURE 11–10. Work request form. *(Courtesy Office of Naval Facilities)*

Whenever possible, use boxes to indicate answers in any section of a form. For example, see Sections 5, 7, 14, 15, 19 and 20 of Figure 11–10. Boxes organize specific responses and reduce the time it takes to complete the form.

7. Size. Most equipment used for filing business documents is of a standard size. Some common sizes for small records are $3'' \times 5''$, $4'' \times 6''$ and $5'' \times 8''$. Large documents, including correspondence, reports and some forms, are either $8\frac{1}{2}'' \times 11''$ (letter or standard size) or $8\frac{1}{2}'' \times 14''$ (termed legal size).

A form should be designed to accommodate standard sizes or equipment available in the organization. Odd-sized forms may not fit into existing filing cabinets or may create problems when filing or retrieving.

8. *Properties of Paper Forms.* Some important qualities to consider when designing a form are the weight, grade and color of the paper used. If a form is used frequently and retained for a long time, a thick (or high pound, as paper is described in pounds, such as 16-pound, 20-pound, etc.) paper should be used. If a form has multiple copies, such as the carbon or carbonless types described earlier in this chapter, then lighter weight paper would be required so every copy of the form can be read.

A paper with a high fiber content lasts longer than one with high sulphite (wood pulp) content. A high grade paper contains more fiber but is more expensive and would be justified only if the form has a long retention.

Colored paper may be used in a variety of ways: to separate sections of a single-page form or to show distribution of copies for a multiple-copy form. This quality can help the user of the form (by using highly visible colors) and reduce filing and retrieval errors as a misplaced color-coded form is easily detected.

Forms Design Checklist

This chapter has presented a variety of principles and guidelines to use in forms design and control. To summarize some of the points, a checklist such as the following one could be used to see if a form is needed and is correctly designed. The checklist has a variety of questions, but not all organizations may find *all* of them appropriate. Rather, the checklist may be viewed as a starting point upon which to construct a checklist that incorporates specific needs of the organization and its personnel.

Form Control	Yes	No

1. Does the form duplicate existing standard forms in use? _____ _____
2. Can existing forms be adapted for the same purpose? _____ _____
3. Is the use of the form justified by getting work done more quickly, more accurately and more economically? _____ _____
4. Can this form be consolidated with other forms? _____ _____
5. Can some other form be eliminated? _____ _____
6. Have the actual users of the form been consulted for possible suggestions or improvements? _____ _____
7. Has everyone responsible for policy and procedures approved the form? _____ _____
8. If a written procedure for the use of the form is necessary for efficiency in its use, has it been written? _____ _____

Form Design and Arrangement	Yes	No

9. Will the wording of the text be understood by all? _____ _____
10. If serial numbering will aid identification, has space been provided for the numbering? _____ _____
11. If routing, handling, or other instructions can be printed on the form, is it so designed? _____ _____
12. If copies of the form are required, are the number of copies justified? _____ _____
13. Does the form, by title and arrangement, clearly indicate its purpose? _____ _____
14. Has the form been tested to ascertain if the spacing is adequate for entries by hand, typewriter or other office machine? _____ _____
15. If the form is to be typed, are items arranged horizontally when possible for speed in completion? _____ _____
16. Are the more important items prominently placed near the top, if practical? _____ _____
17. Are there items of major importance necessary for sorting and reference, and if so, are they placed near the upper right-hand corner? _____ _____
18. If a check system can be used, has it been? _____ _____
19. If the form is to be sent from one person to another, are proper spaces for *"To"* and *"From"* provided? _____ _____
20. Is there proper space for date, number, and signature? _____ _____
21. Have adequate margins been provided for binding, filing, and machine limitations? _____ _____
22. Is the proposed size right for inserting in file folders or binders, as well as office machines? _____ _____
23. Are the quality and weight of paper correct for the purpose of the form? _____ _____
24. If colored paper is proposed, is it necessary in order to expedite handling of the form? _____ _____
25. If the form is to be reproduced after entries are made, are the paper and ink used for the printing suitable for the method of reproduction desired? _____ _____

REVIEW QUESTIONS

1. Why are forms used so widely in business today?
2. What are the main purposes of forms?
3. What are some of the advantages and disadvantages of the following types of forms: (a) unit-set forms, (b) continuous forms, (c) carbonless forms, (d) MICR and OCR forms?
4. What are the major advantages of a forms control program?
5. What are some problems of developing and maintaining a forms program?
6. Who should assume responsibility for controlling forms? Justify your answer.
7. Why is it important to control forms at their creation?
8. What is the value of specified standards for designing new office forms?
9. What is the purpose of a Forms Questionnaire and Analysis Sheet?
10. What information would normally go in the "origination data" section of a form?
11. What is the difference between a form design and a forms control program?
12. How is a records manager likely to be involved in a forms control program?

LEARNING ACTIVITIES

1. Allen Manufacturing Company, a small tractor parts plant, was troubled with a seemingly endless number and variety of forms. A quick count indicated the following numbers by department:

Production	23	forms
Quality Control	16	"
Inventory Control	44	"
Accounting	42	"
Personnel	29	"
Purchasing	14	"
Miscellaneous company-wide forms	23	"
Total	191	forms

Mr. Shaw, the records manager, knew that 191 forms were too many, but he didn't know exactly how to go about reducing or eliminating these forms.

What steps would you recommend Mr. Shaw take in solving this problem?

2. Each department at Midwest Supply Company is allowed to design and create its own forms. According to the president of the company, letting each department create its own forms insures that each meets the function for which it was created. He also thinks that centralized forms control, although it might reduce the number of forms, would not be helpful because "only department heads really know what forms they need and how they will be used."

   a. Do you agree with the president of this company? Justify your position.

   b. How could a centralized control program overcome the president's fears?

   c. Describe how you, the records manager, would approach the president about this problem.

12

Inactive Records

A record is worth keeping and possibly valuable only when it is used by someone in the company. As already discussed in Chapter 3, records have a life span which extends from birth or origin to destruction or permanent storage. They vary in usefulness during this time. The ordinary record goes through several phases in its life span from active to inactive or nonessential. That is, there is a time when a record is referenced often, even hourly; for example, a stock market quotation. Then as new events occur and new information enters the situation, it is used less and less and becomes inactive. The question is, what should be done with it? Should it be destroyed?

Not all inactive records are destroyed. Some, such as copyright documents or original incorporation papers, need to be kept as evidence even though rarely used (inactive) because they are classified as vital to the business. Other records such as old correspondence of founders, minutes, checks,[1] or engineering drawings may, although inactive, be kept for historical value.

A big problem when processing inactive records is to sort the useless from the useful and to keep reducing the bulk of the records that accumulate in a company by eliminating the nonessential so that they don't swamp the "ship." The situation may be compared to keeping a ship free of barnacles. Unless barnacles are scraped off periodically, a ship loses operational efficiency. In the same way, unless a company's files are kept free of useless records, the organization loses operating efficiency. Supervising the separation and ultimate disposition of inactive, nonessential records is an important records

---

[1] One corporation has an eighty-year old check for $500,000 framed and hanging on the wall in its New York board room. It was issued in a historical transaction.

management responsibility. When nonessential records are retained but not used, they waste resources in the same way that shelves of unused inventory do. The records manager must lead the way in an aggressive program that helps the organization identify and dispose of useless, duplicate and nonessential records. This is a very important part of the total service that a records manager can perform for a company.

This chapter contains information about separating inactive records—vital and essential—from operating and transient ones, and about transferring these records to storage areas; to both company and off-site storage centers.

Retained information can be compared to compound interest in that each percentage of annual increase is added to a larger base of company records. If a company's records collection (known also as a *data base*) increases 5 percent a year, the quantity will double in four-teen years. Companies must use records management to control the quantity of records they keep and to slow the growth rate of their collections.

Part of a records manager's duty is to control (manage) the quantity of records (the size of the data base) retained. Agreements among those in authority must be negotiated. Policies and procedures need to be set that specify which records to keep, where, in what form, and for how long. Guidelines and authorization signatures are needed to control the disposal of records.

RECORDS DISPOSITION

The federal government originally highlighted the need for organized and controlled records disposition. A Federal Disposal Act (1939) required the United States archivist to submit regularly to Congress lists of records that government agencies *should* destroy, because, theoretically, no federal records could be destroyed without congressional approval. In spite of this legislation, vast stores of records grew at alarming rates in Washington and at government centers throughout the country. In 1943, further legislation was enacted requiring that destruction schedules be developed for all government files and that each agency should have a records manager who would monitor the results. Reenforced by legislation in 1950, each agency was required to establish an active records-disposal program in order to keep inactive records moving out of high-cost, active office areas. More recent legislation has strengthened the process, but the overall problem of keeping active records free of inactive material continues because it is one thing to have legislation and another to make it work.

Business followed the government's lead as many organizations were burdened with large collections of records in warehouses as well as office buildings. A study in the 1950s by the National Records Management Council estimated that less than 10 percent of a company's records needed to be kept permanently, that only 20 to 25 percent were operating records, that 30 to 35 percent could be transferred to less expensive areas outside the offices, and that 35 percent could be destroyed immediately after initial use because they were transient records. Over the years, other studies postulate that 90 percent of the requests made for retained records are for material less than six months old; 9 percent for material between six months and a year; and only 1 percent for files more than a year old, thus suggesting that many retained records are useless. This does not mean, however, that 99 percent of a company's records that are over a year old can be destroyed. The problem is not that simple. It is not possible to predict in advance whether a record has future use. Part of the solution to the problem, however, lies in maintaining an up-to-date, company-wide records disposition program. And, as already stated, the initiation and maintenance of this program is a records management responsibility.

Records Disposition Checklist

The following checklist should be reviewed periodically because a records disposal program is a basic part of a total records management program.

1. Are all records covered by a retention schedule?
2. Were existing files analyzed recently for an update of the retention schedule?
3. Are manuals with current schedules available to company personnel designated to use them?
4. Are retention/disposition procedures clearly defined and understood by those involved?
5. Are the schedules being used in the company? Who is not using them? Why?
6. Is disposition of records supervised and controlled? Does it follow the procedure set for it?
7. Is an audit made periodically to see whether records are transferred to storage or destroyed according to standard operating procedures?
8. Is the total volume of records in the company monitored periodically? How often?
9. What records are in high-cost work areas? Which are in storage?
10. Have vital records been identified? Are they adequately protected?

ANALYSIS OF RECORD VITALITY

The frequency with which records are used serves as one index of their potential economic value. Where possible, a user study should be made—at least a sampling. How much are they used, by whom, and why? Such studies help determine whether dollars invested in maintaining records can be justified by the dollar value of their use. Further analysis also may show when certain types of records usually become inactive, which ones are duplicate or nonessential and can be destroyed and which ones should be transferred to another location or into another medium such as microfilm.

Checklists

Checklists are helpful when making a usage study. They assure thoroughness and keep one from overlooking various phases of the investigation. Factors that can be checked out in this way when analyzing record vitality are enumerated in the Record Utility Checklist on page 264.

Top Management Support

Records may constitute the greatest intangible asset a business has. Records management is easily one of the most important administrative services of an organization. Therefore, even small companies should have a knowledgeable person in charge and should study and classify their records systematically. No extensive study should be undertaken or expect to succeed without being supported by the authority and whole-hearted backing of top management. If good results are to be achieved, executive management must understand and support records management programs that determine what records are stored where; what is to be destroyed, and when; attempt to get compliance from all divisions of the company; and attempt to operate a functioning records center with qualified personnel. A records management program will not succeed without the informed backing of company executives and the cooperation of department heads and departmental representatives whose records are involved. Cooperation throughout a company is most likely when evidence of top management support is shown.

Communication

Involve company personnel at all levels as much as practical in making record utility studies and in making related decisions about storing or destroying records. Keep those concerned informed about prog-

ress and especially about matters relating to their departmental records. Do what you can to enlist ongoing cooperation from at least one representative in each department. Communicate personally with that representative, having however first obtained from the supervisor authority to work directly with him or her. Participation from departmental employees helps provide acceptance and access to departmental records. It helps with special terminology and with other problems that arise. It helps to avoid noncompliance.

RECORDS CENTERS

Where should the various types of inactive records be kept for the length of time that they are to be retained? The answer to this question should be handled by records management with, of course, the informed participation of those authoritatively involved. Obviously inactive records should be separated from working files. Selecting a place for them involves decisions about security, costs, type of building, space, and back-up equipment such as microfilm viewers or copiers. There are several types of records centers: (1) security storage centers, (2) central files storage centers, and (3) general archives. These may be within the company (in-house) or at a separate location.

In-House Locations

On the whole, in-house centers have cost advantages, provide easy access and retrieval, and better control. They may include either vaults or rooms. Unfortunately, when selecting storage room locations, compromise decisions often become necessary. For example, cost factors usually take precedence over accessibility. Many companies locate the storage center in the lowest possible cost-per-square-foot area, such as in basements. This may introduce problems because cost is only one factor in selecting a location. Other factors to consider are fire resistance, security or limited access for certain types of records, air filtration, and general housekeeping. All these factors must be considered by the records manager.

Storage Vaults

The word *vault* often conjures up the image of a small, dark area or a walk-in bank vault lined with safety deposit boxes. This is not true, however, where records storage vaults are concerned. They vary in size and location depending on the type and quantity of records being safeguarded and the nature and location of the business.

Record Utility Checklist

Authority. What is the basis of the authority for conducting the records study? Is it clearly defined and understood by all concerned? Is there executive support?

Administrative value. How valuable is the record as a basis for future decisions and action? Which decisions; what action? On what is the "value" based? How was it decided?

Duplication of content. How easily can the content of the record be assembled from other sources if needed? How expensive would it be?

Federal, state, and local government requirements. Which documents are needed to comply with government regulations?

Historical value. Does the record have historical value?

Investigational value. Is the company subject to many types of suits and investigations? Do the records contain supportive data in case of suit?

Legal value. Do the records provide legal proof?

Physical duplication. How easily can the records be duplicated?

Policies. Does the company have policies that might affect the disposition of these records? If yes, who is responsible for implementing them?

Procedures. Has a schedule for the implementation of the study been prepared with written instructions and a time frame?

Research value. Does the record provide possible research data about the company or its products? (This aspect is especially important when evaluating scientific records.)

Special records. What provisions need to be made for special records such as tapes, computer printouts, and microfilm?

Supporting value. Does the record provide back-up information for future programs, research, development plans, etc.?

Update. When was the last study made of these records? Was it updated? Who took it?

Volume. How much space does the record occupy? How fast is it accumulating? (Many calculated risks about disposing of records are taken because the original records become too bulky.)

In large metropolitan areas, vaults may be rooms three or four stories below ground, sometimes reinforced with thick concrete walls and lined with three- or four-inch steel plates. Steel doors to large vaults may weigh over a hundred tons. One of the most elaborate vaults in the world was built in Tokyo for the Bank of Japan before World War II to withstand bombing shocks.

Many companies have their own in-house vaults which are safe enough, except in the event of atomic warfare when their entrances could be buried under thousands of tons of debris and become inaccessible. Since few companies want to build outlying bomb-proof records centers to counteract this, they rent space in commercially maintained ones. Examples of this type of security storage facility are the Underground Vaults and Storage, Inc., and the Iron Mountain Underground Security Vaults.

Underground Vaults

Underground Vaults and Storage, Inc., is in Kansas. It includes 128 acres about 650 feet underground. The "ceiling" is rock salt, shale, and sandy soil. Part of the area is divided into large rooms where it is possible to maintain company headquarter facilities, if necessary. (See Figures 12–1 and 12–2).

Iron Mountain Underground Security Vaults is located 125 miles from New York City in an abandoned iron ore mine; its vaults are overlaid with iron ore from 75 to 150 feet deep. It provides some 150,000 cubic feet of storage space.

Supplies that might be stockpiled with data stored at a security center include a flashlight and batteries, a gasoline lantern, first-aid kit, fire extinguishers, maps and a map measurer, rations, a portable radio, a camp cookstove, an easily inflatable mattress or sleeping bag, and rope or twine.

FIGURE 12–1. Record storage areas 650 feet below the surface of the earth. *(Courtesy Underground Vaults & Storage, Inc.)*

FIGURE 12—2. Overview of underground records storage. *(Courtesy Underground Vaults & Storage, Inc.)*

Many urban commercial records centers are outside heavily populated areas but are not underground. People today are more concerned with protection against nuisance bombings, arson, and urban rioting than with atomic disaster so that space in more accessible commercial storage centers is being rented even by small companies. Riots and attacks on business establishments during this past decade have made people aware of things that can happen to their records. For example, most data processing managers understand the importance of having back-up tapes of data and programs at several storage locations.

Off-Site Security Center Features

Features for which a records manager should look when selecting an off-site records center include accessibility to related equipment, such as microfilm viewers, copiers, or computers. Does the center maintain around-the-clock security or accessibility? What is the retrieval time? May input materials (microfilm, tapes, documents) be updated daily, if necessary? How far is the center from population congestion? Is there air conditioning and humidity control in order to maintain ideal conditions for stored materials such as tapes and microfilm? Is there a stand-by generator in case of power failure? When selecting a center, insist on an on-site inspection. Get names of other users and discuss the facility with them.

Security Center Selection Checklist

Key factors to consider when selecting a security storage are covered by the following checklist items.

1. Does the facility offer protection against theft, unauthorized access, flood, fire, quakes, hurricanes, explosions?
2. Does it have an alarm system? fire suppression system? fire hoses? sprinklers (how many)? How do these systems work?
3. Have records vital to continued company operation been identified and procedures for handling them at the storage center been established?
4. How are records packed, carted, handled, retrieved? What types of storage are there?
5. Is the center up-to-date on data processing access, microfilming, and facsimile transmission of documents?
6. Are the personnel competent and agreeable? Are personnel available at off hours?
7. Is there room for expansion?
8. Is there periodic monitoring of the facilities? Periodic inspection of stored media?
9. Is there pickup and delivery service? What special services are there?
10. What is the protection against humidity, temperature extremes, dust, etc.?
11. What provision is made for the destruction of outdated records?
12. What will the company's responsibilities be about off-site records during a catastrophe? Have the responsibilities been assigned? Is there a written plan to handle the procedure?
13. Was the final decision made objectively? Were the facilities of alternate centers or storage areas studied?

Archival Centers

Another type of records center is the *archive*. The term means a collection of historical materials and is not used extensively in business although this does not mean that business is not concerned with keeping historical materials. When historical records are maintained by a business, they are usually kept merely as a part of a company's business records in either an in-house or off-site location. Government, public agencies, libraries, and state historical societies use the term *archives*; specialists in preserving and displaying historical materials for them are called archivists.

The history of business in the United States has not yet been adequately written and as American business and industry become older, there is more interest in preserving documents that have historical significance. The problem of selecting, preserving, and possibly displaying them has become a concern of many records managers, especially those employed by old, established organizations. In some instances then, business records managers also act as archivists and are concerned with archival procedures. Because of this, and because historical materials are from a business point of view *inactive* records, the following information about business archival records and about archival practices is included in this chapter. For more in-depth information consult literature of the American Archival Society available through your local library.

Early Business Archival Collections

First efforts to preserve historical documents that reflected the development of American business related primarily to the development of the textile industry in the Northeast and were donated to the Baker Library at Harvard University by some eastern based organizations. As a result of the Baker collection and of a growing interest by university schools of business administration in business history, university libraries were encouraged to collect historical documents about industries indigenous to their regions. For example, the University of Michigan (Ann Arbor) has a collection tracing the development of the lumber industry in the Great Lakes region, and a southern university has archival records about the tobacco industry. Railroad historical documents are housed in the Newberry Library and records about farm machinery as developed by the International Harvester Company (McCormick family) are with the state historical society in Madison, Wisconsin. In 1953, on the occasion of its 50th anniversary, an archive was established at Fair Lane, the former home of Henry Ford. DuPont and Firestone have also developed business archives. Many schools of business administration now offer business history courses that use archival resources.

Business Archive Procedures

Business archival records should be listed and indexed separately. Special attention should be given to the care and preservation of individual items. Some items may need to be laminated with transparent, removable plastic sheeting applied under heat. Some should be accumulated in special notebooks or binders by date, project, or individual person. For example, all historically significant documents pertaining to the founding fathers and original manufacturing efforts of the company might be preserved in a series of numbered, dated and color-coded binders. Some selected items may be photographed, framed and hung in the company's boardroom. Microfilm of the contents may also be kept in an off-site storage center.

Early archival records are primarily paper documents but more recent ones are tapes—movies and sound tracks or cassettes. Special temperature and humidity precautions need to be taken with them; duplicates are usually made. In all archival situations, special attention should be paid to protecting contents from disaster, excessive people handling, exposure to strong or prolonged sunlight, vermin, fungus, heat, and moisture. Common sense is a good guide in such situations, but specialists should also be consulted. Local professional librarians are usually knowledgeable about archival procedures, but for special problems, consult the state archivist at the state capitol.

Here again a word of caution about trying to do it all alone. Be sure to confer with appropriate authoritative company personnel about the decisions to be made and problems involved in preserving inactive archival materials. Review the situation with them from time to time. Keep them informed and aware. Good communication is important even about such mundane procedures as where to keep archival materials.

Guidelines for Retrieving Inactive Records

1. Get the exact title under which the inactive records you seek have been stored.
2. From the transfer inventory card, get the number of the storage container, its date, and location.
3. Check the authority and procedure needed for retrieving the records. If they are vital, this may mean a security release.
4. Determine the condition under which you can use them. Can copies be made? May they be taken from storage? May they be taken home or to a meeting?
5. Prepare the necessary requisition form accurately.
6. Follow the retrieval procedure carefully. Is it outlined in the Records Manangement Manual or is it a special regulation?
7. If the record is off-site, check transportation regulations. Get special authorization if needed.
8. Allow adequate time for retrieval. Avoid rush situations. They cause tension and breed unpopularity.

(continued on next page)

Guidelines for Retrieving Inactive Records (Cont'd.)

9. Ascertain carefully the time and manner by which the items are to be returned. Are there any special regulations to observe when returning inactive records?

10. Exercise caution while the items are in your hands so they do not become lost or misplaced.

11. Be courteous, patient and explicit at all times. Avoid asking for favors and be a dependable teamworker.

VITAL RECORDS

"Vital" means supporting or necessary to life. Vital records are those necessary to the survival or continuity of a company; the company could not conduct business without them. They include the incorporation certificate, bylaws, stock record books, board of directors' meeting minutes, certain corporate finance records, engineering drawings and specifications, and work processes or formulas.[2] Every organization has records containing information without which it could not function, although the specific information differs depending on the type of business and its complexity. Each organization must analyze its own operations to determine what is vital to its continued existence and a card record should be made for each. (See Figure 12–3 for a sample form of a vital records inventory card.) Naturally, a records manager must take extra precautions to identify and protect vital records.

Classification of Vital Records

Not all vital records have the same degree of importance. The classification *vital* designates materials which have a range of urgency to the survival of a company; that is, some records such as patents, copyrights, and important documents may be 90 to 100 percent vital while others such as minutes of meetings or computer programs may be nice to have as a reference but on a scale of 10 to 100 would be rated as 60 percent vital.

To differentiate the importance of so-called vital records, records managers often refer to less vital ones as *essential* and treat that category as a subdivision of vital records. Essential records are slightly

---

[2]For further definition of vital records, see Chapter 3, p. 42.

VITAL RECORDS INVENTORY	DATE	INVENTORY CONTROL NUMBER		

ORIGINATING OFFICE (DIVISION, DEPARTMENT, SECTION)

OFFICIAL PRIMARILY RESPONSIBLE	TITLE	BUILDING	ROOM	PHONE

CLASS TITLE OF RECORDS	DATE SPAN OF INITIAL TRANSFER	VOLUME

DESCRIPTION OF RECORDS

FILING ARRANGEMENT	METHOD FOR PROVIDING COPIES ☐ EXTRA COPY ☐ MICROFILM ☐ (OTHER)

DISPERSAL POINT ☐ VITAL RECORDS CENTER ☐ (OTHER)	FREQUENCY OF FUTURE TRANSFERS

DISPOSITION
☐ KEEP INDEFINITELY   ☐ INTERFILE FUTURE ACCESSIONS   ☐ REPLACE WITH FUTURE ACCESSIONS

REMARKS

APPROVED BY	TITLE	DATE

FIGURE 12–3. Form for vital records inventory.

less important than vital ones, yet they are "vital" in that they would be difficult to reconstruct in an emergency. If destroyed, their loss might not disrupt the organization. For this reason, essential records may not be given the same amount of security protection as vital records.

The degree of importance and the security given vital records should be established by the records manager in consultation with proper authority in the company.

Vital records may be further classified according to chief operations of a company: fiscal, sales, engineering, legal, manufacturing, administrative, or real property management. Records classified specifically as "vital," although differing among companies, generally relate to the following:

1. *Accounts:* accounts receivable (vendors will supply duplicate copies of accounts payable), loans, money transactions, and government-contract cost records.

2. *Deeds and capital investment records:* property claims and leases.

3. *Documents law requires:* social security, tax, payroll records, charters, bylaws, franchises, licenses.

4. ***Manufacturing records:*** production specifications, engineering drawings, inventories, patent rights, and research data.
5. ***Minutes of directors' meetings.***
6. ***Negotiable instruments:*** stock shares, notes, bonds, and checks.

Of course, records other than those named above may be vital or essential to an organization. There is no pat way to identify them. Each must be considered in relation to the overall function of the company. An inventory list of vital records should contain the following information:

1. Title and brief description of the record or file; date range.
2. Name of person in charge; extension number.
3. Location of file: building number, filing arrangement.
4. Location of duplicate or closely related information.

Vital Record Emergency Precautions

Some attention should be given to protecting vital records in case of an emergency, such as a fire. For example, who is responsible in case of an emergency? What should they do? Who should do what? Specific personnel should be assigned and coached about their responsibilities; for example, to carry out certain records if time permits, to close vault doors, and what to do with the records which have been removed. That is, a well-rounded program of vital records protection includes instructions to operating personnel about what to do with vital records in the office or with those they may be working with if an alert is sounded or a catastrophe occurs.

Fire Damage

The greatest enemy of vital records is fire. (See Figures 12–4, photographs of fire damaged records and 12–5, computer room fire damage.) According to insurance records, losses amount to millions of dollars a year. Fires in computer centers have destroyed equipment and difficult-to-replace data banks.

When safeguarding against fire, consider the additional threat of water damage. Precautions for tapes are especially important because tapes withstand less heat than paper—only about 150 degrees Fahrenheit, depending on the tape material.

Precautions against fire damage in vital record centers should include the following:

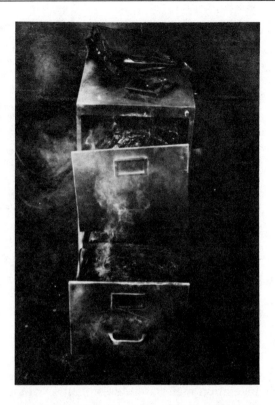

FIGURE 12—4. What a fire does to improperly protected records. *(Courtesy Victor Systems & Equipment)*

1. Air ducts should be kept clean; their locations should be studied. Can they be closed off?
2. Duplicate copies of vital records should be kept in off-site centers.
3. Smoking should not be permitted in sensitive areas.
4. Sprinkler systems and smoke detectors should be installed.
5. Storage areas should be equipped with fire extinguishers. When magnetic tape is involved, extinguishers should not contain carbon tetrachloride because it damages magnetic tape.
6. Clutter should not be allowed to accumulate in corners or aisles of the storage area.
7. Electrical outlets should be checked carefully.

Damage-Resistant Storage

There are many ways to make storage areas fire resistant by insulation. Not to be overlooked, however, are storage boxes themselves. Corrugated storage boxes, especially double-thickness ones, stand up

FIGURE 12–5. Computer room fire-damaged records. *(Courtesy Diebold, Inc.)*

quite well under the effects of sprinkler systems and controlled fires. Their insulation material holds moisture which, during a fire, steams and arrests the rise of temperature within the boxes. (More information is given about storage boxes in Chapter 9.)

Vital Records Procedures

Systematic standardized procedures should be used when maintaining and processing vital records because standardization lessens confusion, simplifies the procedures used, and usually fixes responsibilities. For example, when processing them for storage, the storage containers should be uniform in size, composition, and marking. Their contents should be labeled. A serial numbering system for each type of record is recommended. The box number acts as an address and assures the correct relocation of retrieved boxes. "Addresses" can be keyed to a layout diagram. An address can identify (1) type of container, (2) year assigned to storage, (3) accession in its series, and (4) authority, originator, or jurisdiction. For example, B-80-26-Ac identifies the 26th box of material stored by the accounting department in 1980.

Or, consider the procedure for controlling access. Limited access to vital storage areas is essential; only authorized personnel should be admitted. A procedure for controlling access to essential or vital records can be very important to a company. Is there a standard procedure, in writing, for this situation? Is it included in the overall manual of standard procedures in records management?

Specific techniques for inspecting and coding records for retention, methods of transferring records, records disposition, and control activities for the records cycle have already been discussed in Chapter 3. The same methods and techniques apply to inactive records of all types, including vital records. The sample Records Retention Schedule given in Chapter 3 includes inactive and vital records such as administrative records, contract administration records, corporate documents, legal and taxation papers. Phases the transfer method, shown earlier in Figure 3–5, can encompass might differ only in the care that should be taken when destroying vital records.

ADMINISTERING INACTIVE RECORDS

To be successful, a program for administering vital and inactive records must be actively administered. To administer is to lead; to function effectively throughout an organization, the records manager should be alert to new trends and ideas. Ideas are invisible when first conceived, but like oxygen in the air, when blended with the proper ingredients of courage, conviction, leadership ability, communication skills, and resources, they materialize and can at least be tried out. Administrators know how to utilize and administer good ideas.

As a staff person, a records manager should take the initiative in administering programs that meet the problems of changing times and that involve authoritative and related support. This must be done patiently, yet vigorously and purposefully; there is no one else to do it.

Specific phases of a program for handling inactive records are easy enough and may be summarized as follows:

1. Make an inventory of records.
2. Classify them as vital, essential, active, or inactive; legal, administrative, or operative; paper documents, tapes, films, or others.
3. Develop a retention schedule.
4. Select or create suitable storage facilities: in-house, off-site underground vault, or off-site commercial storage center.
5. Develop and monitor procedures for transferring items to storage for the periods designated in the retention schedule.
6. Supervise the destruction of records when their storage periods end.

These phases are further shown in Figure 12–6.

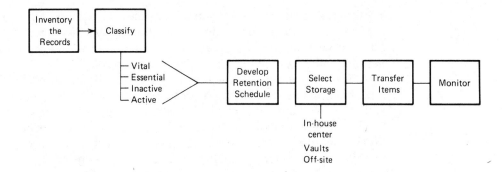

Figure 12—6. Processing inactive records.

There are other aspects of this program that cannot be identified so clearly because they are taken for granted. For example, it is assumed that the records manager will be a knowledgeable, competent professional who is backed by company executives, and who knows how to work cooperatively throughout the company. It is hopefully assumed that the records manager knows how to identify problems, assess resources, consider risks, develop plans, seek cooperation of key people, get results, look to the future, and develop ways to measure success or failure.

To develop effective, on going programs for the various facets of a total records management program, records managers must think and function *administratively*. They must be self starters. They must promote programs that focus on and meet company needs. They should look for feedback—both good and bad—about their programs. They should conduct utility studies.

Effective records managers must show confidence when marketing their programs. There is too much of a tendency for them to view their program as a secondary function within the company. How others view records managers reflects how they view themselves.

REVIEW QUESTIONS

1. How can a records manager provide for the systematic movement of inactive records from active to storage areas?

2. What factors need to be checked when considering the operating value of retained records?

3. What is the value of the department participation approach when making decisions about inactive records?

4. What are records-use studies? What do they reveal?

5. List some questions that should be answered when deciding the legal, operative, historical, and research value of records.

6. What are vital records? How are they identified?

7. What checklist items are especially useful when making an inventory of vital records?

8. Why is executive backing for a vital records program important?

9. What should be considered when selecting a vital records center?

10. What is the archival problem in business records management?

11. What precautions should be taken in preparing business records for archival preservation?

12. What are some advantages of underground storage centers?

13. What features should a records manager check when selecting an off-site storage center?

14. Why should systematic standardized procedures be used when processing inactive records for storage?

15. What precautions can be taken against fire in a vital records storage area?

16. What methods are used to destroy confidential or vital records?

LEARNING ACTIVITIES

1. For the following exercise, *match* each word with a definition.

Word		Definition
1. Procedure	_____	a. A concentration of records often maintained by file specialists.
2. Vital record	_____	
3. Central file	_____	b. Identifiable, standardized items, or pieces of information.
4. Retention schedule	_____	
5. Destruction schedule	_____	c. The storage of data and information.
		d. The movement at stated intervals, at a definite time, of inactive files out of active files.
		e. A schedule showing how long records should be kept.
		f. An item that is necessary to the life or continuity of a company.
		g. A list of things to keep in company archives.
		h. Instructions to follow when sending material to central files.

2. The San Bernardino Electronics Corporation, a young but rapidly growing company, has accumulated a big quantity of records. The farsighted young managers who started the company three years ago established a policy that each division of the company—Research, Production, Marketing, Finance, and Administration—should classify its records every 6 months as either (1) vital, or essential, (2) active, (3) essential but inactive, and (4) inactive and nonessential. Category No. 3 was to be moved to a central storage and No. 4 was to be destroyed. These responsibilities had been delegated to the divisions themselves; it was hoped that personnel from each division would be responsible for evaluating and processing records according to the standing policy.

At this time, however, several things indicate that the San Bernardino Electronics Corporation needs to make changes in its records handling policy. For example, there have been problems about retrieving important records, in providing adequate storage space for records that have been sent to central storage, and in identifying specific personnel in the divisions who will assume responsibility for records.

At a recent executive meeting where the records problem was discussed, it was decided that, because many of the company's records will likely have research and historical value when the history of the electronics industry is written, that the manner in which these records are being preserved also needed to be studied, that conditions in the storage center need to be reviewed, and that some new way of coordinating and controlling records needs to be developed.

1. What recommendation(s) will you make to help the San Bernardino Electronics Corporation achieve better control over its records maintenance program?

2. What organizational change(s) would your recommendations necessitate?

3. List two problems you foresee in implementing your recommendations.

IV

MICROGRAPHICS AND AUTOMATION

13

Micrographics

Processing, storing and distributing vast quantities of records have created widespread interest in the use of micrographics. As technology increases our ability to produce and process information, records managers look to micrographics as a way to save space and provide better service to records users.

The technology of micrographics has increased tremendously in the past few years. Although microfilming operations began in the 1920s, widespread use of reduction processes did not occur until the past two decades. Major improvements in filming operations, equipment to process and store records, and a greater appreciation of the merits of micrographics have led many organizations to use some form of document reduction. Today, a variety of organizations—including government, business, and educational institutions—find some adoption of micrographics to be of benefit in their operations.

DEFINITION OF TERMS

A variety of terms are used today to describe the processes and records produced through reduction of documents. *Micrographics* is frequently used to describe the overall process of filming documents and reducing them into a different format. A formal definition of micrographics is:

> Micrographics combines the science, the art, and the technology by which information can be quickly reduced to the medium of microfilm, stored conveniently, and then easily retrieved for reference and use.[1]

[1]National Micrographics Association, *Introduction to Micrographics*, Silver Spring, Maryland, 1974.

The process of micrographics can be compared to any information processing system. The micrographics "system" includes various activities and procedures, beginning with the determination of what records are to be microfilmed through the final production of a specific type of reduced record.

The reduced record may be identified as a *microrecord* or *microform*. While both terms may be used interchangeably, microform appears to be the more popular word. Microform is the generic term for any record, either film or paper, which contains reduced images or microimages. It is composed of several specific types of microrecords:

1. Microfilm
2. Microfiche
3. Ultrafiche
4. Microcards (or micro-opaques)
5. Aperture cards
6. Jackets

Each of these microforms is described and illustrated later in this chapter.

USING MICROFORMS

The decision to use micrographics in some form is an important one and must be carefully weighed before any purchase of equipment and supplies is made. Although micrographics has widespread application, not all firms may find this process beneficial. A feasibility study should be conducted to determine the need for microfilming before any commitment is made. This study should focus on:

advantages to be obtained through microfilming
costs involved
changes in work operations and procedures
increased efficiency and effectiveness of records storage and use

If the feasibility study indicates microfilming can be of benefit, exploration into converting to this process can begin. An organization may choose to develop a micrographics operation within the firm, or it may desire to have records microfilmed by a commercial firm commonly called a service bureau. A large firm, because of its desire to control microfilming operations and the volume of records maintained, may set up its own center and organize it into a separate department. Other firms may wish to contract with a service bureau that will perform all microfilming operations for a specified fee. Those businesses which do not wish to incur the initial expense of obtaining microfilming cameras and other equipment may find using a commercial firm to be financially beneficial.

The next concern in using microforms is to train personnel in the use of these records. Some initial resistance may be evident since changes will occur and personnel may not accept the changes quickly or openly. However, if records personnel are adequately trained and persuaded of the merits of using microforms, most resistance can be avoided.

The major focus on a training program for micrographics personnel should be on demonstrating the use of the equipment, on explaining new records processing procedures, and on showing employees how micrographics can improve records operations. Employees should be given ample opportunity to learn their new responsibilities with the assistance of qualified supervisors or training specialists.

Advantages of Using Microforms

Of all the reported advantages in using microforms, space saving is the most widely mentioned. Typically, an organization can reduce the space needed to store and maintain records by up to 95 to 98 percent—a tremendous reduction. Since the costs of office space, filing equipment and storage facilities have risen appreciably over the years, a major reduction in space required for microforms yields a considerable cost savings.

Microforms also provide excellent preservation of records along with ease of duplication. Unlike some paper documents which have a limited life, microforms can be preserved for an indefinite time. They can be reproduced quickly and easily—and at a low cost. For example, a duplicate copy of one $4'' \times 6''$ microfiche can be obtained for as low as 25 to 35 cents.

Another advantage of using microforms is the reduced distribution costs. Mailing microforms offers a considerable cost savings over that required for paper documents. Also, they can be carried conveniently. Many business people enjoy the convenience of carrying microrecords with them as they travel—be it by car, train, plane or other mode of transportation. Furthermore, this ease of carrying may allow for use of the records while travelling, especially with the advent of inexpensive, small, and portable readers that can also be hand-carried.

With microforms, the time required to retrieve documents can be shortened considerably, thereby giving prompt user service and increasing the efficiency of the records personnel. Firms such as retail stores, catalog order houses, banks and utilities find that microforms increase customer service capabilities and customer satisfaction. For example, one large midwest power company, after the adoption of microfiche, reported the average time necessary to locate and retrieve customer records was reduced to 20 seconds from a previous time of 1 minute. Coupled with a computer, microforms offer even greater retrieval possibilities and are more efficient than manual operations with paper documents.

Disadvantages of Microforms

As mentioned earlier, not all firms find microforms advantageous. For those organizations that decide to purchase micrographics equipment, the initial cash outlay is substantial. Microfilming cameras, for example, cost from $3,000 to over $12,000, depending on the type of camera and its capabilities. Other equipment (such as film processers, duplication equipment, reader-printers, and enlarger-printers) may also be required and will increase initial costs considerably. Thus, the changeover step of converting paper documents to microforms represents a major commitment.

As with equipment of any type, micrographic equipment needs maintenance and periodic repair. If a piece of equipment is inoperable for some time, the delay may affect records operations and result in inefficiencies. Finding reliable repair personnel who will promptly fix broken equipment is essential and represents another type of expense.

Using the equipment can create other limitations of microforms. Since only one person can use a piece of equipment at a time, other records personnel may have to wait unless additional equipment is available. (Because of the expense involved, many firms may not be able to justify purchasing additional equipment.) Further, in some organizations equipment is centrally located, requiring operators to travel to and from the location in order to use it. Hopefully, the distance operators must travel will be minimal; but if not, some delays or possible employee dissatisfaction may result.

User resistance, if it is substantial, can be an important concern in using microforms. For whatever reason, some people reject photographed records, preferring instead to use only paper documents. They prefer traditional processing methods and shy away from using (or learning to use) equipment associated with microforms.

TYPES OF MICROFORMS

The selection of microform involves choices regarding what will best meet the needs of records management. Each type of microform has distinct advantages and disadvantages; each can contribute to specific user requirements. Primary factors to consider in selecting appropriate microform can include the nature of information to be stored, the format this information is in, and how the microrecord will be used. Other considerations could include:

ease and speed of document retrieval
necessity to update or change records
method of accessing information
cost of equipment and related supplies
requirements to make duplicate copies of records
degree of automation used or proposed

Each of the various types of microforms is described and illustrated in the following sections.

Microfilm

The oldest type of microform is microfilm. It has a wide variety of applications and is still a popular choice because large quantities of information can be stored on a microfilm roll. The beginning of most photographic operations consists of microfilming a paper document. Once developed, the microfilm can be repackaged ("packaging" is the process of deciding the form in which the film is to appear) into other types of microforms.

The standard microfilm is a 100-foot roll that can contain up to 30,000 images. The larger the documents to be filmed, the fewer images that can appear on each roll. For example, approximately 2,500 images of letter-size correspondence ($8\frac{1}{2}'' \times 11''$) can be placed on a single 100-foot roll of 16 mm microfilm whereas up to 30,000 smaller documents, such as receipts, checks, payroll cards, etc., can be filmed on a roll.

Microfilm is available in several sizes: 16 mm, 35 mm, 70 mm, and 105 mm. The 16 mm and 35 mm are most popular, with 16 mm used primarily for images from standard stationery sizes and 35 mm for larger documents such as newspapers, engineering drawings or maps.

Although microfilm is produced in a roll format, it can be packaged onto reels, cartridges or cassettes, as shown in Figure 13–1. Microfilm reels offer a high degree of protection of images and are particularly desirable when the documents being filmed are sequential. Some examples of sequential documents would include books, newspapers, checks or purchase orders.

Cartridges and cassettes provide even greater protection, keeping images free from fingerprints or possible tearing. Both provide ease in locating desired images and in rewinding back to the original frame or the beginning of the roll.

Microfilms can be produced with a minimum of document preparation. Duplicates are easily obtainable also. Microfilm can be viewed on a variety of readers and coded to ensure quick retrieval of a specific image. Some limitations of microfilm include: (1) the difficulty in updating or changing film, (2) the necessity to scan sequentially until a desired frame is accessed and (3) the requirement of coding the film to allow for identification of reel contents.

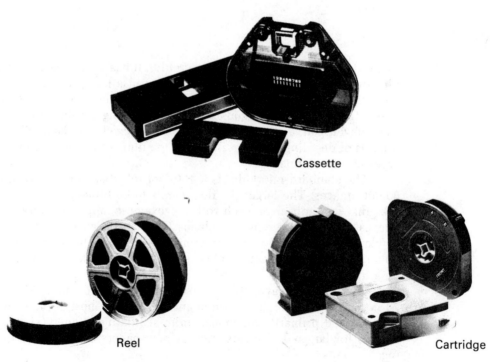

Cassette

Reel

Cartridge

FIGURE 13–1. Microfilm formats. *(Courtesy National Micrographics Association)*

Microfiche

An increasingly popular microform today is microfiche or fiche. This microform is sometimes termed a "unitized" record because film images are placed on a grid format in a predetermined pattern. For example, microfilm images may be cut and sequenced into rows and columns and then duplicated as a microfiche.

The standard size for microfiche is a $6'' \times 4''$ sheet of film containing 60 or 72 microimages arranged in rows. (The number of images on each card may vary depending on the size of the document photographed and the film reduction ratio used.) An example of a fiche is given in Figure 13–2. Images are arranged sequentially and each card is coded (at the top) to identify the contents of the microfiche.

Microfiche has increased in popularity due to the following reasons:

FIGURE 13–2. Microfiche.

1. Fiche uses a unit-record approach in which only desired documents of a single category are placed on one card.
2. Fiche-to-fiche reproduction is economical and can be produced on a variety of equipment.
3. Fiche is easy to handle and can be mailed cheaply with a minimum of packaging.
4. When correctly indexed, specific images can be quickly located on a microfiche reader.
5. Fiche can be viewed on a variety of portable or nonportable readers.
6. Fiche can be used to film all types of documents, including pictures or other visuals, in both black and white or color, if desired.

Because of its ease of storage and retrieval speed, microfiche is becoming more popular than microfilm, if it has not already done so. As technology increases the capacity to produce microfiche directly from the initial photographing process, more consideration will be directed toward using this microform.

Perhaps the greatest limitation in using fiche is in the processing steps required to produce it. Most microfiche is produced from microfilm images that are arranged in the desired format. Although some photographing operations (step-and-repeat camera, computer output microfilm) are simplifying the processing, it can still be time-consuming and expensive to produce a master copy.

Microfiche must be carefully coded and stored to ensure easy retrieval and file integrity. Fortunately, a variety of excellent equipment and supplies are available to protect microfiche records. Security of microfiche can be another concern as the susceptibility of fiche to theft or "souveniring" is high because of its compact size and portability.

Ultrafiche

Ultrafiche is simply a type of microfiche which uses an ultrahigh reduction ratio. While microfiche images are reduced in a range of 18 to 48 times, ultrafiche images are reduced 150 to 400 times or more. Thus, a $6'' \times 4''$ ultrafiche may contain hundreds of images (up to approximately 4,000, depending on the size of the documents being filmed) on which, for example, an entire book or catalog may appear. Although ultrafiche offers the greatest storage density of any microform, few organizations either need or can justify using ultrafiche. In comparison with microfiche, ultrafiche is more expensive to prepare and requires more sophisticated readers capable of enlarging very small images.

Microcard (or Opaque Card)

Unlike other microforms that are transparent, a microcard is a special type of microrecord that contains images on both sides of the card. Figure 13–3 illustrates this microform. It is also called an opaque card because of the type of reader used to view the images on the card.

Several standard sizes of microcards are available: $3'' \times 5''$, $4'' \times 6''$, and $5'' \times 8''$. These sizes are identical to standard index cards used in offices today. Therefore, filing and storage equipment which is used for other purposes is readily adaptable for microcards.

Although not used extensively in business, microcards have features which make them attractive for storing public documents or special publications:

1. They are easily coded and therefore quickly filed and retrieved. (Since microcards consist of black images on white stock, any coding on either face of the card is quickly visible.)
2. Microcard images are on a durable paper stock, coated with a plastic lamination which offers good protection and preservation.
3. Images can be placed on both sides of the card and can be viewed by inexpensive opaque readers.

Aperture Cards

Aperture cards are a combination of microfilm with a punched card that allows data to be stored with the microimage. This format offers a degree of standardization since it uses the standard tab card ($3\frac{1}{4}'' \times 7\frac{3}{8}''$) which most companies use for data processing. The aperture card has a slot (or several slots) into which microimages can be placed. These cards normally hold 35 mm microfilm, although 70 mm film can be used. The tab card itself can be coded to facilitate computer retrieval and storage.

Aperture cards possess the following advantages and disadvantages:

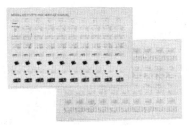

FIGURE 13–3. Opaque (or micro) card ($3'' \times 5''$).
(Courtesy National Micrographics Association)

Advantages

unit record approach is used, thereby storing information relating to one subject or topic

eye-readable headings identify each card

documents can be easily updated or revised

cards are easy and economical to mail

the image size is ideal for certain documents such as engineering drawings

Disadvantages

the coded master is expensive to produce

they offer low storage density since a maximum of only eight page-size images can appear on one 35 mm frame

they offer limited use since most documents are more easily stored in other microforms

An aperture card is illustrated in Figure 13–4.

Jackets

This final microform is a plastic unitized record similar in size to a microfiche. The jacket is composed of single or multiple channels into which film is inserted. A 6″×4″ jacket, for example, can contain five channels with 12 images in each, for a total of 60 images (using 35 mm film).

The major advantage the jacket has over other microforms is that it can be easily updated. The jacket "pockets" protect the microfilm and allow records personnel to organize images in any desired sequence. Each jacket can be easily coded for retrieval and storage efficiency. An example of this microform is shown in Figure 13–5.

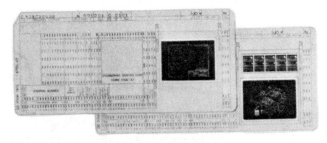

FIGURE 13–4. Aperture card. *(Courtesy National Micrographics Association)*

FIGURE 13–5. Microfilm jacket. *(Courtesy National Micrographics Association)*

THE MICROFILMING PROCESS

Using—or deciding to use—micrographics encompasses several steps, beginning with determining what documents to film up through using specific microforms. Each of these steps should be carefully planned so that they are efficiently and effectively implemented.

What Documents Should Be Microfilmed?

Historically, microfilm was thought appropriate as a way of reducing space and preserving inactive records—those that an organization decided they should retain but that were not used in day-to-day operations. Today, microfilming has broadened its role and has applications for active records and automated retrieval systems.

In business today the question is: What documents should be microfilmed? All records, or just some specific categories? Answering these questions involves several concerns:

1. What is the retention period of the record(s)?
2. Can microfilming be done without incurring undue problems or reduced efficiency?
3. Is the quality of the original document sufficient to produce a good microimage?
4. What volume of records will be microfilmed?
5. What are the legal requirements regarding microfilming documents?

Generally, microfilming should not be considered on the basis of saving space alone. If it is, the cost of microfilming may exceed the savings in space—not a reasonable economic choice. Rather, microfilming of documents should be based on how it can contribute to the organization's operations (user satisfaction, effectiveness of operations, work flow, etc.) in addition to cost or economic analysis.

Microfilming appears appropriate for records that are used in large volume and/or are retained for some time, perhaps five or more years. The bulk of records today are termed "transaction" documents—letters, memos, invoices, purchase orders, payroll forms, etc.—which have a relatively short life compared to vital documents or reference material that may need to be retained permanently. These transaction records rarely justify being microfilmed, even if the company owns its own equipment.

But other records that must be retained for long periods can justify the expense of microfilming, particularly if a large volume of such documents are used frequently. Banks, for example, microfilm customer checks, the largest volume record they process. If they didn't, they would become overwhelmed with "paper" checks and run out of storage space. Based on retention schedules as discussed in Chapter 3, each company can decide which records lend themselves to microfilming.

Legal Concerns of Microfilming

Laws regarding the microfilming of documents support the use of photographing documents with some restrictions. The Uniform Photographic Copies of Business and Public Records as Evidence Act of 1946 defines legal requirements and guidelines for this process. This Act states:

> If any business, institution, member of a profession, or calling, or any department or agency of government, in the regular course of business or activity has kept or recorded any memorandum, writing, entry, print, representation or combination thereof, of any act, transaction, occurrence, or event, and in the regular course of business has caused any or all of the same to be recorded, copied or reproduced by any photographic, photostatic, microfilm, micro-card, miniature photographic, or other process which accurately reproduces or forms a durable medium for so reproducing the original, the original may be destroyed in the regular course of business unless held in a custodial or fiduciary capacity or unless its preservation is required by law. Such reproduction, when satisfactorily identified, is as admissible in evidence as the original itself in any judicial or administrative proceeding whether the original is in existence or not and an enlargement or facsimile of such reproduction is likewise admissible in evidence if the original reproduction is in existence and available for inspection under direction of court. The introduction of a reproduced record, enlargement or facsimile, does not preclude admission of the original.

In interpreting this act, the main provisions to be met in order to satisfy these legal requirements are:

1. That the copy was made in the regular course of business. (Intention is to prohibit photographing documents in order to avoid using the original documents—for whatever reason.)
2. The photographed copy must have been made by a process that completely guarantees the accuracy or authenticity of the record.
3. Processed copies must be clearly identified. (This may involve having records officials certify them.)

With some exceptions, photographed copies of documents may be satisfactorily used in replacement of original copies. If this is true, then the original documents may be disposed of without any harm to the firm. However, to be safe, it is advised that each company carefully review existing local, state, and federal laws before destroying documents.

Records personnel should also be aware of federal laws prohibiting the copying of some types of documents. For example, documents such as government securities, postage stamps, passports, licenses, and draft cards may not be reproduced under any circumstances. Furthermore, copyrighted material is protected from being reproduced (with some exceptions), and an individual or organization who violates this law is subject to prosecution.

Preparing Documents to be Filmed

An important goal of micrographics is to have the microrecord clearly visible and easy to read. To meet this goal, documents to be filmed must be carefully prepared and coded as needed. Some guidelines to follow in completing this step include:

1. Remove all staples, paper clips or other fasteners from the document prior to filming.
2. Erase or correct any writing, coding, smears or other marks that are not a part of the original document. (Erasing marks that are a part of the original will result in obtaining an invalid record.)
3. Repair any parts of the document that are torn, creased or may in any way produce unwanted marks on the microfilm.
4. Correctly code the original document with whatever identification is required or desired. Be sure that coding is placed in a position on the document that does not interfere with the information on the original.

The Filming Operation

Only qualified and experienced personnel should be given the responsibility for filming documents. The process requires careful attention and planning—along with a good knowledge of photographic principles and practices.

Once documents are ready to be filmed, one of three microfilm cameras may be used: the *rotary*, *planetary* or *step-and-repeat* cameras. An illustration of each of these cameras is shown in Figure 13–6. The rotary camera is used most frequently to film standard-size documents. This camera is highly efficient as hundreds of documents can be filmed per hour. An operator may hand-feed documents into the camera or an automatic feed device may be used, which speeds up the filming process considerably.

Step-and-Repeat
(Brookeades (Aust.)

Planetary (Bell & Howell)

Rotary (Terminal Data Corp.)

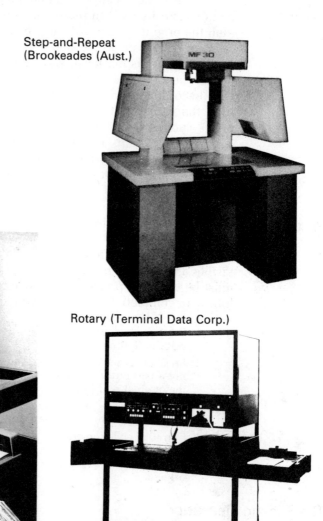

FIGURE 13—6. Microfilming cameras.

The planetary camera is especially appropriate for filming large documents or records which cannot be easily fed into a rotary camera. This camera also permits lighting to be changed to correspond to the requirements of each document being filmed. Although the film quality of a planetary camera will usually exceed that of the rotary camera, the filming speed of a planetary camera is slower, because each document must be manually positioned and filmed.

The step-and-repeat camera is used to produce microfiche. It is designed to film images in a patterned grid of rows and columns to produce the 6″ × 4″ standard microfiche.

The processed film obtained from any of the cameras described above should pass two tests to be of acceptable quality. The film's *resolution*, that is, the measure of the sharpness of the lines of the images on the film, should meet prescribed standards. Clear images will make the microform easy to read and thus reduce eye strain or fatigue. If the resolution is not within standards, documents should be refilmed.

The second test of film quality is to examine its *density*. This is measured by a *densitometer* that measures the contrast between reproduced images and the background film. Proper contrast makes the microform easier to view and ensures compatibility with whatever microform reader is used.

Packaging the Microrecord

After the film is processed, a decision must be made regarding the form in which the film should appear. It may be produced as microfilm in either a reel, cartridge or cassette package. It may be further processed and placed into a unitized format such as microfiche, ultrafiche, jackets, aperture cards or micro-opaques. Whatever choice is made should be based on factors such as costs, convenience, user satisfaction—and other factors discussed earlier in this chapter.

If additional copies of a microform are desired, specialized equipment is available to meet this need—regardless of the number of duplicates requested. Roll-to-roll, fiche-to-fiche, roll-to-fiche, or card-to-card duplication is possible.

MICROGRAPHICS EQUIPMENT

A variety of readers are available for viewing microforms. Selecting the appropriate one will depend on the microform being viewed, the user's needs and the environment in which the reader will be used. Readers have truly become versatile today; models are available as lap readers, portable units, and desk or free-standing units. Figure 13–7 shows examples of the types available.

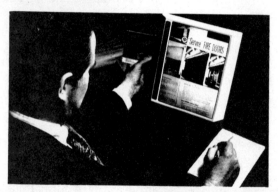
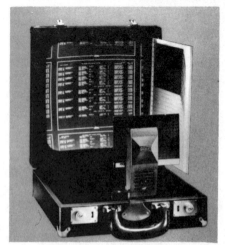

FIGURE 13—7. Microform readers. (*Courtesy Bell & Howell Micro Photo Division*)

Although readers are available for all types of microforms, many companies manufacture portable ones especially for microfiche. These are compact, lightweight, and yet produce acceptable magnification and clear display of documents. These units can be transported within an organization or taken out of the office when travelling.

Some readers have special features: they produce hard copy reproductions from a microform (reader-printers), or they enlarge microimages and produce copies up to 24″ × 36″ (enlarger-printers). These features, available in self-contained units, expand applications of micrographics technology.

Storing active or inactive microforms is also a convenient process today because of the many types of storage equipment available. These include:

For roll microfilm:

storage files and trays
modular microfiles
rotary files
briefcase units

For unitized microforms:

easel binders
rotary stands
desk stands
fiche panels
travel cases
albums
mailers
roll top files

Although it is impossible in this chapter to illustrate all the storage equipment that is available, several items are shown in Figure 13–8. Records personnel who are interested in knowing more about this equipment could consult any of the various companies that manufacture this equipment.

Computer Output Microfilm (COM)

An increasingly important application of microfilm technology is that of computer output microfilm (COM). Organizations that have computerized their data processing requirements can use COM as a way to control paperwork costs and have information available for records users.

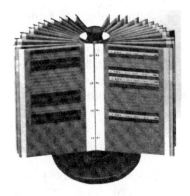

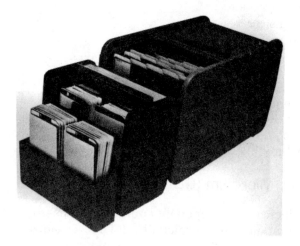

FIGURE 13—8. Microform storage equipment.

The COM process involves taking data from the magnetic storage medium of a computer, usually a computer tape. A COM recorder converts data to microfilm, eliminating the paper printout step. The microfilm can then be displayed on a cathode ray tube (CRT) and can be used by records personnel as needed. If hard copy of a microfilm is required, one can be obtained at the press of a button—if the equipment has this feature available.

In addition to reducing paperwork, COM is highly efficient. The microrecording of data by COM can be as fast as 15,000 to 20,000 lines a minute. Search time for locating information on the microfilm is exceptionally quick when coded with specific identifying information. For example, a single document stored with hundreds of others can be located in a few seconds.

A summary of major advantages of using COM, as given by Reitzfield, includes the following:[2]

1. COM eliminates the purchase and use of expensive, carbon-interleaved forms.
2. COM eliminates the time-consuming decollating of forms.
3. COM eliminates the time-consuming bursting of forms.
4. COM eliminates the time and expense of binding large computer originated reports.
5. COM speeds up the reproduction process of computer generated records twenty times faster than the average computer printer.
6. COM reduces 30% of the cost of reproducing computer generated records.
7. COM reduces 90% of the cost of distributing computer generated records.
8. COM reduces 90% of the space requirements for storing computer generated records.
9. COM reduces 90% of the time and effort to store computer generated records.
10. COM reduces the time and effort to retrieve computer generated records.

SUMMARY OF THE MICROGRAPHICS PROCESS

Figure 13–9 summarizes and consolidates steps that are a part of the micrographics process. Within the micrographic system, each organization has a variety of procedures and equipment it can use to im-

---

[2]Milton Reitzfield, "Microfilm Usage for Systems," *Records Management*, Cleveland, Ohio: Association for Systems Management, 1973.

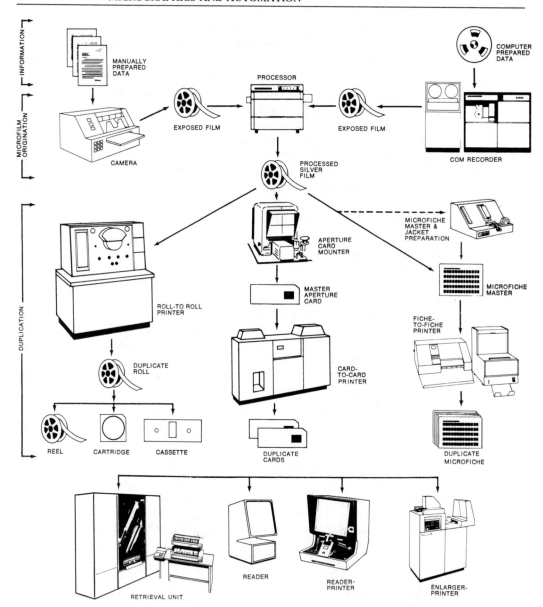

FIGURE 13—9. The micrographics process. (*Source: Introduction to Micrographics.* Published by the National Micrographics Association, Silver Spring, Md., 1974)

prove information processing activities and plans. As technology improves the capability of micrographic equipment to assume new functions, more improvements can be anticipated.

REVIEW QUESTIONS

1. Define the following terms:
   micrographics
   microforms
   microrecords

2. Under what conditions might an organization consider using microforms?

3. Why would a feasibility study be helpful to determine if microforms should be used? What aspects of the organization's activities would be analyzed during the feasibility study?

4. What are some of the advantages and disadvantages of using a service bureau to microfilm records?

5. How can the use of micrographics benefit an organization?

6. What are the major features of the following types of microforms?
   microfilm
   microfiche
   ultrafiche
   microcards
   aperture cards
   jackets

7. In what ways can microfilm be packaged?

8. What is a microform reduction ratio?

9. When might an organization find it feasible to microfilm records?

10. Under what provisions can documents be microfilmed and satisfy legal requirements regarding photographing records?

11. Can all business documents be photographed? Why or why not?

12. Why should documents be carefully analyzed prior to being photographed?

13. Discuss the features of rotary, planetary, and step-and-repeat cameras. Under what conditions would records personnel prefer to use each type of camera?

14. Define the terms *density* and *resolution*. Why are they important aspects of film quality?

15. What is COM? Why is it an efficient way of processing and using information?

LEARNING ACTIVITIES

1. The Phoenix office of Modern Merchandise, Inc., is presently facing a problem: too many records and no place to put them. This office, among other things, has maintained sales, inventory, purchasing and payroll records for eight western outlets since 1965. They find they have no storage space for current records and there is confusion in finding and using inactive records.

   Current retention schedules specify retaining sales and payroll records for seven years, and inventory and purchasing records for three years. Management is considering some way of microfilming records to reduce space and improve their use of inactive records. However, when discussing this interest with records personnel in the firm, the president of the company noted a slight reluctance by the employees to have microfilmed documents. Yet, the president still thinks the change would be beneficial and wishes to proceed immediately.

   a. Based on this limited information, do you think the company should change to micrographics? Justify your response.
   b. What microforms would you recommend they use?
   c. What might you recommend this organization do to overcome the perceived employee reluctance?

2. Two years ago, Southern Machine Company hired a micrographics service bureau to film their active and inactive records. Since this firm manufactures, stores, and sells hundreds of car and truck parts, they find the convenience of using microfiche helpful to their operations. However, the records supervisor at this firm thinks the fee charged by the service bureau is excessive and that an in-house operation would be cheaper. A feasibility study is recommended to analyze the possibility of doing the microfilming internally.

   a. What economic factors should be analyzed as part of the feasibility study?

   b. In making the decision, what factors other than economic ones should be considered? Explain your answer.

14

Automated Information and Records Systems

Automating the transmission and storage of information is of concern to all of us but especially to records managers. New technological developments for processing information give records managers a chance to form new ideas and to use new devices for working with problems inherent in handling, moving, storing, and destroying paper records. Devices that give the greatest promise of revolutionary results are those that substitute electronic images for paper work. These devices take records management several steps into the electronic age.

Making the changes necessary to take records management into the electronic age involves many problems, not the least of which is the tendency of people everywhere to resist change, particularly when it relates to something as revolutionary as the elimination of paper documents. People are comfortable with paper documents because they are used to them. Even when they know that paper-oriented information processing and communication are inefficient, they cling to old routines because it is easier for them psychologically to struggle along with avalanches of paper records rather than to adapt to technological developments that include devices they do not understand too well. Electronic mail, electronic document distribution, electronic message centers, paperless offices, electronic document identification, telecommunication networks—these are disquieting terms because they involve a whole new series of devices, methods, and procedures.

Devices capable of storing, sorting, sending, and receiving records electronically will very soon be installed in most companies; they presage *the office of the future.* The office of the future relates to the concept of providing office workers with automated and electronic tools so they can work more effectively with less effort. These "tools" include electronic components, processes, and systems that interface (link) and integrate, thus creating a new office work environment. The automated and electronic office of the future is a *combination* of the typewriter keyboard with new electronic hardware such as the magnetic storage typewriter, automatic word processing with text editor, telecommunicating networks, and CRT (Cathode Ray Tube) screens. (See Figure 14–1.)

ELECTRONIC DATA PROCESSING AND WORD PROCESSING

The distinction between word and data processing operations is that one is better adapted to handle words than the other although both, of course, can process either words or numbers. That is, *word* processing is primarily a qualitative process; data processing is quantita-

FIGURE 14–1. Electronic devices at an office work station. *(Courtesy Wang Laboratories, Inc.)*

tive.[1] Data processing is traditionally associated with computers; word processing with magnetic storage typewriters and text (word) editing equipment.

Word Processing

Word processing refers to an electronic processing system that was first introduced by the International Business Machines Corporation (IBM) in 1964 as the Magnetic Selectric Typewriter (MTM). As typists typed, the keystrokes were stored on a magnetic tape cartridge. Corrections could be overlaid on the tape and a new, errorless copy automatically produced at 150 words a minute. At first considered to be revolutionary, the concept of capturing keystrokes on magnetic media soon became an accepted practice. Word processing is an office system that grew out of the typewriter—a universal office machine. It is, therefore, user oriented because people are comfortable with it. With it, they do not have the feeling of bewilderment that often confronts them when using a computer.

Computer Hookup –

Although early word processing was thought of as a centralized Administrative Support (AS) system, or an automated typing pool for handling typing production, evolutionary changes in the equipment gradually changed the original stand-alone MTM to type-editing equipment with automatic readability when linked with a CRT (Cathode Ray Tube where a typist can see copy on the screen before it is printed). Linking this type-editing equipment to a company's computer memory capability, high-speed printers, and off-line storage has moved word processing technology a giant step forward, putting it right into the company's mainframe companywide computer network. Sharing the logic of mainframe computer systems permits huge amounts of text from the text editing equipment to be stored in computer access "files" for future use, thus also taking over some traditional filing and document storage functions. Today's word processors, therefore, as a result of their ability to be linked to computer systems, can share computer data banks and even be hooked into telecommunication networks that extend across the country or around the world, or they can queue onto a computer printer/copier such as Computer Output Microfilm (COM).

---

[1]Records can be quantified by *counting* the *number* of files stored, the unit *time* it takes to access them, or the *cost* of labor spent in retrieving a file, but the substance of the documents filed is qualitative—*words* and *concepts*.

The relatively low-cost magnetic storage word-processing typewriters and text-editing equipment together with several shared computer and telecommunication systems have the potential, then, of becoming part of an overall shared system[2] for an entire corporation. Most experts agree that combined word and data processing is the future technology of the office. They believe word processing will be the common interfacer in the whole of information management on a companywide basis and that the huge storage (data bank) capability of a mainframe company computer system will take over the text or document storage function. Because of the nature of the equipment, this stored text will be electronically retrievable and can be "delivered" to CRT units at individual work stations as needed.

System Capability

In addition to the capabilities of a word processing *system* when linked to a computer system, it can process dictation, typewriting, copying, mail distribution, and filing. Its text-editing capability will automatically delete items; insert copy; move lines, paragraphs, or pages; justify margins; number pages and paragraphs; underline; tabulate; insert end-of-line hyphens; align columns; vary type faces (pica, elite, proportional), generate forms for statistical tables and reports; scroll rapidly up/down, right/left; use sub- or superscripts; input text from cassettes, floppy disks, cartridges, OCR (Optical Character Recognition), COM or network hookups; and output to high-speed printers, typesetting machines, tape, or network lines. Some text-editing machines will repage copy when producing a manuscript and handle automatic searches for designated items. As word processing installations become a more common part of a company's machine installations, they may be placed around a company as data processing terminals are now. (See Figure 14–2.)

Basic Types of Word Processing Installations

There are four basic types of word processors: (1) stand-alone, (2) hybrid, (3) shared logic, and (4) distributed.

1. A *stand-alone* word processor may have one or more magnetic storage typewriters and text-editing machines in a central location.

---

[2]The word *system* does not belong exclusively to computer technology. Any plan (manual, automatic, or electronic) for processing repetitive information is a system. The total system anticipated in the office of tomorrow is a combination of interlocking subsystems, some of which are computer systems.

FIGURE 14—2. A communicating word processor. This word processing configuration has multifunction capabilities on a text file or data base. It contains a working memory, simplified keyboard with a numeric keypad, disk drives, and programmable commands. It can also go on-line to a shared system. (*Courtesy Royal Oak Business Machines, Inc.*)

The term "stand-alone" usually means that the equipment is not linked to other units, especially the computer.

2. A *hybrid* installation has access to a data processing terminal. With such a hookup, for example, an accountant can use the same terminal to prepare both a written report and perform the related calculations.

3. A *shared-logic* equipment configuration usually includes a mini computer which maintains a data bank[3] of pertinent correspondence and documents. The configuration might also be hooked to such peripheral equipment as printers (for batches of form letters) or an OCR reader for automatic input from forms.

4. A *distributed* word processing configuration refers to a big, disbursed installation in a large company or government bureau. It includes a variety of systems joined in a network that might even interconnect offices in different cities or government offices in different countries. Such installations, although geared predominantly to high-volume word processing tasks can also handle forms processing, *file*

---

[3]Computer technology has monopolized some terms such as *data bank*. Actually, data bank may refer to *any* accumulation of "data" whether qualitative (words) or quantitative (numbers) held in electronic memory. Generically speaking, it would even be possible to refer to a library (non-computerized) as a "bank" of data.

inquiries, and file transfers through their linkage to mainstream computer systems. All new word processing installations have the capability for such transmissions.

Communication Networks

The automated flow and transmission of information among electronic devices in offices coincide with new developments in communication network technology. Communication network technology is speeding up transmission and leaving behind the era of bulky cable hookups and unsightly wires. For example, fiber optic cables (strands of glass as thin as hair) can carry 10,000 times as much information as the same diameter copper wire. One glass fiber can carry 800 conversations, tens of thousands of messages, 20 TV programs, or 50 million bits of data per second. With this new technology, 40,000 typically sized books can be transmitted from coast to coast in an hour, or the contents of a 24-volume encyclopedia in 3 minutes. Hundreds of glass fibers can be formed into a cable.

The merging of data/word processing technology with the new telecommunication technology where impulses are bounced off satellites also provide another wide array of information storage and information processing combinations. For example, terminals linked via telephone lines to CRT devices and mini computers provide instant access to information of all types: documents, pictures, and graphic displays. These systems can be reinforced by satellite communication devices (extraterresterial equipment) *for storing information* for down-to-earth business data.

Extended telecommunication networks make it possible to interface voice, video, facsimile, or data/word input that access or transmit from huge data banks of all types: daily news, market data, biographies, property records, etc. They make business teleconferencing practical, thus saving travel time and costs. They make electronic mail a reality. These services are likely to change the very structure of offices and the way information is processed.

Small Computers

Small computers, most of them desk-top size and known as mini computers, are being produced by a variety of new as well as old established companies. For example, IBM[4] produces a shared-logic[5] mini-

[4]Other manufacturers: Olivetti, Cannon, Compucorp, Macrocomputers, and Randall Data Systems, to name a few.
[5]May go on-line with mainframe computers, thus having the capability of sharing their logic (data banks and programs).

computer word processor that will address, store, prioritize, and distribute documents to any department, individual, or division of a company or to any distribution list recorded in its system. The message can already have been stored in the system's memory or may be newly entered. It can be displayed on a 24-inch CRT screen for a final edit. An IBM displaywriter desk top text-editing machine that uses floppy disk storage media checks the spelling of about 50,000 words via an electronically stored dictionary which it can access.

Xerox, another established office equipment industry, has produced a mini computer that can select, sort, and automatically report data contained in typical office records. Connected to an office communications network called *Ethernet* (Xerox tradename), it links office devices within one location or externally across a city.

With mini computer systems such as these, business departments and government agencies can send and receive electronically processed records, storing them in various classifications for current or future use. This, of course, introduces problems for records management. Automated and electronically processed records management are in their infancy, but it already behooves records managers to become involved.

Another category of small computers that is impacting office work is the microcomputer. Manufacturers of microcomputers include Texas Instruments, Radio Shack, Apple, and Wang, to name a few.

Data Banks

Hundreds of data banks maintain a wide scope of information. Some are privately developed, others commercially. Data banks are large "files" or accumulations of data held *electronically,* usually on magnetic tapes, discs, cylinders and microfilm which can be accessed and processed by computers as needed. A company's accumulation of data about production, inventories, sales, finances, etc. can be referred to as its data bank, or specialized areas of data such as that held by Social Security or Internal Revenue can be called data banks. In general, the term *data bank* is computer terminology for stored ("filed") data that has been accumulated and is ready for use when needed. To be called a data bank, it should be organized and programmed in such a manner that retrieval is efficient. When efficient retrieval is not a characteristic, the so-called data bank is in effect a heterogeneous mixture and competes with the proverbial Fibber Magee's closet or the "miscellaneous" section of a manual file.

A trend in the current development of data banks that are commercially prepared and to which access may be rented is to accumulate data of special interest to individuals in the private sector; for example, sports, news, encyclopedic information, property records, history, legislation, etc. With new technology it will even be possible for individuals to compile and own data banks to be used personally; for example, private collections of music, poems, family mementos, and personal records. It will be possible to access such data bases via personal (portable) terminals, an adjusted television set, or even via a dial telephone. Prepared in England, the following two systems—Viewdata and Prestel—illustrate general use data base "files."

Viewdata

An interaction information system for home or office use, *Viewdata*, developed and regularly updated by the British Post Office, accesses a data base of approximately 200,000 pages of information ranging from airplane time tables, news, and encyclopedia information to advertisements. The system can use 96 different upper/lower case characters, symbols, graphics, and 7 colors.

Prestel

Another BPO service is *Prestel* (tradename) that permits subscribers to access a computer data base using their existing telephones as the instruction carrier medium and a modified television set as the receiver, either at home or at work.

Microfilm Retrieval

Traditionally microfilm has been considered as merely an economical way to store information, thus reducing bulk in active office areas and also providing security for copies of documents; however, with its marriage to computers, new applications have emerged. Easy access to stored information is accomplished through COM and CAR (Computer Assisted Retrieval). (See Figure 14–3.) With this device, five years of bulky computer printouts, when converted to 4 by 6-inch microfiche cards, occupy only a small box that can be kept on a desk; also, several cards can be mailed in an ordinary envelope whereas the original bulky computer printouts would probably need a box. Other forms of microfilm include reels, aperture cards, microjackets[6] and cartridges. (See Chapter 13 on micrographics.)

---

[6]Microthin transparent jackets that serve as a file for individual pieces of small sequences of images inserted into channels of the jacket.

FIGURE 14—3. A microfilm reader/printer. *(Courtesy Bell & Howell)*

An Era of Televised Images

With the capabilities of new technology, information we store *today* may not need to be stored at all. It may be cheaper, for example, to reconstruct a report from basic elements held in electronic memory whenever the information is needed. We need in this respect to adjust our thinking from a world of paper and print to an era of televised images. (See Figure 14–4.) In the new image (or data base) storage technology, if a paper document (hard copy) is thought to be essential (for example, a printout of a schedule of payments) it may be printed on demand. In fact, phototypesetters as well as high speed printers can now interface directly with computer systems and type-editing machines in word processing systems.

Rising paper and office labor costs mean that we can no longer afford the luxury of processing paper-based information and performing office work as we have in the past. The technological developments described above are making it possible to change office paper work procedures quite drastically. Alert records managers must keep up on these new developments, thus helping their companies survive and prosper in the present highly competitive business environment.

As we get rid of paper for storing information and substitute

Figure 14–4. Electronic images become a part of the manager's desk. (*Courtesy Administration Management, July 1969.*)

electronic capabilities that can retrieve images from data banks or from microfilm storage and project them on CRT screens, we expand the power of data bases for both business or government and for private access. The future potential of these technical developments is exciting and is likely to affect not only the office of tomorrow but the personal information storage and retrieval procedures of all of us.

Saving Filing Space

In business micro-retrieval systems combined with word processing devices allow typewritten documents to be filed and indexed automatically on microfilm. In word processing, a microfilmed document can be accessed from its file via a text-editing machine with a typewriter-style keyboard. Systems that use micro or mini computers with access to mainframe computers have further extensive storage capabilities, especially when COM is used. Since filing cabinets take up valuable space, are awkward and time consuming to access, and often accumulate contents without due consideration for their future value,[7] many organizations are converting to mini or micro computers

---

[7]This unfortunately can also be a problem in developing and managing certain types of business data bank files (i.e., financial, inventory, or materials maintenance data).

and microfiche terminals. These conversions involve knowledge about and experience with emerging electronic data and image processing technology. Feasibility studies need to be made in order to convert records management from paper to microfilm or electronic data bases. Principles which will serve as company guidelines for the management of electronic and microfilm data base systems should be developed by records managers. Some questions which might be used in developing these guidelines and which should be asked in the transition from paper to electronic storage are as follows:[8]

1. What is the validity of an electronically retrieved record from an operating and legal point of view?
2. Must there always be a paper or microfilm backup to electronic records?
3. How can physical security be provided for electronic records?
4. How can privacy be provided and assured for electronically stored records?
5. How do we assure record integrity—that the record has not been altered?
6. How do we verify the authenticity of electronically generated records?
7. What equipment or system of access should be used for storing and retrieving the records?
8. What provision will be made for personal data bases, especially among a company's top executives?
9. Who is responsible for managing electronically stored records?
10. Who is responsible for seeing that only essential data is stored; for example, seeing that data banks contain only a minimum of nonessential items or material which can be easily computed from elsewhere?

ELECTRONIC MAIL

Electronic mail (EM) does not have a single meaning. The basis of the concept is stored information, telecommunication media and devices such as dial phone networks, microwave or satellite transmissions, cable TV, a television or radio broadcasting system, or a data communication network. Still somewhat in the early evolutionary stages, it is an application of image transmission technology; the concept is appreciated, but the best way for implementing it is yet to be evolved.

---

[8]Adapted from John J. Connell, "The Records Manager in the Office of the Future," *Information and Records Management*, February, 1980, p. 49.

There are currently four types of EM installations: (1) facsimile transmission, (2) TWX and Telex, (3) communicating word processors, and (4) computer-based message systems.

Facsimile Transmission

Facsimile transmission is hard copy communication by phone; that is, it requires two facsimile machines—a sender and a receiver—connected by phone. The sending unit electronically scans typed, handwritten, printed, or graphic copy and converts it to electronic signals that are transmitted to the receiving unit over telephone lines by a procedure that is similar to the dial-tone concept. Virtually anything on paper can be transmitted by facsimile equipment.

First introduced in 1842, facsimile did not have a real impact until computers and telecommunication networks were developed. Today desk top scanners hooked to computers can feed facsimile input to central units and the "data" may be accumulated and stored for as long as the originator desires. Users can send to this central data bank whatever information they wish, retrieving it when needed, and further transmitting copies to designated facsimile terminals upon request.

Facsimile equipment can operate unattended at night, thus reducing costs because it operates at low phone-line rates during that time. If instructed, it can also produce a self-monitoring report of what it sent, to where, and when, which can be checked the next morning.

Equipment of this type can be cost-justified on its own unique capabilities. For example, facsimile transmission can eliminate postage costs and delivery delays. The cost for one minute of cross-country transmission has been estimated at about 75 cents a page. Other benefits are quick and certain delivery because delivery is accomplished in minutes instead of days as with postal services. Facsimile transmission of correspondence and other routine business communications saves labor as well as processing and distribution time. Nor is there the risk one sometimes has with postal services of losing valuable original documents. An electronic mail log automatically keeps track of mail sent and of information (files) pertinent to it.

Facsimile mail transmission is one new concept that takes electronic technology right to the office worker's desk. Because of it, one can really see the beginning of structural changes among jobs of office knowledge workers: secretaries, accountants, managers, statisticians; also, teachers and librarians. It is anticipated that about 70 percent of the American work force will be affected by electronic mail and related technology as it develops. EM eliminates much paper shuffling and manual clerical tasks and provides think-time, thus giving office employees more time to use decision-making skills and to develop personal abilities and identification, increase problem-solving techniques and improve communication.

TWX and Telex are often referred to as teletypewriters. They can send or receive messages (mail) to compatible equipment via telephone lines at up to one hundred words a minute.

A *communicating word processor* can send final copy as it appears on a CRT screen to any other similarly equipped word processor or to a computer terminal for printout. Hence, it too can be used for transmitting electronic mail. A system known as electronic document distribution (EDD) is linked with text editing and data processing.

A *computer-based system* displays messages on CRT screens and can route instant copies to addressees listed in the system or print them out at computer speeds for postal mailing to those outside the system. It is estimated that 70 to 75 percent of all company correspondence is internal.

Electronic Message Centers

It is a natural step forward from computer mail to electronically maintained appointment calendars, message, and tickler services. When managers keep appointment calendars and tickler files on a computer, they can view the material at any time on a CRT screen, correct and update items on sight, and file or retrieve them instantly. (See Figure 14–5.) When an executive tells his personal desk computer that he wants to see a schedule of the day's appointments, a printout is not necessary because the list can be retained on the CRT screen or recalled whenever necessary. The list prepared by the computer may be used during the day and destroyed later, because the same information is available from the computer any time it is needed until it is deleted or erased from electronic memory.

AUTOMATION AND ELECTRONICS

As we learn from the contents of this chapter, many "filing" changes are resulting from advances in electronics. Some records are no longer maintained in anything but magnetic form. They are received, used, stored, and retained all in machine readable form. A large computer system can handle hundreds of users, each with a personal terminal. Each user can, from the personal terminal, create, change, or electronically eliminate stored data "files." Yet, how is it that most computer systems are still backed with some paperwork?

FIGURE 14–5. A personal desk terminal.

Some manual or semiautomatic, machine-assisted office activities will no doubt continue to be needed for a long time as a backup or for get-ready and put-away work in spite of the rapid development of electronic image retention and transmission. For each element of computer processing, there remain at least two distinct elements of manual work—the *before* processing or make-ready activities and the put-away activities *after* processing.[9] No matter how automatic and sophisticated a program is, there is the need for human intervention and related manual activities. Manual workflow activities will be merged, of course, as much as possible with the new technology. That is, the best of old methods will surely be combined with the new as human beings learn more and more about interfacing with the machines and technology which have been, after all, created to serve them. Some examples of interfacings between manual (human) and semiautomatic or electronic methods are described below.

---

[9]Basically *all* work, whether manual or electronic, is made up of three phases: (1) get ready, (2) *do,* and (3) put away. For example, when a student is about to study there are the "get ready" activities of finding the assignment, paper, pen, a place to sit, etc. The *do* activities involve actually preparing the assignment. "Put away" activities include returning paper, pen, books, and finished assignments to their proper locations, pushing the chair up to the desk, and perhaps even turning off the light. In modern technology, *get ready* activities could include requisitioning tapes and programs from storage. *Put away* activities could include notes for program changes or tape updates and memos or phone calls about *do* activities.

Automated Indexing

As documents are transferred, updated, cross-referenced and retrieved, manual indexing is cumbersome, especially as the volume grows. An automated indexing system makes it easier to inventory, classify, and control them and such an index can be created either by an in-house computer programmer or a consultant. When ready, the system can handle routines for generating notices about records that are due for destruction, tally the number of referrals made to stored records during a given time, maintain an inventory of storage boxes, thus helping determine when and where additional space is available, and facilitate cross referencing in many ways.

File Management

To assist in the control and orderly storage of centralized files, computer lists can be electronically generated for each department, division, or branch office, automatically preparing lists of file folders which are to be discarded directly from on-site file cabinets, those which are to be prepared for storage, and those now in storage which are scheduled for destruction. Such lists would be very time-consuming to prepare manually and would be prone to human error, but when computerized, are quite accurate and are available in minutes. Accurate and easily available computerized indexes of this type facilitate file management throughout a company.

Bar Code Index

Another automated procedure that saves much manual work is the bar code index. For example, in large business organizations or government agencies, OUT files can be traced through electronic identification by using a bar code of a series of light and bold lines printed on the outside cover of a folder (similar to the bar codes used on groceries and merchandise in your local shopping center) (See Figure 14–6.) and can be read automatically by a computer. Or, the departmental identification can be printed on the folder in a typeface that can be read by OCR equipment. The marriage of automatically read file identification data with computer processing has many potential applications for indexing, tracing, and managing files.

Labels

Labels for recurring files, especially where the periodic transfer method is used, can be printed from computerized lists for each department, branch, or division. This saves manual typing time.

FIGURE 14—6. Bar code.

Unit Records

Automated files that include movable aisles save time and space and are easy to operate because they are motorized and move electrically. Although not yet interfaced with electronic equipment, the automated files concept is widely used with open shelf files. (See Chapter 9.)

INFORMATION RESOURCE MANAGEMENT

Records managers should make a strong effort to adapt the new technology throughout their companies, thus reducing paper flow, paper shuffling, and paper stacking and hoarding. Information is a key resource in business, government, and industry; paper is the vehicle generally used for storing, moving, and retrieving it. As handled in the majority of offices, "paper" processing is cumbersome and costly. In the face of constantly increasing paperwork and rising labor and other costs, we must turn to technology to improve office efficiency and bring costs under better control. Records managers should reevaluate the way they conduct operations, take advantage of the new technology, and look for improvements in basic procedures, even though they run into situations where supervisors and managers are reluctant to adopt new concepts. It is better to move ahead slowly than not at all.

As we move from paper to nonpaper records, records managers should take advantage of the opportunity to become *change agents* in developing methods and procedures for the office of tomorrow. Cumbersome past practices survive only when no one steps forward to bridge the gap between the past and the present. There is a large gulf to span between the old, habitual thinking and established work routines of yesterday, and the new emerging ones of tomorrow's electronic age. To bridge the gap, new concepts, feasibility studies, long-range planning, and a constant input of information about new procedures are essential. It is not just enough to be up-to-date; it is better in a situation of this type to be ahead of the times as much as possible, because the new technology is impacting office procedures quite fast.

Looking Ahead with Records Managers

As previously stated with the new records processing technology, information on one machine can be available to others interconnected into the same telecommunication network. Information keyed into one machine can be *moved* electronically to a variety of office machine "satellites"; high-speed printers, text-editors, microfilm terminals, electronic message centers, or electronic mail. (See Figure 14–7.) All information, whether contextual, quantitative data, graphic, or voice can be moved, processed, stored, or retrieved in electronic form. In this new framework, information processors, office employees and executives can use a personal electronic memory CRT screen instead of working with files of papers. For example, in this new environment, a central data bank can file correspondence automatically, address lists, retrieve data (including graphs), and destroy (automatically erase) unwanted items.

Today people still feel comfortable with paper records, but experience shows that those who try the new devices for even a few months and get over initial uneasiness with them are reluctant to go back to the old. The nervousness felt when confronting a new experience of this type can be overcome by active participation and first-hand exposure.

The Records Management Challenge

Automation of records has a leading priority with those concerned with information processing and related office procedures. The person finally responsible for automating and integrating an organization's records management with the electronic age will be either the data processing, word processing, administrative services, or records manager. Which one it will be depends largely on how much initiative records managers take and how forceful they become in the transition. The greater the exposure of today's records managers to all aspects of the new technology, the more chance they have to survive and to have a significant part in the transition; to have a place on the company's mainframe information resources management team. To enter the new electronic age as a member of this important team, a records manager must take the initiative, move energetically, and without delay.

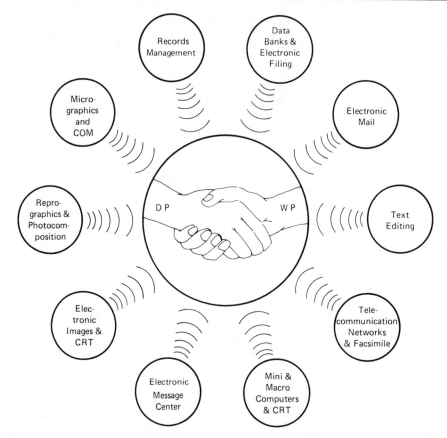

FIGURE 14–7. Office automation satellites.

The modern age has a false sense of superiority because of the great mass of data at its disposal. But the valid criterion of distinction is rather the extent to which man knows how to form and master the material at his command. (Goethe, 1810)

REVIEW QUESTIONS

1. What electronic devices promise revolutionary changes for records management?

2. What are some problems records managers face in converting to electronic information processing systems?

3. What can electronic word and data processing devices do that cannot be done manually?

4. What are some unique capabilities of electronic information processing devices?

5. Describe four types of word processing installations.

6. What does a text-editing machine do?

7. What are the component parts of a word processing configuration?

8. How can a word processing installation become part of a mainline computer system? What are the advantages of this?

9. How do the following affect records management?

a. word processing	h. data banks
b. COM	i. electronic mail
c. EM	j. electronic message centers
d. computer data bases	k. facsimile transmission
e. mini computers	l. electronic appointment calendars
f. CRT	m. bar-code indexes
g. microfilm	

10. How are telecommunication networks affected by

a. glass fiber optics	c. data banks
b. satellites	d. data transmission

11. What is the function of a mini computer?

12. How are business data banks prepared?

13. What is the function of a CRT?

14. What questions should a records manager ask in making the transition from manual filing systems to electronic devices?

15. Describe four types of EM installations.

16. What is an automated index and how is one used?

17. What is a bar code index and how does it work?

18. What is the modern records manager's role in electronic information resource management?

19. What qualifications does the future records manager need?

20. What is records management's main challenge in this era of office technology evolution?

Campaign Headquarter Records

1. You are state office/records/personnel manager for the campaign headquarters of a major political party. The office is preparing for a presidential election and at this time there are plenty of funds available. You have a permanent staff of six full-time paid employees, two part-time, and a large group of volunteers who are in and out of the office, especially as the campaign progresses. Phones ring constantly. At this time, you have the following records:

   1. Biographical material to be used in press and television releases.
   2. Campaign promotion materials: leaflets, buttons, banners, etc.
   3. Financial records including pledges, contribution records, expenses, and contribution goals.
   4. List of names, addresses, and phone numbers of important campaign supporters.
   5. List of volunteer workers:
      a. political science majors
      b. office helpers
      c. rally helpers
      d. people who will hold coffee-hour meetings in their homes
      e. people willing to work at the polls
      f. people willing to transport voters to and from the polls
      g. potential speakers
   6. Speaking schedules and personnel
   7. Personnel records: job descriptions, salary schedules
   8. Voting registers by precincts

   Write a recommendation to the party regional director covering the following items:

   1. What systems you plan to develop for the records and materials in the headquarter office and the supplies and equipment you will need. The records are currently in poor shape, mostly in boxes.
   2. A description of electronic devices you recommend for the headquarter office to tie in with other state and the national headquarter office.

2. Prepare a reference file about electronic office equipment by consulting the phone directory or newspaper for names of electronic equipment manufacturers and writing their marketing departments for brochures or other explanatory material about their latest office electronic devices.

   When the materials arrive, organize them for future use. Enrich the materials received by mail with summaries of articles from office magazines such as *Data Processing Digest for Office Automation*.

Appendix A

The Certified Records Managers Program

Robert L. Bailey

INTRODUCTION

The information and technology explosion of the past two decades has created a significant challenge for all sectors of our society. Rapidly multiplying records coupled with steadily increasing costs of personnel, equipment and supplies have placed a tremendous strain on administrative operations, demanding that records be handled more efficiently, economically, and ethically.

The Institute of Certified Records Managers (ICRM) was created in 1975 in recognition of the need for dynamic leadership in the field of records management. Sponsored by the Association of Records Managers and Administrators (ARMA), the Society of American Archivists, and the National Association of State Archivists and Record Administrators, ICRM is an independent, non-profit educational institution administered by a ten to fifteen member Board of Regents who represent private industry, federal, state and city government, and the academic community. The *Constitution and By-Laws,* Article II (January 7, 1975; October 7, 1978), states ICRM's objectives:

1. To define, promote and advance the concept of records management and related fields and to support the professional recognition of records managers.

2. To work with educational institutions in developing and improving records management curricula and courses of study.

3. To promote the value of certification of records managers to the various national, state and local governments and the private sector.

4. To develop and administer a program for the professional certification of records managers, including the granting of appropriate recognition.

5. To develop and administer certification examinations in records management with complete responsibility for the scope, complexity, and integrity of such examinations.

ICRM membership is open to those individuals who are designated Certified Records Managers (CRM). According to David Stevens, ICRM Headquarters, representation through the spring of 1981 includes 265 Certified Records Managers in the states and the District of Columbia, Australia, Europe, Israel and the Republic of South Africa. Membership growth since 1975 not only reflects professional status through certification with its implications for career advancement but underscores the vital role of records managers in the evaluation of current office needs while preparing for the office of tomorrow. Records managers, educated and certified in available technologies and organizational strategies, are best suited to coordinate the activities of those groups responsible for planning and monitoring the future flow of information.

BECOMING A CRM

To become a Certified Records Manager you need *not* be a member of one of the sponsoring ICRM organizations but must satisfy certain education/experience and examination requirements:

A. You must hold a baccalaureate degree from an accredited four-year college or university with at least three years of full time or equivalent professional experience in records management prior to certification. Professional experience involves conducting studies and surveys, or developing, designing and complementing records systems in two or more of the following categories:

I. Records management principles and program organization;

II. Records generation and control;

III. Active records retrieval, systems and equipment;

IV. Records retention, scheduling, protection, and records centers;

V. Technology of records management.

Professional experience may also be defined as having direct management or operational responsibility in two or more of the above categories or as serving as an accredited college/university instructor with responsibility for teaching records management in two or more of the above fields on a full time basis. At the discretion of the ICRM Board of Regents, experience may be substituted for education according to the following table of equivalents:

Educational Requirement	Work Experience
Four years (B.A./B.S. Degree)	Three years
Three years	Five years
Two years	Seven years
One year	Nine years
-0- (secondary school graduate)	Eleven years

B. You must pass, within five years of application, the Certified Records Management examination, which is designed to test (1) knowledge of subject matter, (2) the ability to apply that knowledge to different situations and to organize data, and (3) communication skills.

APPLICATION PROCEDURES

If you are interested in becoming a candidate for Certification by Examination, request applications from ICRM Headquarters, P.O. Box 89, Washington, D.C. 20044. Since the examinations are offered only twice a year and require very careful advance planning, the application forms must be returned no later than 60 days prior to the selected examination dates.

1981–82 Example Dates and Deadlines

	1981		1982
Test Date	Application Deadline	Test Date	Application Deadline
May 7–8	March 6, 1981	May 20–21	March 19, 1982
November 18–19	September 18, 1981	November 18–19	September 17, 1982

The application form for the CRM is composed of the following sections:

Part I—Personal Data
Part II—Records Management Experience

Part   III—Education
Part   IV—Honors
Part   V—Publications
Part   VI—References
Part   VII—Examination Sections and Dates Requested

You must certify that you have reviewed the *ICRM Constitution and By-Laws* and understand that good character and sound business ethics are a part of earning the CRM designation. Send a current job description with your application, particularly if you want to substitute experience for education.

When ICRM Headquarters receives your completed application, the $10.00 registration fee and the $15.00 fee for each part of the examination you plan to take, they will send you examination instructions and the name and address of the proctor. It is your responsibility to telephone the proctor for the address of the examination site located as close as possible to you. The examination instructions include the time schedule for the CRM exam as well as the number of multiple choice questions included in Parts I–V, exam conditions and the appropriate format for answering all questions. You must use number 2 pencils for the multiple choice questions and use ink or ball point pen to answer essays.

You will be notified by mail of your "Pass" or "Fail" status within 60–90 days. If you fail to pass any portion of the examination you may reapply for a second test on the specific section, paying only the $15.00 fee.

PREPARATION FOR THE CRM EXAMINATION

The designation "CRM" is to records management what "CPA" is to accounting. Fulfilling the qualifications to become a CRM require application and considerable preparation. In her excellent article, "Strategies for Passing the CRM Examination," in the *ARMA Records Management Quarterly,* Dr. Mary I. Robek, President of ICRM, states that general intelligence, knowledge provided by experience in records management and by intensive review over a period of time are three necessary conditions for success in completing the examination. Candidates should make note of Dr. Robek's strategies which actually apply to any formula for success:

1. ***Goals.*** Are you taking the CRM examination for personal recognition as a professional, satisfaction in having been certified as knowledgeable in records management, or with expectations of monetary gain as a result of certification?
2. ***Personal assessment.*** The honest review of character traits, per-

sonality and motivation helps you to persist in the preparation to become a CRM. Reviewing the Study Guide should certainly prove invaluable to the objective analysis of strengths and limitations.

3. **Attitude.** Professionalism includes striving for excellence. Approach the examination with confidence because the assessment means that you are ready to demonstrate knowledge and growth in records management.

4. **Realistic expectations.** By reviewing the Study Guide, books, journals and other materials, and participating in different types of study programs you will acquire further understanding of the types of issues on which you may be questioned.

Preparing for the CRM examination through extensive review depends on your circumstances. You may live near an accredited college or university that offers records management courses. ARMA and ICRM recently sponsored a joint study of institutions that provide either a complete program or isolated courses in records management. Initially published in the January 1981 *Records Management Quarterly,* the "Directory of Collegiate Schools Teaching Records Management" is reproduced in Appendix B. Additions to the Directory appear in the April 1981 *Records Management Quarterly.* You may obtain additional copies of the material by writing to the *Records Management Quarterly,* Association of Records Managers and Administrators, Inc., 4200 Somerset Drive, Suite 215, Prairie Village, Kansas, 66208. Single copies of the *Quarterly* are available.

If college-level coursework is inappropriate or simply impossible for you, consider attending the study groups which are organized by Certified Records Managers or by regional ARMA chapters. The San Francisco Golden Gate Chapter, for example, circulates a questionnaire asking candidates for preference in study topics and location and frequency of meetings. In addition to working with certified managers, candidates may invite special speakers to group meetings. A roster of potential speakers, all of whom have extensive training in records management, is provided in the ARMA Manual *Organization Concepts to Information Management Programs.* Speakers are classified alphabetically by location and by subject. It is also possible, of course, to design your own study plan by securing descriptive material from ICRM Headquarters, reviewing texts recommended in the sample bibliographies (Appendix B), or by following the ARMA *Records Management Correspondence Course* guide available from ARMA, P. O. Box 281, Bradford, Rhode Island, 02808.

Preparation for the CRM examination will be incomplete if you do not consider the elements of test taking itself. A few tips are certainly in order! You should know in advance that the multiple choice questions require selecting the *one best* answer. Read each question carefully, paying particular attention to such cue words as "always," "never," or "totally." Use intelligent guessing. Record your answers within the space provided on the optical scanning sheet with a heavy, dark pencil mark. Don't change your answer unless you are sure that it was wrong in the first place. The essays, worth varying numbers of points, are essentially short answer questions. Answer each question as clearly, fully and concisely as possible in the time allotted. Although essay questions are graded primarily on content, organization, clarity, spelling, mechanics and literary style are also taken into account. Edit, check and proofread your work! Do the same with the case studies. As indicated in the examination outline, case studies may be comprehensive in scope or may address a specific aspect of records management. You are given a choice of case studies to analyze. Choose the one for which good solutions come to mind immediately and for which you can demonstrate some special expertise. Read the cases critically focusing on gathering all the data, organizing and interpreting the material, considering all solutions, selecting the best, and determining the appropriate action for putting the solution into effect.

Although potential questions are submitted prior to the exam to the ICRM Examination Committee for review, standardization and possible use, candidates are encouraged to provide feedback on their test taking experience. Constructive criticism regarding the consistency of wording and terminology, noting questions that may appear unfair because of use of an unknown brand name or commenting on those multiple choice items for which there may actually have been more than one correct answer assures fairness and ongoing quality in CRM exam design.

In addition to satisfactorily completing the examination, you must subscribe to the Code of Ethics which is an ongoing requirement to maintain CRM status.

THE CERTIFIED RECORDS MANAGEMENT EXAMINATION— STUDY GUIDE

The CRM examination, administered by ICRM in May and November, consists of six parts—five of which correspond to the desired categories of professional experience. The sixth part focuses on case study problems that interrelate all elements of the first five parts. Two full days are required to conduct the series. You may sit for selected portions or may complete Parts I–V during the two-day period. You may not take Part VI until you have passed Parts I through V. The examinations combine multiple choice and essay questions with two hours allotted for I, II, III, IV, and V and four hours for the essay discussion in Part VI.

The following outline contains material that you may find on an ICRM exam. Since test content changes with each administration, not all subjects or topics may appear on future exams; moreover, some information not listed yet germane to sound records management could be covered. Also, ICRM publishes and updates frequently the study guide, so be sure you obtain the latest copy.

OUTLINE FOR CERTIFIED RECORDS MANAGEMENT EXAMINATION[1]

Part I—Management Principles and Program Organization

You should be knowledgeable about generally accepted theories of management and organization, taught in most introductory business management courses. Topics include:

A. Management Principles and Techniques
   1. Planning
      a. Program scope
      b. Policy and authority guidelines
      c. Office/space planning
      d. System planning and techniques such as:
         1. Record surveys
         2. System analysis
      e. Program justification
         1. Techniques of selling management
   2. Organization
      a. Types of business organization
      b. Organization concepts such as:
         1. Centralization vs. decentralization
         2. Lines of authority and communication
         3. Span of control
      c. Records management function
         1. Alternatives for organizational placement
         2. Internal organizational structure
   3. Staffing
      a. Job descriptions
      b. Personnel selection

[1]© 1980 Institute of Certified Records Managers. Reprinted by permission.

       c. Staff sources

       d. Personnel appraisals

       e. Salary administration

       f. Training

    4. Directing

       a. Leadership

       b. Delegation

       c. Coordination

       d. Goal setting

       e. Work scheduling

       f. Resource utilization

       g. Specific techniques or theories such as:

          1. Management by exception

          2. Management by objective

          3. X–Y theory

       h. Directives

    5. Control techniques including:

       a. Budgeting

       b. Status reports

       c. Audits

       d. Standards

       e. Procedure manuals

B. History and Philosophy of Records Management

    1. Early origins

    2. Development of modern profession

    3. Current issues and legislation

    4. Necessity for records management

    5. Definitions of concepts and terminology such as:

       a. Records

       b. Records management

       c. Life cycle of records

       d. Information management

ICRM Sample Review Questions[2]

MULTIPLE CHOICE

Choose the alternative that best completes the following:
The person in charge of the records management training function
should

---

[2]The sample review questions after each part of the outline are from the ICRM handout,
"CRM Examination Sample Questions."

a. know enough about human behavioral patterns to realize that trainee's response is enhanced by accepting things as they are
b. not attempt to completely remold the new employee's personality
c. not strive to significantly alter the new employee's behavioral patterns
d. all of these
e. none of these

Answer: d

ESSAY QUESTION (10 MINUTES)

1. Compare each of the following requisites of good records management, depending upon whether an active or an inactive storage area is involved.
   a. equipment
   b. the storage location
   c. filing procedures utilized

ESSAY QUESTION—SAMPLE ANSWER

In both active and inactive storage areas, appropriate equipment, an adequate and accessible storage location, and efficient filing procedures are essential. Features of an active file area include:

a. Sufficient aisle space for banks of drawers, or lateral files
b. Systematic coding, indexing, cross referencing, and checkout procedures.
c. The handling of all records as specified by the records manual
d. Adequate equipment which will not injure employees, i.e., files that tip, shelves that wobble, stools that slip
e. Adequate controls (checkout), indexes, fire protection
f. Well-trained personnel

Features of the inactive storage center include:

a. Clean, dry, low cost storage
b. Systematic procedures for transfer-in and transfer-out of storage
c. The handling of all records disposal procedures as specified by the retention schedule
d. Low cost file carton or similar containers as well as other low cost storage supplies
e. Adequate controls (e.g., control cards and an adequate labeling system, for ready retrieval of records, good fire protection, adequate shelving units, well-trained personnel)

Part II—Records Generation and Control

(Note: Word Processing is included in Part V.)

The second part of the CRM examination may contain questions pertaining to system control and expenditure and to the creation of documents that become records.

  A. Correspondence Management
   1. Definition
   2. Objectives
   3. Standards, studies and systems control including:
       a. Form letters and guide letters or paragraphs
       b. Plain letter writing, 4-S writing program and training plans
       c. Signature authority, reviews and copy reduction
       d. Stationery, format standards and correspondence manuals
       e. Correspondence procedures to improve quality and reduce costs
   4. Equipment evaluation and controls
  B. Directives Management
   1. Definition
   2. Objectives
   3. Standards, studies and systems control including:
       a. Approval authority and coordination process
       b. Formats, revision and field tests
       c. Historical or record set and issuance case files
       d. Loose-leaf filing and updatable systems
       e. Distribution codes and controls
  C. Forms Management
   1. Definition
   2. Objectives
   3. Principles and practices of forms improvement including:
       a. Approval authority and cost justification
       b. Forms and procedures analysis and design
       c. Standards for format, production and materials
       d. Printing specifications, controls and review
       e. Forms case files and functional files
  D. Mail Management
   1. Definition
   2. Objectives
   3. System standards, studies, policies and procedures including:
       a. Mail management versus mail operations
       b. Mail receipt, sorting, controlling and redistribution

        c. Post office liaison, schedules, rates, weights and fee considerations

        d. Mail routing guides, office codes and special equipment

        e. Special messengers, classified materials and registered mail

  E. Reports Management

    1. Definition

    2. Objectives

    3. Program standards, studies and controls including:

        a. Reports inventories

        b. Information requirements

        c. Approval authority

        d. Reports control symbols

        e. Format, systems and distribution controls

  F. Reproduction Management

    1. Definition

    2. Objectives

    3. Operational and systems management including:

        a. Printing plant versus self-service quick copy installations

        b. In-house vs. off-site facilities

        c. Systems analysis, cost justification, and lease vs. purchase

        d. Copying and printing requirements vs. equipment and service options

        e. Jurisdictions, regulations, guidelines, and training

  G. Records Creation Control Programs

    1. General concepts

    2. Systems improvements vs. equipment and manpower expenditures

Review questions provided by ICRM, which again include both multiple choice and essay responses in a two hour time frame, are:

MULTIPLE CHOICE

Form paragraphs and letters should be developed by:

  a. the records manager

  b. the head of the Word Processing Center

  c. designated correspondence employees

  d. department managers

  e. the mail room supervisor

Answer: c

ESSAY QUESTION (10 MINUTES)

1. List 7 benefits of a forms control program.
   a. eliminate unneeded forms
   b. produce efficient forms (eliminate unneeded items)
   c. reduce inventory of forms
   d. eliminate duplication of effort
   e. streamline requisition and ordering procedures
   f. reduce the cost of purchasing forms
   g. reduce the cost of processing paperwork within and between departments
   h. improve the quality of forms
   i. evaluate forms according to their need and value
   j. reduce processing time
   k. combine similar forms
   l. reduce the tendency towards errors on forms

You may encounter other such essay questions as:

1. State five reasons for using a forms analyst (10 points)
2. When installing a quick copy service as a segment of a records management program, state five things to be considered prior to implementation (10 points)
3. Name at least three rationale for housing directives in a three-ring-binder (6 points)

Part III—Active Records Retrieval Systems and Equipment

Each candidate for CRM certification should be aware of the generally accepted rules governing storage and retrieval of information as well as of the desirability of centralized, decentralized and uniform filing systems. Don't be too surprised to find some overlap with other sections when completing questions related to the following areas:

A. Filing Systems
   1. Identification of record series
      a. Records surveys and inventories
      b. System analysis
   2. System selection/design including:
      a. Alphabetic systems
      b. Numeric systems
      c. Color systems
      d. Combination systems
      e. Index, cross-reference and charge-out systems

   3. System implementation, operating techniques and procedures
      a. Records acquisition
      b. Indexing, classification, cross-referencing and coding
      c. Sorting
      d. Filing methods
      e. Reference service and research
      f. Folder and label preparation
   4. System maintenance and control including:
      a. Centralization vs. decentralization
      b. Charge-out and follow-up procedures
      c. Status/activity reports
      d. Procedure manuals
B. Equipment Evaluation, Selection and Use
   1. Equipment
      a. Drawer files
      b. Open shelves
      c. Power and movable units
      d. Safes/security files
      e. Stools and ladders
      f. Visible card files
      g. Other
   2. Standardization
   3. Safeguard for confidentiality and privacy
   4. Reviewing equipment requests
      a. Costs comparison and economic studies
      b. Space and load considerations
C. Evaluation and Control of Supplies
   1. Filing supplies
      a. Folders
      b. Guides
      c. Forms
      d. Other supplies
   2. Standardization
   3. Evaluation and control

ICRM Sample Review Questions

MULTIPLE CHOICE

A filing system that has been devised to permit accounts to be kept
in alphabetic sequence and still be filed by number is called:

    a. alpha-numeric filing
    b. duplex-numeric filing
    c. numeric-name filing
    d. triple-check automatic filing
    e. none of these

Answer: a

ESSAY QUESTION (10 Minutes)

1. What is meant by the terms "color accent" and "color code" when used to designate phases of color usage in filing systems? What is the purpose of each technique?

A. Color Accent
   1. Gives additional identity to a particular section or segment of a filing system to make it easier to locate that segment or section.
   2. Assists in filing and finding by such means as showing contrasting colors on various types of folder and guide tabs.
B. Color Coding
   1. Each of a series of colors is identified with a particular alphabetic section in the system thereby giving it a positive color code by which identification of a given alphabetic section can be made easier.
   2. Uses color on guides and folders according to a scheme in which a color is always associated with the same alphabetic designation within a system—thus a code (a systematized pattern of identification).

Part IV—Records Protection and Disposition

A. Records Inventory
   1. Pre-planning
      a. Scope
      b. Forms selection/design
      c. Code development
      d. Facility layouts
      e. Authorization clearance
   2. Methods
   3. Consolidation
      a. Categorizing
      b. Standardizing terminology
      c. Summarizing
B. Inventory Analysis
   1. Organization of data

    2. Records appraisal
       a. Organizational requirements
       b. Governmental requirements
    3. Authority approval
 C. Scheduling
    1. Type of schedules
    2. Formats
    3. Procedures
    4. Maintenance
    5. Disposition
 D. Vital Records Systems
    1. Definition
    2. Scope
    3. Objectives
    4. Identification procedure
       a. Selection
       b. Justification
    5. Methods of protection and preservation
 E. Record Centers
    1. Definition
    2. Objectives
    3. Physical characteristics
    4. Equipment
    5. Layout
       a. Space conservation
       b. Accessibility
       c. Lighting
       d. Load considerations
    6. Procedures
       a. Acquisition
       b. Indexing
       c. Operations
       d. Control
    7. Economics including:
       a. In-house vs. commercial facilities
       b. Site selection
       c. Justification
 F. Archival Management
    1. Definition
    2. Objectives
    3. Criteria for selection of records

> 4. Storage requirements and methods of preservation
> 5. Control
> G. Security
> > 1. Types
> > 2. Security classification of records
> > 3. Methods of protection
> > 4. Control procedures

ICRM Sample Review Question

MULTIPLE CHOICE

The records manager differs from an archivist in that the archivist's primary concern is:

a. nonrecurrent records

b. interpretation of records

c. current records

d. exhibiting material effectively

e. all of the above

Answer: b

ESSAY QUESTION (4 MINUTES)

1. Should an archivist preserve the original order in which records are accessioned? Discuss briefly. (4 points allotted)

Yes, the archivist should preserve the original order in which records are accessioned.

Discussion:

All records are assigned to record groups. These groups are numbered in the order in which the first transfer of each record group was received. Accession of archival material is arranged first according to department of transfer and thereunder by accession number except when the accessions have been combined. After each entry is entered, the number of the record group to which the records belong is listed.

Part V—Technology of Records Management

Virtually every office in the public and private sector today directly or indirectly uses micrographics and the computer. Knowledge of available technologies including data communication systems, word processors, and the minicomputer, for example, is vital to one's success in records management. You should therefore be prepared for questions on any of the following topics:

A. Micrographics
  1. Microforms
     a. Film sizes
     b. Film material
     c. Film polarity
     d. Reduction and magnification ratios
     e. Quality control
     f. Storage considerations
  2. Equipment
     a. Camera types
     b. Film processors
     c. Reading and reproduction devices
     d. COM devices
     e. Other
  3. Applications
     a. Cost studies and economics
     b. Specifications and procedures
     c. Legality
  4. Retrieval
     a. Indexing
     b. Commercial systems
B. Data Processing
  1. Basic definitions such as:
     a. Automated data processing
     b. Electronic data processing
     c. Information
     d. Data
     e. Data collection/data entry concepts
     f. Hardware
     g. Software and programming
     h. System
  2. System analysis
     a. Problem solving
     b. New system development
  3. Data processing methods/criteria for selection
     a. Manual
     b. Electromechanical
     c. Electronic computers
  4. Hardware-functions and capabilities

      a. Central processing unit
      b. Input/output devices
      c. Other peripheral hardware
      d. Hardware evaluation
      e. In-house vs. off-site facilities

   5. Software
      a. System software
      b. User programs
         1. Specifications
         2. Design
         3. Coding
         4. Testing
         5. Documentation
         6. Procedures

C. Word Processing
   1. Definition
   2. Objectives
   3. Justification
      a. Office evaluation
      b. Economic/cost studies
   4. Equipment
      a. Dictation
      b. Electronic typewriters/storage devices
      c. Computer
      d. Text editing
      e. Other
   5. Software requirements
   6. Application Procedures
   7. Control

You may be asked to define a planetary camera, and to indicate the size film required and for what type of documents it is used, to define "information vs. data" and show their relationship to each other, or to name five types of microforms, stating their characteristics and appropriate use.

ICRM Sample Review Question

MULTIPLE CHOICE

A Management Information System (MIS)

   a. may be operated either manually or through mechanical or electronic means

  b. encompasses all the communications within and external to an organization by which data are recorded and processed for operational purposes

  c. processes data obtained by telephone, by contact with other people, by studying an operation, and from data processing units

  d. exists to provide information that supports top managers in directing the total enterprise in the accomplishment of its objectives

  e. all of these

Answer: e

ESSAY QUESTION (10 MINUTES)

  1. How do you account for the increased use of data communication systems in modern office procedures?

Essay Question—Sample Answer

Factors accounting for the increased use of data communications systems include:

  a. Increased size of business organizations covering a wide geographic area

  b. The centralization of management and therefore of the business information

  c. The improvements of electrical and mechanical equipment

  d. The increased cost of wages, which makes it possible to substitute higher priced equipment

Part VI—Case Studies

The case studies represent the application portion of the CRM examination. As such, they presume that you have acquired the competencies measured in all preceding parts. The case studies are fictitious "real life" problems that a records manager or a consultant specializing in records management or micrographics would be likely to encounter in the course of his or her work. You must read the problems posed in the case studies carefully, and develop a written answer based on the action instructions provided in each case. It is important that you understand that some case problems in Part VI may be comprehensive in scope, and thus the solution may draw from several areas of records management. Thus, your response must be based on your comprehension of the several aspects of the records management problems involved. Other cases may describe problems involving only one element of records management.

Examination—Part VI

CASE STUDIES

Read the following instructions carefully

1. In these case studies you are an analyst or consultant dealing with top management on a stated problem. Your response is to be in that vein.

2. Read the case "problem" and required "action" of the attached four cases. Complete three out of four to fulfill the requirements of this part of the examination.

3. Prepare your answers to include an explanation of how and why your response can solve the problem and fulfill the action requirements. Answers should be complete and concise. Complete sentences are preferred to outline replies. Use of phrases like "creation control" are meaningless without elaboration. Illegible writing and lack of clear expression will adversely influence the evaluation of the examiners. Statements such as "establish a V.R. Program" are unacceptable without some explanation as to what a V.R. Program is or how it operates and how it will help in this case.

4. For this portion of the examination, ball point or ink is preferable to pencil and use of pencil will adversely influence evaluation. (Pen and ink reports to top management are standard when typewritten reports are not possible. Pencil reflects poorly on the analyst and frequently eliminates his recommendations from management consideration.)

5. Place your candidate number (not your name) at the top right corner of each answer sheet you submit. Begin each new case on a new sheet and identify it by its company name and case study number. When finished, arrange your answer sheets in case number order and number all of your answer pages in one sequential order, in the lower right corner in a circle (X).

6. Since a total of four hours is allotted to this portion of the examination you may wish to spend the first half hour reading your five cases, and allot the remaining time proportionately for your answering.

Failure to follow these instructions may adversely affect the grading of your answers.

REVIEW CASE STUDY—JANOBEK JEWELERS, INC.

Problem

Janobek Jewelers, Inc. has maintained a File Department for centralized filing of active material since 1950. However, prior to 1970 few departments took advantage of the facilities and service offered.

As for active records, the departments originating them had complete control, making arrangements individually for space in vacant areas of company-owned buildings in which to store them when they were no longer needed in the offices. To rid offices and/or storage areas of obsolete material, most departments depended on sporadic housecleaning, rather than systematic destruction schedules. The practice followed by departments in transferring records from office to storage area and eventually destroying them was usually set forth in informal intra-departmental memoranda. Thus the volume of paperwork in storage grew steadily. By 1968, inactive records occupied a total of 8,000 square feet of space divided among seven locations all in the same geographic area. In addition, there were many inactive records in the office area.

Availability of space, rather than systematic arrangement, had governed where records were stored. Although it was generally known where a particular document might be found, all documents of a specific classification were not necessarily in the same location. In fact, an employee frequently had to visit several of the seven locations in order to get a complete, running story on one project. Records removed from storage for reference were seldom returned to the package from which they had been taken. Since no one was responsible for keeping the files in order, bundles, boxes, and transfer cases in the storage area were often left open with their contents spilled about on the floor. The company had begun to grow rapidly after 1960 and the space available for record storage was depleted. The comptroller, whose records represented a large portion of the inactive documents in storage, became concerned that many important records were inadequately protected and were hard to find when needed. It was evident that a new approach to records storage was required.

Action

You have been hired as a consultant to aid Janobek Jewelers, Inc., by making a complete study of their files and filing practices and how they might be improved.

List and discuss the steps you would follow and the recommendations you would make, as well as the rationale behind those recommendations.

Case Study (Answer)

There is no standard answer for case studies. Individual approaches are taken into account in evaluating answers. Each case study has a series of elements essential to a proper response. These account for 30 points in the grading. For the Janobek Jewelers, Inc., case study, the following elements are among those that should be considered in the answer:

1. Prepare for the survey by meeting with the officers
2. Prepare by reading company regulations on files
3. Prepare by studying existing retention schedules
4. Study vital records and archives program
5. Study equipment and supplies procedures
6. Conduct survey of central files area
7. Survey files in decentralized departments
8. Survey seven storage areas
9. Interview workers in files and file users
10. Collect facts on file ages and volumes
11. Analyze disposal of obsolete records
12. Consider centralized versus decentralized files
13. Consider records centers and vital records needs
14. Analyze disposal of obsolete records
15. Check commercial records centers and equipment vendors
16. Check absence of total records management program
17. Discuss findings and proposals with officers
18. Prepare final report, audit and follow-up

Recommendations should include:

1. Establish a total records management program
2. Provide for records manager position and staff
3. Inventory all records, active and inactive
4. Prepare records retention schedules
5. Coordinate schedules and obtain necessary approvals
6. Establish central records center vital records program
7. Develop records center operation procedures and facility

In addition to the requirements for the above elements your answer is also judged on:

Professionalism Your understanding of principles and practices of records management, management concepts of organization, technology, awareness of history and literature sources.

Logic Construction of answer follow-through continuity, facts and required calculations.

Completeness Full response to all of the specific actions required in the question. Avoidance of both too short and too wordy an answer.

Condition, neatness, format Presentable, readable. Acceptability of spelling, grammar and punctuation. Arrangement of information.

Reader's reception of reply Persuasion, conviction, tact, managerial tone, reasonableness.

Miscellaneous ability indicators Cost consciousness, efficiency, resourcefulness.

It is important that you read the case studies very carefully. Make certain that you understand the requirements. Jot down some thoughts before you put the final answer together. Case studies are similar in terms of the degree of information required in the answer, so each should be given equal time.

CONGRATULATIONS—YOU'VE BECOME A CRM!

As any futurist knows, technology is advancing by the second. One punch of the button and information becomes immediately accessible. The responsibility inherent in the role of records manager is tremendous. The CRM examination is a challenging assessment of competency to deal with the myriad issues, decisions, and situations with which the manager is perennially concerned. Passing the CRM examination is an honor truly worthy of congratulations, yet the individual designated CRM must constantly keep abreast of changes within the field. Continuing education, whether through university coursework, special seminar or professional conference attendance is strongly encouraged.

Records managers tend to be an accomplished lot; through their own professionalism, they should serve as mentors for individuals whose personal attributes and aspirations would make them well-suited to records management careers. Having become a CRM, one should be alert to talents in others and foster greater awareness of career potential within one's community. Educational institutions which do not already offer instructional programs in records management may be most responsive to curriculum development based on occupational projections. Course syllabi on the "Introduction to Records Management," "Modern Archives Management," and "Forms, Design, Analysis and Control," published by the ARMA National Education Committee, are specifically designed for integration on the two- and four-year college, vocational, and secondary school levels. Records management is an exciting, dynamic science that offers the unique attraction of upward career mobility within an organization as well as skills which are transferable from the academic environment to the industrial area and from the private sector to the public sector. The Certified Records Managers Program certainly merits each CRM's continuous support.

Appendix B

Records Management Publications and Organizations

PUBLICATIONS

Administrative Management
Geyer-McAllister Publications, Inc.
51 Madison Avenue
New York, NY 10010

Information and Records Management
250 Fulton Avenue
Hempstead, NY 11550

Microfilm Techniques
250 Fulton Avenue
Hempstead, NY 11550

Modern Office Procedures
614 Superior Avenue West
Cleveland, OH 44113

The Office
73 Southfield Avenue
Stamford, CT 06904

Management World
AMS Building
Maryland Road
Willow Grove, PA 19090

Records Management Quarterly
4200 Somerset Drive
Suite 215
Prairie Village, KS 66208

The Secretary
Crown Center G–10
2440 Pershing Road
Kansas City, MO 64108

Systems and Procedures
24587 Bagley Road
Cleveland, OH 44138

Today's Secretary
330 West 42nd Street
New York, NY 10036

Infosystems
Hitchcock Publishing Co.
Hitchcock Building
Wheaton, IL 60187

ORGANIZATIONS

Administrative Management Society
Maryland Road
Willow Grove, PA 19090

Association of Records Managers
and Administrators, Inc.
4200 Somerset Drive
Suite 215
Prairie Village, KS 66208

National Microfilm Association
Suite 1101, 8728 Colesville
Road
Silver Springs, MD 20910

National Secretaries
Association
World Headquarters
Crown Center G–10
2440 Pershing Road
Kansas City, MO 64108

Appendix C

1978 Bibliography for Certified Records Manager Examination[1]

Institute of Certified Records Managers
P.O. Box 89, Washington, D.C. 20044

The books listed below are suggested for study for the CRM examination. The list is neither all inclusive nor restrictive. Books not listed may be equally good. Review of two or three books selected for all the parts, or one or two books selected for each part of the examination should, in most cases, be adequate preparation.

Parts
1 Records Management Principles and Program Organization
2 Records Generation and Control
3 Active Records Retrieval, Systems, and Equipment
4 Records Disposition/Protection
5 Technology of Records Management

Covers
Parts

1 2 3 4 5 ARMA. *Correspondence Course.*

1 2 3 4 5 Johnson, Mina M. and Norman F. Kallaus. *Records Management, 2d Ed.* Cincinnati: South-Western Publishing Company, 1972. ISBN: 0-538-11670-6.

---

[1]Reprinted by permission, ICRM.

1 2 3 4 5   Maedke, Wilmer, Mary F. Robek and Gerald F. Brown. *Information and Records Management*. Beverly Hills, CA: Glencoe Press, 1974. ISBN: 0-02-476360-8.

1 2 3 4 5   Neuner, John J W., B. Lewis Keeling and Norman F. Kallaus. *Administrative Office Management*. *7th Ed.* Cincinnati: South-Western Publishing Company, 1978. (6th Ed, ISBN: 0-538-07510-4).

1 2 3 4 5   Quible, Zane K. *Introduction To Administrative Office Management*. Cambridge, MA: Winthrop Publishers, Inc., 1977. ISBN: 0-87626-4003.

1 2 3 4 5   Terry, George R. *Office Management and Control, 7th Ed.* Homewood, IL: Richard D. Irwin, Inc., 1975. ISBN: 0-256-0157-7.

1 2 3 4 5   Weaver, Barbara N. and Wiley L. Bishop. *The Corporate Memory*. New York: John Wiley & Sons, 1974. ISBN: 0-471-92323-0.

1 2 3 4 5   NARS-GSA Records Management Handbooks (see attached current listing)

1 2   4 5   Benedon, William. *Records Management*. California State University-Los Angeles, Trident Book Store, 1969.

1   3 4   Place, Irene, Estelle L. Popham and Harry N. Fujita. *Fundamental Filing Practice*. Englewood Cliffs, NJ: Prentice-Hall, Inc. 1973. ISBN: 0-13-332742-6.

   2 3 4   Surgen, Olive. *Records Management Fundamentals*. Information and Business Systems, Inc., P.O. Box 635, Gaithersburg, MD 20760.

      3 4 5   Bassett, Ernest D. and David G. Goodman. *Business Filing and Records Control*. Cincinnati: South-Western Publishing Company, 1974. ISBN: 0-538-11100-3.

      3 4 5   Clark, Jesse L. *Records Management by Clark*. Newton, MA: Paperwork Systems, 1971.

1   5   Lazzaro, Victor (Editor). *Systems and Procedures: A Handbook for Business and Industry*. Englewood Cliffs, NJ: Prentice-Hall, Inc., 1968. ISBN: 0-13-581425.

1   Hodgetts, Richard M. *Management: Theory, Process, and Practice*. Philadelphia, W.B. Saunders Co., 1975. ISBN: 0-7216-4708-1.

1   Sisk, Henry L. *Management and Organization, 2d Ed.* Cincinnati: South-Western Publishing Co., 1973. ISBN: 0-538-07410-8, G-41.

1   Glueck, William F. *Personnel: A Diagnostic Approach.* Dallas: Business Publications, Inc., 1974. ISBN: 0-256-01574-0.

2   Knox, Frank. *The Knox Standard Guide to Design and Control of Business Forms.* New York: McGraw-Hill Book Company, 1965. ISBN: 0-07-035251-8.

2   O'Steen, Carle. *Forms Analysis: A Management Tool for Design and Control.* Stamford, CN: Office Publications, Inc., 1969. ISBN: 0-911054-01-4.

3   ARMA. *Alphabetical Rules for Filing, Revised.* Association of Records Managers and Administrators, P.O. Box 281, Bradford, RI 02808. 1972.

3 4   National Fire Protection Association, *Protection of Records* 1975. NFPA No. 232, 470 Atlantic Avenue, Boston MA 02210.

4   Kish, Joseph L., Jr. *Records Retention Step-by-Step.* Bronx, NY: System Press, 1972.

4   Mitchell, William E. *Records Retention—a Practical Guide (Revised).* Ellsworth Publishing Company, Box 3162, PO Annex, Evansville, IN 47731. 1968.

4   *Retention and Preservation of Records with Destruction Schedules.* Records Controls, Inc., 3920 So. Michigan Avenue, Chicago, IL 60653.

4   Schellenberg. T. R. *Modern Archives: Principles and Techniques.* Chicago. University Press, 1975. ISBN: 0-226-73684-9.

5   Awad, Elias M. *Business Data Processing, 4th Ed.* Englewood Cliffs, NJ: Prentice-Hall, Inc., 1975. ISBN: 0-13-093864-5.

5   Murach, Mike. *Business Data Processing and Computer Programming.* Chicago: Science Research Associates, Inc., 1973. ISBN: 0-07-051640-1.

5   Sanders, Donald H. *Computers in Business: An Introduction, 3d Ed.* New York: McGraw-Hill Book Co., 1975. ISBN: 0-07-051640-1.

5   Costigan, Daniel. *Micrographic Systems.* Silver Spring, MD: National Micrographics Assn. 8728 Colesville Road. RS16-1975. $16.50.

5   Nanney, Thomas G. *Using Microfilm Effectively.* New York: Geyer-McAllister Publishing Co., Inc., 1968.

5   Association for Systems Management. *Business Systems.* Cleveland: Association for Systems Management, 1970.

5   Burch, John G. and Felix R. Strater. *Information Systems: Theory and Practice.* Wiley-Hamilton, 1974. ISBN: 0-471-12323-4.

5   Optner, Stanford I. *Systems Analysis for Business Manage-ment, 3rd Ed.* Englewood Cliffs, NJ: Prentice-Hall, Inc., 1975. ISBN: 0-13-881276-4.

5   McCabe, Helen M. and Estelle L. Popham. *Word Processing: A Systems Approach to the Office.* New York: Harcourt Brace Jovanovich, Inc., 1977. ISBN: 0-15-596666-9.

5   Rosen, Arnold and Rosemary Fielden. *Word Processing.* Engle-wood Cliffs, NJ: Prentice-Hall, Inc., 1977. ISBN: 0-13-963504-1.

GOVERNMENT PUBLICATIONS

Personal Privacy in an Information Society. (The Report of the Privacy Protection Study Commission). No. 052-003-00395-3.

Protecting Federal Records Centers and Archives From Fire. No. 022-002-00049-0.

GSA PUBLICATIONS

Order from: Superintendent of Documents, U.S. Government Printing Off., Washington, DC 20402.

SB-247
Records Management Handbooks   May 23, 1977

Communications. Policy and Procedure, Managing Directives. 1967, reprinted 1974. 67 p. il. GS 4.6/2:C 73. 022-002-00009-1. $1.15.

Correspondence Management, Managing Correspondence. A guide to efficiency and economy in letter and memo writing that can be employed effectively in private industry as well as government. This manual presents a complege program to cut correspondence costs. 1973, reprinted 1975. 35 p. GS 4.6/2:C 81/973. 022-003-00899-3. 85¢.

Forms Management. 1976. 40 p. GS 4.6/2:F 76/3. 022-002-00014-7. 85¢.

Managing Current Files, File Stations. 1968, reprinted 1974. 52 p. il. GS 4.6/2:F 47/3. 022-002-00012-1. 85¢.

Managing Current Files, Files Operations. 1964, reprinted 1976. 76 p. il. GS 4.6/2:F 47. 022-002-00013-9. $1.05.

Managing Correspondence, Form and Guide Letters. 1973, published 1974. 45 p. il. GS 4.6/2:L 56. 022-003-00903-5. 80¢.

Managing Forms, Forms Analysis. Rev. 1960, reprinted 1974. 62 p. il. GS 4.6/2:F 76/960. 022-002-00015-5. 90¢.

Managing Forms, Forms Design. Rev. 1975. 96 p. GS 4.6/2:R 24/4. 022-002-00028-7. $1.35.

Managing Information Retrieval, Information Retrieval. 1972, reprinted 1975. 132 p. il. GS 4.6/2:In 3/2. 022-002-00036-8. $1.65.

Managing Information Retrieval, Information Retrieval Systems, 1970, published 1971. 150 p. il. GS 4.6/2:In 3. 022-002-00030-9. $2.25.

Managing Information Retrieval, Microfilming Records, 1974, published 1975. 168 p. il. GS 4.6/2:M 58/2. 022-001-00056-6. $2.35.

Managing Information Retrieval, Microform Retrieval Equipment Guide. 1975. 92 p. GS 4.6/2:M 58/974. 022-002-00034-1. $1.50.

Managing the Mail. 1971. 94 p. il. GS 4.6/2:M 28. 022-002-00033-3. $1.40.

Plain Letters, Managing Correspondence. 1973. 51 p. il. GS 4.6/2:L 56/2. 022-002-00041-4. $1.10.

PERIODICALS

Administrative Management. Geyer-McAllister Publications. 51 Madison Avenue, New York, NY 10010.

American Archivist, The Monumental Printing Co., 3110 Elm Avenue, Baltimore, MD 21211.

Business Graphics, Graphic Arts Publishing Company, 7373 N. Lincoln Avenue, Chicago, IL 60646.

Computer Decisions, Hayden Publications Co., Inc., 859 Third Avenue, New York, NY 10022.

Corporate Systems. United Technical Publications, Inc., Division of Cox Broadcasting Corp., 645 Stewart Avenue, Garden City, NY 11530.

Datamation. F. D. Thompson Publications Inc., 35 Mason Street, Greenwich, CN 06830.

FORM. National Business Forms Association, 300 N. Lee, Alexandria, VA 22314.

FORMAT. Association of Business Forms Manufacturers. (ABFM), John R. deMasi, 19034 Mills Choice Rd., Gaithersburg, MD 20760.

Information and Records Management. Information and Records Management, Inc., 250 Fulton Rd, Hempstead, NY 11550.

Infosystems. Hitchcock Publishing Company, Hitchcock Building, Wheaton, IL 60187.

Journal of Data Management. Data Management Association, 505 Busse Highway, Park Ridge, IL 60068.

Journal of Micrographics. The National Micrographics Association, 8728 Colesville Rd., Silver Spring, MD 20910.

Journal of Systems Management. Association for Systems Management, 2487 Bagley Rd., Cleveland, OH 44138.

Management World. Administrative Management Society, AMS Building, Maryland Rd., Willow Grove, PA 19090.

Microfilm Techniques. Microfilm Techniques, Inc., 250 Fulton Avenue, Hempstead, NY 11550.

Modern Office Procedures. The Industrial Publishing Co., 614 Superior Ave. West, Cleveland, OH 44113.

The Office. Office Publications, Inc., 1200 Summer Street, Stamford, CN 06904.

Office Products News. United Technical Publications, Inc., 645 Stewart Ave, Garden City, NJ 11530.

Prologue: The Journal of The National Archives. Prologue: The Journal of The National Archives, National Archives Building, Washington, DC 20408.

Records Management Quarterly. Association of Records Managers and Administrators. P.O. Box 281, Bradford, RI 02808.

Systems. United Business Publications, Inc., 200 Madison Avenue, New York, NY 10016.

Word Processing Report. Geyer-McAllister Publications, Inc., 51 Madison Ave, New York, NY 10010.

Word Processing World. Geyer-McAllister Publications, Inc., 51 Madison Ave., New York, NY 10010.

Words. International Word Processing Association, AMS Building, Maryland Rd, Willow Grove, PA 19090.

office Admin and Aud Ma

The periodicals listed above are representative of those which contain articles on records management. Only a few periodicals give complete attention to records management, but most office magazines contain occasional articles that specifically apply to one or more of the records management activities. Most articles are indexed in the Reader's Guide to Periodical Literature or the Social Sciences and Humanities Index. Also check the magazine's accumulative indexes or the table of contents of each issue.

Appendix D

Standard Divisions for Alphabetic Guides

60 Divisions

A	Cr	H	Li	Pe	St
Am	D	He	M	Pi	Su
B	De	Ho	Mar	Q	T
Be	Do	Hu	Mc	R	To
Bi	E	I	Me	Ri	U
Br	F	J	Mo	Ro	V
Bu	Fi	K	Mu	S	W
C	G	Ki	N	Sch	We
Ch	Gi	L	O	Se	Wi
Co	Gr	Le	P	Si	XYZ

100 Divisions

A	Cl	Fr	John	Ni	Sp
Al	Co	G	K	O	St
Am	Con	Ge	Ke	P	Sto
Ander	Cor	Go	Ki	Pe	T
Ar	Cr	Gr	Kn	Pi	Tho
B	Cu	Gro	L	Pr	Ti
Bar	D	H	Le	Q-R	Tr
Be	De	Ham	Li	Ri	U
Ber	Di	Har	Lo	Ro	V
Bi	Do	Hat	M	Ros	W
Bo	Dow	He	Man	S	War
Br	E	Hi	McA	Sch	We
Bro	El	Ho	Me	Se	Wh
Bu	Et	Hon	Mi	Sh	Wi
C	F	Hu	Mo	Si	Wo
Car	Fi	I	Mu	Smith	XYZ
Ch	Fo	J	N		

150 Divisions

A	Co	Gar	Jones	Mu	Sp
Al	Con	Ge	K	N	St
Am	Coo	Gi	Ke	Ni	Sto
Ander	Cor	Go	Kel	O	Su
Ar	Cr	Gr	Ki	Or	T
At	Cu	Gre	Kn	P	Te
B	D	Gro	Kr	Pe	Tho
Baker	Davis	H	L	Pet	Ti
Bar	De	Hal	Lar	Pi	Tr
Be	Del	Ham	Le	Pr	U
Ber	Di	Har	Lei	Pu	V
Bi	Do	Harr	Li	Q-R	Ve
Bl	Dow	Hat	Lo	Re	W
Bo	Du	He	Lu	Ri	Wall
Bon	E	Hen	M	Ro	War
Br	El	Her	Man	Ros	We
Bro	Et	Hi	Mas	Ru	Wei
Bu	F	Ho	McA	S	Wh
Bur	Fe	Hol	McD	Sch	Wi
C	Fi	Hon	McK	Schm	Williams
Car	Fl	Hu	Me	Se	Wilson
Cas	Fo	Hun	Mi	Sh	Wo
Ch	Fr	I	Miller	Si	Wr
Che	Fri	J	Mo	Smith	XY
Cl	G	John	Mor	Sn	Z

200 Divisions

A	Con	Green	Lar	Or	Sn
Ad	Coo	Gri	Le	P	Sp
Adams	Cor	Gu	Li	Par	St
Al	Cr	H	Lo	Pat	Stone
Allen	Cu	Ham	Lor	Pe	Str
Am	D	Har	Lu	Per	Su
American	Davis	Harr	M	Ph	Sw
Ar	De	Has	Mah	Pi	T
As	Dem	He	Man	Po	Th
B	Di	Hen	Mar	Pr	Ti
Bal	Do	Her	Mart	Pu	To
Bar	Dor	Hi	Mas	Q	Tr
Bas	Dr	Ho	Mc	R	Tu
Be	Du	Hom	McD	Re	U
Ben	E	Hos	McI	Ri	United
Bi	Ed	Hu	McM	Rid	V
Bl	El	Hun	Me	Roc	Ve
Bo	En	I	Mer	Ros	Vo
Br	Es	J	Mi	Ross	W

Bre	F	Je	Miller	Ru	Wal
Bro	Fe	Jo	Min	S	War
Brown	Federal	John	Mo	San	We
Bu	Fi	Jon	Mor	Sc	Wel
Bur	Fl	Jones	Mos	Sch	Wes
C	Fo	K	Mu	Schu	White
Cam	Fr	Ke	Mur	Se	Wi
Car	Fri	Kem	N	Sh	Wil
Cas	G	Ki	National	Sher	Wils
Ch	Ge	Ko	Ne	Si	Wo
Che	Gi	Kr	Ni	Sim	Wr
Ci	Gl	Ku	No	Sk	X
Cl	Go	L	O	Sm	Y
Co	Gold	Lan	Ol	Smith	Z
Collins	Gr				

GLOSSARY

ACTIVE RECORDS. Records that are referenced at least once a month.

ALPHABETIC FILING. Any system that arranges names or topics according to the sequence of letters in the alphabet. Materials may be classified by subject, name, place, or organization.

ALPHA-NUMERIC. File coding system made up of combinations of letters and numbers.

ANALYSIS. A study of the parts of a system in relation to the whole; in business, considers costs, objectives, resources, alternatives, and results.

APERTURE CARD. Data processing card specifically designed so that a microfilm may be mounted in it.

ARCHIVE. A collection of items that has historical value.

ARCHIVAL STANDARDS. Standards set by the U. S. Bureau of Standards to assure quality in microfilm images.

ASSOCIATION OF RECORDS MANAGERS AND ADMINISTRATORS (ARMA). A national group devoted to the development of records management as a profession.

AUTOMATION. An automatic procedure or device replacing human effort and using information feedback so that it may be self-correcting. Sometimes used to describe mechanization in a factory or office; also as a synonym for electronic data processing or computerization.

AUXILIARY EQUIPMENT. Supplementary equipment at a work station; for example, a movable tub file next to a desk.

BATCHING. Grouping records by a common factor such as function or time.

BINDER. A semi-permanent holder of papers.

CAPTION. Information on the tab of a guide or folder that identifies material contained therein; a label.

CARD DESIGN. The arrangement of constant items and lines on a card form; designed to facilitate the recording of variable input data.

CARD FIELD. A column in a fixed position on a punched card into which certain information is punched regularly.

357

CARD FILE. An orderly arrangement of selected items of information recorded on separate cards. Sometimes called unit files.

CARRIER FOLDER. A folder used to transport records from files to wherever they are needed. It is made of heavy Kraft or Manila and may be color coded.

CARTRIDGE. A container that facilitates loading and unloading film or tape into equipment.

CATHODE RAY TUBE (CRT). Office equipment that looks like a TV set equipped with a typewriter keyboard. It is a computer's window to the world. See "Video Display Terminals."

CENTRALIZED FILES. Files of several organizational units grouped physically in one location.

CHARACTER SENSING. Mechanical reading of symbols or marks made with special ink or pencil.

CHARGE-OUT. A procedure that substitutes a card or sheet, with identification data, for records loaned out. Its function is to ensure that items removed can be located and returned.

CHRONOLOGICAL FILING. Filing in sequence by date. When records are filed chronologically, the latest date should be in front.

CLASSIFICATION PLAN. A predetermined arrangement of the contents of a file according to key items and relationships. It identifies groups and standardizes information into a cohesive whole.

CLASSIFYING. The act of determining by analysis groups into which records should be categorized.

CLEARANCE SESSIONS. A series of meetings with different levels of management to decide about new records management procedures or systems.

CODING. Act of writing file designations on records as they are classified.

COLLATING. Often called "gathering." It is the operation of putting sheets or documents into a desired sequence.

COMMERCIAL RECORDS CENTER. Privately operated companies that store records for different companies. Charges are based on cubic feet plus various service fees.

COMPRESSOR. That part of a follow block at the back of a file drawer that holds folders upright by compressing them.

COMPUTER OUTPUT MICROFILM (COM). Microfilm produced by computers from magnetic tapes. Special electronic processes and equipment are used for this conversion activity.

CONFIDENTIALITY. Privacy of records; the issue of who should have access to information, especially that relating to personal affairs and held in data banks.

CONVENIENCE FILES. Personal or unofficial files located near the point of use for convenient reference.

CORRESPONDENCE MANAGEMENT. A management control function used to regulate volume of correspondence processed, analyze use, and establish uniform systems for filing, maintenance, and retrieval.

CROSS FILE. The practice of filing vertically across the width rather than the length of a drawer.

CROSS REFERENCE. Notation in a file or on a list showing where else a record is stored or referenced. Also called "cross filing."

CUT. The dimension of a folder tab. For example, a one-third cut means that the tab takes up one third of the folder's back flap width.

DATA BANK. Accumulation of facts and figures; usually identifies vast stores of data held for computer processing.

DATA PROCESSING. Any method by which facts are collected, classified, stored, and retrieved.

DECENTRALIZED FILES. Records maintained near the point of origin rather than under one control in a centralized area. May also be called departmental files.

DECIMAL FILING. System for classifying records in units of 10 and coded for numerical order.

DESCRIPTOR. A broad heading that characterizes the main features of a class or type of records.

DESTRUCTION NOTIFICATION. General letter or detailed information sent departments about the scheduled destruction of records. May also be called a *directive* or *standard operating procedure.*

DICTIONARY PATTERN. An arrangement of items in strict alphabetical sequence regardless of relationships.

DIE CUT. A folder that has been shaped by a cutting mold.

DIRECT ACCESS FILE. A system that can be referenced without using a relative index.

DISPERSAL. Act of placing copies of vital records in locations other than those housing the originals.

DISPOSAL, DISPOSING, DISPOSITION. Destroying or eliminating records that are no longer needed.

DISPOSITION SCHEDULE. A plan for the preservation or orderly disposition of records; an itemized list specifying disposition intervals.

DIVIDER. A metal plate or stiff guide that separates groups of files and helps to keep them upright.

DOCUMENTS. Printed or written records that are relied upon to prove something.

DUO MODE. The process of microfilming on one half of a film strip and then on the other half.

DUPLEX MODE. The process of microfilming both the front and back sides of a document simultaneously.

EDGE-NOTCHED CARDS. File cards containing a border of holes that may be notched to indicate (signal) items of information. Also called "edge-punched cards"; a manual system.

ELECTRONIC DATA PROCESSING (EDP). Storing and manipulating information through electronic computer equipment devices that use electronic circuitry to perform data-processing operations such as arithmetic. Impulses are transmitted from elements that have no physically moving parts.

ENCYCLOPEDIC PATTERN. Information grouped first by key headings as to content, then by subtopics that are alphabetized under them. An example of this pattern is the Yellow Pages in a telephone directory, which groups businesses as to type and then alphabetizes them within each type.

EQUIPMENT SURVEILLANCE. Action taken under a records management program to review requests for procurement of equipment. Use is analyzed to determine when new equipment is justified or to select proper type.

FACSIMILE. Exact reproduction of a document, usually a photocopy.

FILE. Papers or data accumulated in a container. Also, a large collection of records representing the business of an organization.

FILE INDEX. An ordered list of descriptors indicating where a record is within a filing system.

FILE REQUISITIONS. Requests for filed material usually written on a special form. The form may also be used as a charge-out. See "Charge-Out."

FILES. Containers for storing records, folders, cabinets, shelves, and boxes.

FILES MANAGEMENT. Management function that provides for the analysis of information retention systems and equipment to determine efficient procedures and equipment for given operations.

FILING. Process of arranging and sorting records so they may be found when needed.

FILING RULES. Standards or guides for consistency. They hold to a minimum arrangements that might result from personal choice or inexperience.

FILING SYSTEMS. Planned methods of indexing and arranging records (including guides, folders, and equipment).

FILING UNIT. An item of information, or each abbreviation, initial, or word considered when using filing rules.

FILM SIZE. Film width expressed in millimeters: 16MM, 35MM, 70MM, 105MM.

FLOOR LOAD. Capacity of floor area to support given weight expressed in terms of pounds per square foot.

FLOW CHART. Linear graph depicting steps in a procedure, thus showing linkage of activities and giving an overview of the system.

FOLLOW-UP. Checking to see that materials taken from files are returned or that items requiring later attention are suspended so that they will be called up at the appropriate time.

FORM. A printed record with blank spaces for inserting variable data. Also a form letter.

FORMS ANALYSIS AND DESIGN. Process of deciding what to print on a form, sequence of items, quality of paper, size, cost, and use.

FORMS MANAGEMENT. Management function that assures that unnecessary forms do not exist and that those needed are designed efficiently and produced economically.

FUNCTIONAL CLASSIFICATION FILE. A control file bringing together copies of forms or documents used in an activity, classified and filed according to purpose.

GEOGRAPHIC FILING. Arranging records alphabetically by location: country, state, district, region, city, or town.

GUIDE. Heavyweight and captioned divider used to identify file sections as well as provide physical support for contents.

HARD COPY/LIVE COPY. Paper copies of records as opposed to microfilm or magnetic tape. Such documents are immediately available for use without processing.

IMAGE. Reproduction on microfilm.

INACTIVE RECORDS. Stored records that are seldom used. Sometimes called "noncurrent" or "dead" records.

INDEX. An ordered list (usually alphabetical) of items (names, key words, or topics) within a body of information.

INDEXING. Act of selecting the caption by which a record is to be filed.

INDIRECT FILING. Reference must be made to a backup source before locating desired materials; that is, one does not go directly to the material.

INFORMATION MAINTENANCE. Keeping data and related equipment in a state of repair and usability.

INFORMATION PROCESSING. The manipulation of data through a series of changes in order to put it into a new form for use.

INFORMATION RETRIEVAL. Recalling and repossessing data when it is needed.

INFORMATION UTILITY. The true value to an organization of data maintained by it.

INPUT. Data fed into a system.

INSPECTING. Examining records for filing release marks.

INTEGRATED DATA PROCESSING (IDP). Coordinating information among the various units involved: files, work stations, and machines.

KRAFT. A type and quality of paper used for file folders and dividers, usually tan and heavy weight.

LAMINATING SYNTHETIC. A man-made substance that coats and preserves paper documents.

LATERAL FILE. Side opening file; may also refer to shelf files.

LEADER. Strip of film or paper at beginning of roll of film used for threading.

MAGNETIC CARDS. Cards on which information can be stored in magnetic fields.

MAGNETIC INK. Ink containing an iron ingredient so that it can be read automatically.

MAGNETIC MEDIA. Plastic tape, chips, and other devices used to store data for computer input. Data is "written" in the form of magnetized specks that the computer can read. Thousands of specks can be packed onto an inch of media.

MANUAL. A policy, administrative, or operational reference book.

MAP-AND-TACK FILE. A geographic information system with information represented by pins or tacks stuck into a map. Color coding may be used.

MARK SENSING. The act of marking cards with lead that contains a "metal" ingredient so that they can be read automatically by special machines.

MECHANIZATION. The replacement of human effort with machines.

MICROFICHE. Grid pattern, transparent card of micro images (usually 6 by 4½").

MICROFILM, MICROFORM, MICRORECORD. Microimage records.

MICROPHOTOGRAPHY. Photographic system, reproducing records in miniature, microimage form.

MISCELLANEOUS FOLDER. Folders holding records for a variety of correspondents or subjects.

MOBILE FILE. Any file that is easily transported.

NONSIGNIFICANT NUMBERS. Code numbers that do not have a subject matter meaning; for example, those assigned to forms in sequence.

NUMERIC FILING. Filing records, correspondence, or cards by number.

OUTFOLDER. A folder in which to store incoming records while a regular folder is on loan. It should give the name of the person who has the original.

OUT GUIDE. Used to indicate that an item has been taken from the files.

OUTPUT. Information that comes out of a data processing system; the opposite of *input.*

PHONETIC SYSTEMS. Arrangement of items according to pronunciation.

POINT. A unit of measurement for identifying the thickness of paper.

POLICY. A written statement from management that describes a settled course or defines boundaries of a procedure.

PREFABRICATED SYSTEM. A set of guides and folders designed before the facts and then adapted to the changing conditions of a particular situation; the opposite of tailor-made systems. Also called "commercial" systems.

PRESSBOARD. Used for guides identified by stiffness and thickness. See "Kraft."

PRIMARY GUIDE. First and main guide for a section of stored records.

PUNCHED CARDS. Cards with holes punched in them that translate our language into a coded or machine read language. They are used to store and manipulate information automatically.

PROCEDURE. A series of related steps that achieve a given objective within a system.

READER. Device for viewing microimages; consists of a projector and screen.

RECORDS. Any paper, book, photo, microfilm, map, drawing, chart, card, magnetic tape, or printout that has been generated or received by a company and is used as evidence of activities.

RECORDS APPRAISAL. Analysis of records to establish retention policy; may include review of operational and legal value.

RECORDS CENTER. Low cost, centralized area for housing and servicing inactive or semi-active records whose reference rate does not warrant active office space and equipment. See "Commercial Records Center."

RECORDS INVENTORY. List identifying company records, including information that enables control and evaluation of them.

RECORDS MANAGEMENT. Program of systematic control applied to the creation, organization, maintenance, retrieval, use, and disposition of records so that needless records will not be created and useful ones will be available when needed.

RECORDS MANAGER. Person responsible for development and maintenance of records management program. Other titles used: Records Coordinator, Supervisor of Records, and Records Administrator.

RECORDS RETENTION SCHEDULE. Comprehensive schedule by department and/or type of record indicating how long records are to be kept. May specify transfer date to center as well as final disposition date. See "Disposition Schedule."

REDUCTION RATIO. Measure of how much a document is reduced when microfilmed.

REFERENCE ANALYSIS. Statistical breakdown of reference requests to determine how often retained records are used.

REFILE. Process of replacing charged-out records.

RELATIVE INDEX. Separate alphabetical list of topics otherwise listed; facilitates retrieval.

REPORTS. Written accounts of activities or events prepared for distribution and analysis in statistical or narrative form.

REPORTS MANAGEMENT. The management function that assures that reports are kept to a minimum but that those kept are well presented, accurate, and timely.

RETENTION PERIOD. The time that records must be kept before disposition; sometimes depends on the occurrence of an event such as contract closure.

RETENTION SCHEDULE. Time table specifying how long records should be kept.

RETRIEVAL. The process of locating and removing items from their retention or storage systems.

SCREENING. The act of eliminating unnecessary items before they are filed.

SECURITY CENTER. A location where important records are safely stored. It may be a bomb shelter located outside the city.

SHELF FILING. System that uses open shelves rather than cabinets for storing materials.

SIGNALS. Devices that are fastened to records to get attention. Signals are often used in card and visible systems.

SIGNIFICANT NUMBERS. A number having connotation; an interpretative meaning. For example, license plate 1-69-85 might mean Douglas County, plate issue 69,000 series, 1985.

SORTING. Process of arranging items in the order in which they will later be filed.

SOUNDEX. An indexing system in which names that sound alike (but are spelled differently) are grouped.

SPACE DYNAMICS. Arranging work environment components to provide maximum utility of space and equipment as well as employee comfort. Also known as Ergonomics.

STANDARD. A guide established by authority as a criterion or model. May be expressed as a rule, policy, principle, or written procedure.

STANDARD PRACTICE INSTRUCTION (SPI) or STANDARD OPERATING PROCEDURE (SOP). Written descriptions of procedures to follow, often compiled into a manual or handbook.

STATUTE OF LIMITATIONS. The time limit within which an action may legally be brought upon a contract.

SUBJECT FILING. Arranging records alphabetically by names of topics or things, rather than by individual names.

SUBSYSTEM. A part of a larger system.

SYSTEM. A combination of interrelating parts that interact to achieve some objective. The identity of the parts depends on the type of system. A filing system, for example, might contain the following parts: equipment, supplies, personnel, standard procedures and methods, file supplies, and machines.

SYSTEMS ANALYST. One who studies alternate ways to reach objectives based on rationale, costs, resources, and benefits associated with each alternative.

TAB. The projection on a folder or guide on which the caption is written. Tab sizes vary in proportion to the folder width: a one-third cut is one-third the width of the folder.

TAILOR-MADE SYSTEM. Designed to meet the special needs of a particular business or situation. Opposite of "Prefabricated System."

TAPE LIBRARIAN. One who maintains a collection of tapes.

TERMINAL-DIGIT FILING. A method of filing by the last digits (usually the last two) of a number instead of by the first digits as in traditional left-to-right reading.

TICKLER FILE. A chronological file set up to "tickle" the memory about records or items that need action. A memory aid.

TRANSFER FILE. A file of relatively inactive material that has been or is to be moved from active files.

VARIABLE INFORMATION. Information that is recorded on a form. It changes according to the individual situation; for example, dates, names, and quantities.

VIDEO DISPLAY TERMINAL (VDT). Desktop video screen. These items are replacing both typewriters and file cabinets. Memos, letters, reports, and raw data may be composed on or entered into the machines and the resulting documents or computations can be transmitted to a rate of more than three pages a minute from terminal to terminal around the world.

VISIBLE FILE. Cards or strips arranged in specially designed equipment so that one line of each record is visible at a glance.

VITAL RECORDS. Records essential to resumption or continuation of operations of a company.

VITAL RECORDS CENTER. Repository for housing records classified as vital.

WORD PROCESSING TERMINALS. Typewriter-like machines on which one can add, delete, and reformat an entire article by typing directly over items; then press a button and get a fresh typewriter printout, perfectly spaced and justified. Equipment may be connected with a computer; has a memory bank of its own.

WORK FLOW. The movement of work in process from one work station to another.

WORK STATION. The area where an individual works. In an office, it is usually composed of a desk, a chair, and related equipment depending on the function.

Index